MODERN MILITARY TOWARDS 2000

Two F/A-18 Hornets perform a spectacular vertical climb during a day's "fighting" over RAAF base Williamtown. The immense task of defending the Australian continent and its air and sea space, covering more than a tenth of the earth's surface, demands a high-pitched state of readiness from the nation's three modern services. The high-technology Hornet symbolises the country's need to secure its future with advanced systems, long-range defence capabilities, and the expertise of its armed forces and defence industry.

Australia
1788-1988

AUSTRALIANS AT WAR

MODERN MILITARY TOWARDS 2000

PETER BADMAN

ALUN EVANS

DOUG HURST

BEDE JORDAN

TIME-LIFE BOOKS. AUSTRALIA
in association with JOHN FERGUSON. SYDNEY

Designed and produced by
John Ferguson Pty Ltd
100 Kippax Street,
Surry Hills, NSW 2010

Series Editor: John Ferguson
Consulting Editor: George G. Daniels
Series Director: Lesley McKay
Editor: Tony Love
Picture Editor: Julian Leatherdale
Designer: Jane Tenney
Production Manager: Tracy O'Shaughnessy
Staff Writer: Julian Leatherdale
Assembly Artist: Jane Tenney, Josie Howlett

Time-Life Books, South Pacific Books Division
Managing Director: Bonita L. Boezeman
Production Manager: Ken G. Hiley
Production Assistant: Dimity Raftos

First published in 1989 by
Time-Life Books (Australia) Pty Ltd
15 Blue Street
North Sydney, NSW 2060.

(c) Time-Life Books (Australia) Pty Ltd 1989

This book is copyright. Apart from any fair dealing for the purposes of private study, research, criticism or review, as permitted under the Copyright Act, no part may be reproduced by any process without written permission. Inquiries should be addressed to the publisher.

National Library of Australia
cataloguing-in-publication data

Modern Military.
 Bibliography.
 Includes index.
 ISBN 0 949118 41 9

1. Military art and science — Australia —
 Technological innovations.
2. Australia — Armed Forces — Equipment.
 I. Badman, Peter
 II. Title (Series: Australians at War; 15).

355'.033094

This publication has been partially funded by the Australian Bicentennial Authority as part of its program to help celebrate Australia's Bicentennial in 1988.

Printed in Hong Kong.

The Authors: PETER BADMAN is a senior executive with a computer company who writes in his spare time. He was a regular soldier for 32 years and retains a strong interest in the Australian Army and its history. During his military career he saw active service in Vietnam, and later commanded an infantry brigade in Australia. He lives in Canberra with his wife and one of his three children. Peter Badman acted as a consultant for this title and wrote chapter 5.

ALUN EVANS was born in Tongala, Victoria, in 1933. He entered the Royal Australian Naval College in 1947, and during his 32-year career he commanded a Naval Air Squadron, the destroyer escort HMAS *Yarra* and he paid off the third HMAS *Sydney* in command. He retired in November 1978. He has written one other book concerning the RAN, *A Navy for Australia.* He now lives in the Blue Mountains. Alun Evans acted as a consultant, wrote chapter 2 and co-wrote chapter 1.

GROUP CAPTAIN DOUG HURST has served in the Royal Australian Air Force for 30 years and for 27 of those years he was a navigator. He has written articles for various defence journals and magazines. He is currently working as an airforce officer in the Russell Offices in Canberra where he resides with his wife and two children. Doug Hurst wrote chapter 3, co-wrote chapter 1 and acted as a consultant for this title.

MAJOR BEDE JORDAN enlisted in the Citizen Military Force in 1961 and served in the Infantry until he was commissioned in 1966. In 1986 he joined the Australian Joint Warfare Establishment to develop training materials for the defence forces. In civilian life, he operates one of the academic services units at the University of Newcastle and lives at Coal Point with his wife and two daughters. Bede Jordan wrote chapter 4, co-wrote chapter 1 and acted as a consultant.

CONTENTS

Chapter	1	**To Australia's Defence**	**12**
Picture Essay		Vanguard of the Seas	30
	2	**Building a Modern Navy**	**42**
		The Ultimate Aircraft	69
	3	**From Mustang to Hornet**	**78**
		Special Operations	106
	4	**A Mobile Army**	**114**
	5	**Into the Future**	**150**

Bibliography 164
Acknowledgments 164
Picture Credits 165
Picture Essay Quotes 165
Index 166

In their F/A-18 Hornets, carrying missiles, ground-attack weapons and long-range fuel tanks, a modern RAAF fighter pilot and his wingman have more

striking power than an entire RAAF squadron of World War II.

In modern camouflage gear and armed with the new Steyr assault rifle (left), 6 RAR soldiers track enemy snipers during urban warfare training. Re-organise

and re-equipped for defence of Australia's North, the new-look Army is ready for action.

Two of the RAN's most modern warships, the guided-missile frigate HMAS Canberra leading her sister ship HMAS Darwin, steam in line ahead with

guided-missile destroyer HMAS Hobart and fleet replenishment ship HMAS Success on a Navy battle exercise.

1
TO AUSTRALIA'S DEFENCE

A hostile power gains a foothold in the continent's Top End, putting to the test Australia's military strategy of layered defences combined with joint operations. In retaliation, a coordinated naval and air attack and airborne deployments turn back the enemy threat.

As the heavy cloud cover over the Arafura Sea began to break up 200 kilometres northeast of Darwin, a Royal Australian Air Force P-3C Orion banked at the end of its patrol leg and reversed its track across the top of the Northern Territory coast. The aircraft had been flying for more than three hours with no results — three hours of looking at increasing patches of afternoon rain and the endless, empty ocean.

The Orion's radar operator yawned and glanced at his watch, recalling what now seemed an aptly memorable line from his years of training. War, he was told, was mostly long periods of boredom punctuated by moments of stark terror.

It was time again to transmit. Just a quick sweep or two, then off. Intelligence from one of the Royal Australian Navy's submarines on long-range surveillance duties in the South China Sea had reported a force of naval ships heading through the Indonesian archipelago towards the Australian mainland. The Orion and its crew were on the lookout.

It was no surprise that such a group of vessels

The Australian Defence Forces insignia has RAAF eagle, RAN anchor and Army swords with boomerang and seven-point star.

12

would be heading this way. The whole of the Australian Defence Force was in a high state of alert. A northern regional power had recently challenged Australia's rights to a 200-nautical mile exclusive economic zone, lucrative fishing grounds, and its oil and gas fields. The battle was at first a verbal one, as Australia was accused of greed in a resource-starved world, but the tensions exploded when small raiding parties were landed across Australia's Top End. Several ADF units were already in action.

The intruders had gained a limited foothold a week ago when a small group of ships breached Australia's recently declared Maritime Exclusion Zone, an imaginary line drawn on the ocean as a tripwire, announcing to all nations to stay outside, lest they be treated as an enemy. That first force had then put ashore bands of soldiers near Wyndham in northern Western Australia, and from there the saboteurs had ventured into the Ord River area and were holding out against Army troops of Norforce battling to contain them in some of the continent's harshest terrain. One of the Royal Australian Navy's Oberon submarines, on a routine patrol in the Timor Sea, had then come upon the enemy ships, engaging and attacking them with Mark 48 torpedoes. One destroyer had gone to the bottom, and the others were sent scurrying out of the MEZ.

There now seemed no doubt that the enemy intended further action to perhaps harass population centres, disrupt communications and destroy military installations, with the plan to extract political concessions from the Australian Government.

The approaching ships were certainly the next wave of the conflict, and how far they would pressure Australia's military commanders was the vital question. The Orion's crew could not be too careful. They were a key element in the surveillance of the continent's approaches, and the armada would expect them as surely as the Australians searched for their quarry. No doubt the enemy would be listening for the P-3C's own radar: if it were used continuously the aircraft's position could easily be fixed and tracked. It was now simply a waiting game.

The Orion's radar blinked on, the screen coming to life with a broad line of brightness showing at the top of the picture: the southern parts of the archipelago were under a bank of cloud so thick that radar could not penetrate it. If the enemy had reached the northern edge of the aircraft's surveillance area, he was probably hidden by the weather.

Then the edge of the cloud clutter on the screen firmed up, the image sharpening. It caught the operator's eye, and he adjusted the sensor station controls in front of him.

"Radar contact," he called. "Zero two zero degrees, nine zero miles. At least six contacts close together, probably more."

The P-3C and crew had almost certainly found the ships they had been looking for. The Orion's vast patrolling range and far-seeing radars had been a telling factor, as had been its complex surveillance systems, the aircraft fulfilling its role within the country's planned defence in depth.

Concentrating in the continent's north, where the tentacles of Australia's military power were being positioned more and more, the defence in depth policy placed forces in layers out from the Australian coast when a contingency arose. The Orion was covering the outer reaches.

With such a posture, political will especially could be given definite parameters; maritime and economic exclusion zones determined decision-making lines. And the layers of defence meant that Australia's commanders could best choose where and how to confront the approaching ships. Timely Intelligence, however, was critical to success — and the P-3C had just beaten the enemy to the punch.

The operator at the Orion's sensor station inserted the newly found contact position into his aircraft's computer memory, so that the information was now readily available to other crew members, and switched his aircraft's own radar to standby. Then, 30 seconds later, a radar emission was detected — a long-range, air-search radar of the type Intelligence had briefed

With the Australian Defence Force's evolving strategies of northern based defence, defence in depth and tri-service coordination, bases for all three services are being established in the continent's Top End and on the northwestern coast to give multi-layered surveillance and defence coverage of the nation's region of strategic interest.

the Orion to expect from the enemy's flagship.

"Radar emission. Zero two zero. A Hughes SPS 52C E/F band. It's them alright."

The Orion's own radar had been on standby in the hope of detecting exactly such a radar emission, the P-3C's crew monitoring its own specially designed radar-detection receivers which could analyse and indicate the direction of any radar emissions in the area. The approaching ships had similar receivers, and very likely had detected the P-3C's radar before it was placed on standby.

The enemy had two options: he could have remained quiet, giving the P-3C the hard job of finding him in such open sea; or he could try to locate the Orion. He chose to fire up his long-range radar in the hope of pinpointing the P-3C's position. It was, possibly, a fatal decision — in doing so he had identified himself.

The game of hide and seek that they were playing was the very crux of the airforce's surveillance role. In covering Australia's northern approaches, Orions came across many warships. Just one month before, on a routine deployment based out of Butterworth airbase in Malaysia, the crew had flown patrols over one of the main shipping routes across the Indian Ocean, the "Iron Highway" they called it. Mostly they followed the wakes of merchant shipping, but they sometimes tracked slowly increasing numbers of Indian naval units in Russian-designed vessels to and from their base in the Nicobar Islands. Once they also surprised a Soviet Echo-two cruise-missile nuclear submarine and a Krivac destroyer; the submarine dived, but the Australians tracked it for hours using passive acoustic sensors.

The Navy's submarines also played an important surveillance role, able to sit undetected while monitoring traffic on a shipping route or entering and leaving foreign ports. And on regular patrols within Australia's strategic region, the Oberons could give early detections of approaching enemy forces.

But the area these front-line lookouts had to cover was huge — effectively more than one tenth of the globe. Australia itself is an island of similar size to continental United States of America, and it is situated south of the world's biggest archipelago. That chain of islands begins in the west with Sumatra, and through 1,300 islands of Indonesia parallels the equator for more than 6,000 kilometres, on to Papua New Guinea before spilling southeast through the Solomon Islands into the South-West Pacific. North to south, the area stretches more than 5,000 kilometres from the Asian islands to the Southern Ocean and Antarctica. Unofficially, Australia's strategic interests spread even further, to Japan in the north, beyond India and down the coast of Africa in the west, and out towards the centre of the Pacific Ocean. The task of keeping an eye on all this territory was, in the very least, a daunting one.

Today, back in their own skies, the Orion's crew were very much at war. And their latest discovery had been assessed as enemy — or at least he would be if he kept heading south. Now, the hostile ships were still in international waters, just 50 kilometres north of Australia's declared maritime exclusion zone. If this latest force of uninvited warships crossed into the MEZ, it would be an unambiguous challenge to Australia's sovereignty.

The Orion would expose itself only for the briefest possible bursts, flying random tracks and using its radar sparingly to maintain tracking of the enemy ships. The enemy contact was reported to the joint force commander, the Maritime Commander, at Maritime Headquarters, Garden Island, Sydney. With his Chief of Staff and the Air Adviser, he now considered the fast-unfolding situation. They knew from latest enemy contact reports the ships' position, track and speed, and that if the ships held heading they would penetrate the MEZ very soon. But apart from testing Australia's resolve, the question of what the ships intended to do once inside the zone still remained unclear.

From the enemy's rhetoric of the last few weeks, it was clear that he wished to prove that Australia could not secure its northern 200 nautical mile Exclusive Economic Zone or remote coastal areas. However, he did not have enough ships for a full-scale invasion, and was thought to lack effective airpower. These weaknesses logically should have limited the attack options to a display of strength off the Australian coast or a small landing party or two. But logic did not always apply in war.

The Maritime Commander knew this all too well. He had found his enemy, but still he was uneasy. The ships had been too open in their approach, and furthermore his Intelligence told him that there were more vessels at the enemy's disposal — possibly six or seven more.

The chief of staff was similarly concerned. By his reckoning, two helicopter-capable destroyers may not be in the force being shadowed, nor a converted container ship fitted out to fly recently bought Harrier jump jets. Again there was no conclusive information.

The Air Adviser also was frustrated by a lack of accurate Intelligence, especially on the squadron of Harriers. Although he did not expect the aircraft to be fully operational in the short time that the enemy had owned them, he could not rule out that possibility.

The commanders, without a complete picture of the enemy, were now forced to act on the possibilities. Where were the other ships? Were the Harriers operational and how effective could they be? Was this a feint to draw defending forces away from a thrust involving the other enemy ships? And if so, what were their plans?

A second force with helicopters and Harriers would give the enemy a number of options: he could use the choppers to fly troops on a harassment raid against a coastal settlement like the bauxite mines at Gove or Groote Island; or if the Harriers were available, they could strike several targets. A full-scale invasion was still beyond him, but not an attack serious enough to demonstrate Australia's weaknesses in keeping him out.

Fortunately, the ADF had ample forces to counter the threat, but it was now a matter of waiting until the MEZ was crossed. Until then, all the preparations necessary, and all the Australian military's efforts would have to be concentrated in readiness for battle.

In Darwin, an RAAF squadron of F-111 aircraft was put on 30 minutes alert for a maritime strike. Another Orion was sent out to look for the possible second group of ships. And the Navy was also prepared for its role. Fast patrol boats were scouting the northern parts of the EEZ, and a task force of larger ships led by the FFG guided-missile frigate HMAS *Darwin* with two Seahawk helicopters was operating further out. As well, two submarines lurked below the surface in the western sections of the Arafura Sea and the eastern Timor Sea, each patrolling designated areas so not to cross each other's path, each hoping for a detection.

The Maritime Commander's plan at this stage was simple. If the ships continued on track towards the Australian mainland, he would hit them with aircraft at the outer edge of the MEZ, then with submarines, and then, if they kept coming, with both ships and aircraft closer in. Now, because of his uncertainty as to the enemy's plan, and the probability of a fight looming, he made sure that the Chief of the Defence Force and the Minister knew of the latest developments. As well, the land and air commanders were told of the likely need for extra air defence for the ships at sea and in the Darwin and Tindal airbase area. Generally, all forces in the north were to be strengthened and ready for further action.

Meanwhile, to the east, another of the RAN's guided-missile frigates, HMAS *Adelaide*, was steering across the top of the Gulf of Carpentaria and into the Arafura Sea. She and the task group of ships she was leading were loaded with materiel bound for Darwin, and as they approached their destination in the dark, early hours of the morning, they, too, were suddenly called into a high state of alert against the threat of aircraft, surface vessels, and possibly even submarines of the hostile power.

The extra P-3C sent out from Darwin to hunt for a potential second enemy force had been tracking across the task group's path and gained contact on a group of ships surprisingly quite a distance inside the gulf. The Orion's

Guided-missile frigate HMAS Darwin leads a naval task force on alert in Australia's northern waters. While the frigate's passive sonar listens for an enemy presence, her two Seahawk choppers are on search and destroy patrols further out.

intelligence brief, regarding the enemy's ships, had been spot on — they included the two helicopter-capable destroyers expected by the chief of staff. The enemy's strategy was quickly filling in, but their presence so close to shore was a major headache for Australia's commanders. How did they get this far south without being detected? What were their motives? Was this now the main enemy thrust?

The *Adelaide*'s captain's responsibilities had been suddenly compounded. His task group had formed at Townsville to carry reinforcements of troops and weapons bound for Darwin, and in doing so was undertaking one of the Navy's major roles, that of support for its fellow land forces. With the *Adelaide* was the *Jervis Bay*, an ex-vehicle and passenger carrier commissioned into the RAN as a training ship but currently loaded with military impedimenta, the *Tobruk*, a purpose-built heavy landing ship laden with armoured personnel carriers and troops to support the men and equipment of Norforce already battling the saboteurs in the Kimberlys, and two destroyer escorts, the HMAS *Derwent* and *Swan*, each of which was equipped for close-range air and surface defence with a Seacat missile and radar controlled 4.5 inch guns.

The frigate's captain was only too aware of his duty. Although he was in charge of a complex array of computerised electronic wizardry and weaponry, his first task was to get a $300 million ship and its 190 men, as well as the others in his group, safely to Darwin. But with the enemy so close, and sounding more powerful than the *Adelaide*'s group, such a job would not be so simple, especially if the Orion's report was correct. The frigate's captain decided to turn away from the enemy ships and await further orders.

The enemy had scored a major coup in penetrating this far south and undertaking the next step in his planned challenge, which was to gain another foothold on the continent and this time up the stakes against the Australian Government. The move had been audacious. While the ADF's commanders were concentrating their forces in the north and western approaches to the Northern Territory and Western Australia, the enemy's destroyers had hugged the west coast of New Guinea and ventured into the Gulf of Carpentaria, taking maximum advantage of heavy cloud in the area and using surveillance reports from a submarine that had been sitting undetected at the gulf's opening.

Now they were close enough to launch a helicopter-borne harassment raid on Weipa township and the nearby newly completed RAAF airfield facilities.

The reports of the convoy in the Gulf, close enough to attack Cape York were a shock to the Maritime Commander. The new airbase close to the bauxite-mining town, although virtually unmanned on a regular basis, was an important link in the control of Australia's northern airspace, enabling all of the RAAF's aircraft, including its F/A-18 Hornet fighters, to operate to the continent's northeast. If the airfield fell to hostile hands, there was every likelihood that it could become a major enemy centre. As well, the prospect of Australian forces having to attack the recently completed base facilities to retake it would be a bitter pill to swallow.

The respective ADF air and land commanders were quickly informed of the latest developments. The F-111s at Darwin were readied for takeoff, while the commander of the 1st Battalion of the Royal Australian Regiment based in Townsville, Lieutenant Colonel John Salter, was telexed with the latest information. It appeared from local reports that the enemy had, in fact, not hesitated, landing a raiding party which had quickly begun to harass town dwellers. It was possible, too, that the enemy had surrounded and occupied the airfield.

The 1st Battalion was one of the prime units of the Australian Army's Operational Deployment Force within the 3rd Brigade, on 24-hour notice for action in any contingency. Salter would be able to concentrate quickly a 170-strong unit based on a company of infantry and comprising additionally a reconnaissance party of field engineers, a forward observer party to call down artillery fire, some medium trucks, a signals detachment for rearwards communications, and a small administrative element which included medical support. The CO would also move his small tactical headquarters with the company group should a full deployment be needed.

Normal battle procedures after the first signs of trouble a week ago had the entire 850-strong battalion group coming together, including an artillery battery of six 105 mm guns, utility helicopters, Bell 206B-1 Kiowa light observation helicopters, 60 light and medium vehicles and many tonnes of stores including sandbags, barbed wire, ammunition and fuel supplies. If the enemy remained in control of the airbase, such a move would definitely be on.

Firstly, however, Salter had to make a reconnaissance of the Weipa area. With a recce platoon he flew quickly to the area in the first available RAAF Caribou small transport aircraft, landing at a gravel strip on a nearby cattle station where the local Army Reserve captain had withdrawn to provide a HQ outside the enemy threat area. Awaiting him when he arrived was the news that hostile forces had indeed landed and spread out to take over the town's main facilities. Their number was, however, undetermined. Effectively the intruders had sealed off the community and made their country's political point.

Also at the strip, housed temporarily in one of the station's large sheds, was a Kiowa chopper that had been moved to the district after the current conflict had flared. Salter took it out to reconnoitre the township, and on return to his HQ he decided to fly in as soon as possible an assault force to retake the Weipa precincts. Considering the likelihood that the enemy forces on the ground were mobile, and well-armed, there seemed no doubt that the ODF's arrival would be contested.

Salter, his recce platoon, and a small party of reserves had plenty of work to do the next day before the rest of the company group flew in that night. The platoon was guided by the reserves through the scrub closer to town to keep an eye on the enemy, who seemed well

Inserting troops into a potential "hot" zone, RAAF Iroquois choppers carry litters for possible wounded and have their door-gunners poised to provide suppressive fire before landing. The soldiers quickly seek cover as more choppers arrive.

organised and with brave intentions to secure a perimeter around the area. Also, the Australians needed to prepare an improvised night-landing strip at the station for the battalion's Caribou aircraft — the area was "hot" and the rest of the Diggers would be arriving in the dark.

As the night had come on and the Caribous approached, Salter's men on the ground lit a series of hexamine solid-fuel tablets, usually used to heat the soldiers' food and water, to mark the station strip. From the cockpit of the first of the aircraft, Flight Lieutenant Nigel Murphy strained through the darkness to pick up the flickering yellow lights, judging in the dark where he was on an imaginary extended centre line. Left or right, he thought, and what about the crosswind? Clouds, too, had made things more difficult by masking the horizon. Murphy had clocked up more than 1,000 hours on Caribous, but this mixture of visual and instrument flying, with the potential for attack, was as hairy as he had ever experienced.

With his right hand held up on the throttles and the left on the control column, Murphy now took in the checks and reports on the rate of descent and airspeed.

"Seventy knots, trees above on both sides, 15 feet off so flare now!" the co-pilot called. Murphy brought the stick back and closed the throttle, and with a thud the struts in the undercarriage took the load as the main wheels touched down.

The Caribous were combat loaded, having been warned that enemy soldiers were possibly in the area of their strip. In Murphy's hold, the men of the 1st Battalion lay packed on the floor in their camouflaged uniforms and webbing. It was good to be on the ground safely, and the adrenalin rush eased. Still, the back ramp had to be quickly lowered and the cargo door raised — this could be the enemy's chance to open fire. But the Australians raced away from the aircraft unopposed though sandblasted by the wash of the still-running engines. Once away from the airstrip clearing, the soldiers moved into the scrub and waited for the remainder of the company to fly in close behind them. So far, their arrival had gone by the book.

Kitted for action, soldiers sit on webbing seats in the belly of an RAAF C-130 Hercules, part of a battalion airlift to reinforce the first wave of helicopter-borne troops.

Also during the night, six L5 howitzers of the battalion's affiliated 107 Field Battery, Royal Regiment of Australian Artillery, were brought in. They were versatile and lightweight guns, capable of being stripped quickly to manpack loads, and would provide close fire support if necessary to defend Weipa or to force the enemy from any foothold he had gained.

Next to arrive, and well before first light, were six Bell Iroquois UH1H utility helicopters, ready to carry an assault force inside any enemy-held perimeter. They were soon back in action, their rotors chopping into the early morning air, as they headed for the first flashpoint, the airfield facility. Flanked by two helicopters acting as gunships, the other four choppers were loaded with seven fully-equipped soldiers, each strapped into their seat, grasping their personal weapons and peering forward to catch their first sight of the landing zone.

It was a tense moment for all concerned. Would the insertion be contested? Should there have been artillery preparatory fire to neutralise likely enemy positions? They waited for the crack of a passing bullet, or worse, the crash of a shattered windscreen or panel. They were vulnerable, but the slicks, the manpower carriers that had proved themselves so capably in Vietnam, were tough little workhorses.

Suddenly they went in, as the gunships wheeled in from above to protect the landing. The slicks dropped onto the red, dusty ground just long enough to disgorge their passengers, who ran quickly to each side and adopted firing positions until the choppers had cleared the landing area. It was all over within minutes; the force was down and ready for action.

But all was quiet; without even a sniper to worry about. It seemed that the enemy had not taken over the airfield at all. Or, if he had done so, he had since withdrawn from its vicinity possibly to regroup in strength around the town outskirts. Maybe the invaders had already begun to react to the arrival of the Australian troops, realising that the base was untenable? Perhaps they had, instead, sought to be rescued

and returned to their mother ships waiting in the gulf?

At least the airfield was now free for the remainder of the 1st Battalion if required. Certainly, fire from the artillery and gunships was not yet needed; even so, the choppers buzzed angrily above the gathering soldiers, checking things out before they returned to their holding area at the cattle station. Unopposed, Salter's men quickly secured the airfield's perimeter and dug in.

Back in Townsville, the C-130 Hercules of the RAAF's Air Lift Group were ready to move. Now that the Weipa airfield was known to be secure, the transports would fly in the remainder of the battalion group by a round-the-clock tactical move. It would take 15 Hercules aircraft 10 sorties each over 40 hours. In the end Salter's battalion command post was established with camouflage nets and with radio links forward to his four rifle companies and rearwards to the 3rd Brigade headquarters.

Mapboards showing dispositions and possible enemy locations were marked up by Intelligence staff, and signallers stood by their radios, log books open. A supporting gun battery had moved up and was sited nearby with 1 RAR's six 81 mm mortars, and a light dozer was pushing up a protective bund around the guns. Sandbags were filled for use in strongpoints, machine-gun arcs were interlocked, barbed wire put down and fire lanes cut as required. Elsewhere, a logistic maintenance area to support the operation was being established, and Landrovers and gangling Unimog MC2 four-tonne trucks were working hard to clear stores away from the airfield.

Just two days after the enemy had landed, the battalion was now ready to close in and stop the intrusion. The Army's ODF, based upon the 3rd Brigade, had so far proved that mobility with quick-reacting land forces was the key to the defence of the remote north in such circumstances. Now all that was left was to see what kind of fight the enemy could put up.

However, there was little hope for the saboteurs, as they were now alone on foreign soil, their lifeline destroyed. When the first detection of the enemy naval group in the gulf had been made, the RAAF's F-111s based in Darwin during the alert were quickly brought up to readiness. Squadron Leader Mike Nelson was informed of the Maritime Commander's requirements, then Nelson himself briefed a flight of four aircraft on the tactics they were to use if launched. All that remained was for them to do their pre-flight preparation checks.

On the black tarmac at Darwin, the row of F-111s appeared more menacing at night than usual, the dark punctured by hosts of spotlights. The white of each of the aircraft's Harpoon missiles seemed oddly pristine. A sea breeze tore at the red safety streamers attached to each of the weapons, but as the pre-flight checks proceeded the streamers were removed. The flight could be in the air at any moment.

Nelson had been flying the strike bombers for more than eight years, yet the mission ahead of him still shot a chill into his bones. He mentally double-checked every detail of the briefing: the plan was to fly in two pairs of two, rendezvousing with the P-3C Orion over the gulf for strike direction for a simultaneous, coordinated attack with Harpoon cruise missiles against the enemy ships. Properly planned and timed, such an attack should overwhelm the ships, confusing their defences as they battled in a number of directions to fight off the bombers.

There was, however, a wild card: the lack of solid Intelligence on enemy airpower. So far, no Harriers had been sighted with either convoy. They were most likely not yet operational, but the long shot was that they were being kept in reserve to ward off any air attack.

The *Adelaide*, *Derwent* and *Swan* were receiving constant updates of the track and speed of the enemy ships, but the frigate and the destoyer escorts would have to await developments before their precise role became clear. They were now in the hands of the Maritime Commander — and the fateful tides of war. But with any sort of luck, the RAAF's aircraft would hit the hostile ships, and the frigate, with its helicopters, could then turn its attention to the nearby submarine that had appeared in the enemy's gameplan.

The newly detected underwater opponent was all that the maritime commander needed to finally call the F-111s into the battle. Meanwhile, the P-3C continued to stalk the enemy force, preparing to guide the F-111s to their prey. If the air attack on the enemy ships was successful, the FFG and its two escorts would then be free to turn towards the submarine that had been lying in wait.

The RAN was well equipped to hunt down the sub. The *Adelaide* had its own over-the-horizon targetting capability on board, two Seahawk helicopters that had only recently come on line into the Navy. The Seahawks could leave the ship's flight deck, and with a sophisticated array of sensors, including sonobuoys, detect and target the underwater enemy. They would keep the submarine busy while the naval convoy and its screen got on with its job of getting to Darwin. As well, the helicopters could strike the boat with their own torpedos, or direct the FFG to fire at the submarine if needed.

Back in Darwin, Nelson was already in the air with his three F-111 companions, heading east to the Gulf of Carpentaria. The enemy ships were close to 1,000 kilometres away, but well within range. The flight was timed so that the F-111s would get to their targets just as the sun was coming up over the Cape York Peninsula, making the adjustment from night to day visuals a headache for the ships' defenders, and therefore a great advantage to the strike aircraft. There was also a bit of cloud around the ships' current position, which might, too, prove to be a help for the pilots. But in these days of electronic warfare, weather and time of day were not necessarily decisive — still, for the F-111s, every element would be exploited.

The plan was to fly high and fast to the area, then descend to just above the waves before entering the threat zone. When they arrived over the gulf, the enemy ships had been pinpointed by the Orion. The force consisted of two destroyers and two escorts, all of which carried guided anti-aircraft missiles. The ships had already begun to move to the north, undoubtedly having picked up notice of the approaching aircraft.

The F-111s were not going to make it easy for the vessels — to fly straight at them from their known base at Darwin would be the most expected route and the simplest of all scenarios for the ships' surface-to-air missiles. Instead, Nelson took the latest position reports from the Orion and manoeuvred to begin his strike from the east, out of the low, dawning sun. The other F-111s fanned out to the north and south to commence their multi-directional attack.

Nelson banked into his first run at one of the destroyers, taking his aircraft down to 50 feet above the calm gulf water and getting it out to 600 knots. As he approached the outer reaches of the ships' missile range of 30 nautical miles, he prepared to fire his Harpoon. Needing some more height to drop the missile away from his aircraft, Nelson pulled up the F-111 slightly before firing. Everything was going to plan.

Now, however, the circumstances differed from that of a real battle. In any genuine confrontation, the million-dollar Harpoon missile would have fallen away from the aircraft, the airflow spinning the weapon's own engine, a puff of smoke telling Nelson that the missile was on its way. The ship it had targetted would have had little chance.

This, however, was not a real battle, but an exercise to determine exactly how Australia's interdependent forces would deal with an intrusion in the continent's north. The individual aircraft, ships and army units did everything they would in battle except drop real bombs or fire loaded missiles and guns..

Today there would be no smoke from destroyed ships; just the pilots' and Australia's military commanders' knowledge that the technology that they had at their hands could deliver their intended powerful punch.

The air-sea battle had been four ships versus four aircraft, and with one imaginary Harpoon having put out the first of the enemy ships, the other three F-111s began their attack runs. Their missiles, too, would have found their mark, but

BEYOND THE HORIZON SENTINEL

Chief Petty Officer Jim O'Connor is one of Australia's most unusual coastguards. Stationed thousands of miles inland, he is a member of a small team manning an outback radar station near Alice Springs in Central Australia from where he can "see" Jumbo jets take off and land in Singapore, foreign fishing trawlers trespassing in northern Australian waters or small aircraft illegally landing in remote northern airfields. O'Connor's remarkable long-range surveillance is made possible by the Jindalee over-the-horizon radar (OTHR) system, designed and built by Australia's own Defence Science and Technology Organization (DSTO).

Australia is faced with the enormous problem of detecting and tracking any maritime or aerial threat over millions of square kilometres of air and sea space along its vulnerable northern coast. The expensive solution would be to use hundreds of conventional land-based radar dishes and a large and costly fleet of airborne radars. Confronting this challenge, Australia's DSTO scientists went back to the principles of shortwave radio transmission.

Due to the earth's curvature, shortwave radio transmissions shoot off into the upper atmosphere where an ionised particle layer, the ionosphere, acts as a "mirror" reflecting the waves back to earth from where they "bounce" back again to the ionosphere. Strategically located relay stations can pick up, amplify and retransmit these radio waves so that they are bounced off the ionosphere several times and travel enormous distances. The Jindalee radar system has adapted this old technique for a new defence radar capability. For most defence, air traffic control and maritime purposes, conventional radar operates in the very high (VHF) or ultra-high (UHF) frequency band; these microwave transmissions penetrate the ionosphere and are not reflected. Jindalee however uses high frequency (HF) or shortwave transmissions for an over-the-horizon radar detection and tracking capacity that has an estimated range of more than 3,000 kilometres — about eight times greater than conventional microwave radars.

In the early experimental phase Australian scientists bounced HF signals off the ionosphere and received a faint echo back from a designated target; in this way the bounced radio pulses "illuminated" an area some thousands of kilometres distant. Sophisticated computer programmes had to be written to distinguish quickly and accurately the reflected signal from the "clutter" of static and echoes from land and sea. Two radar stations, a transmitter and receiver, were then built about 100 kilometres apart, 45 kilometres outside Alice Springs. Later versions of Jindalee's programmes became infinitely more sophisticated. After a two year refurbishment programme costing $38 million, the Alice Springs research station became operational in 1989.

Jindalee's complex receiver antennas can be electronically switched to focus on specific areas within the

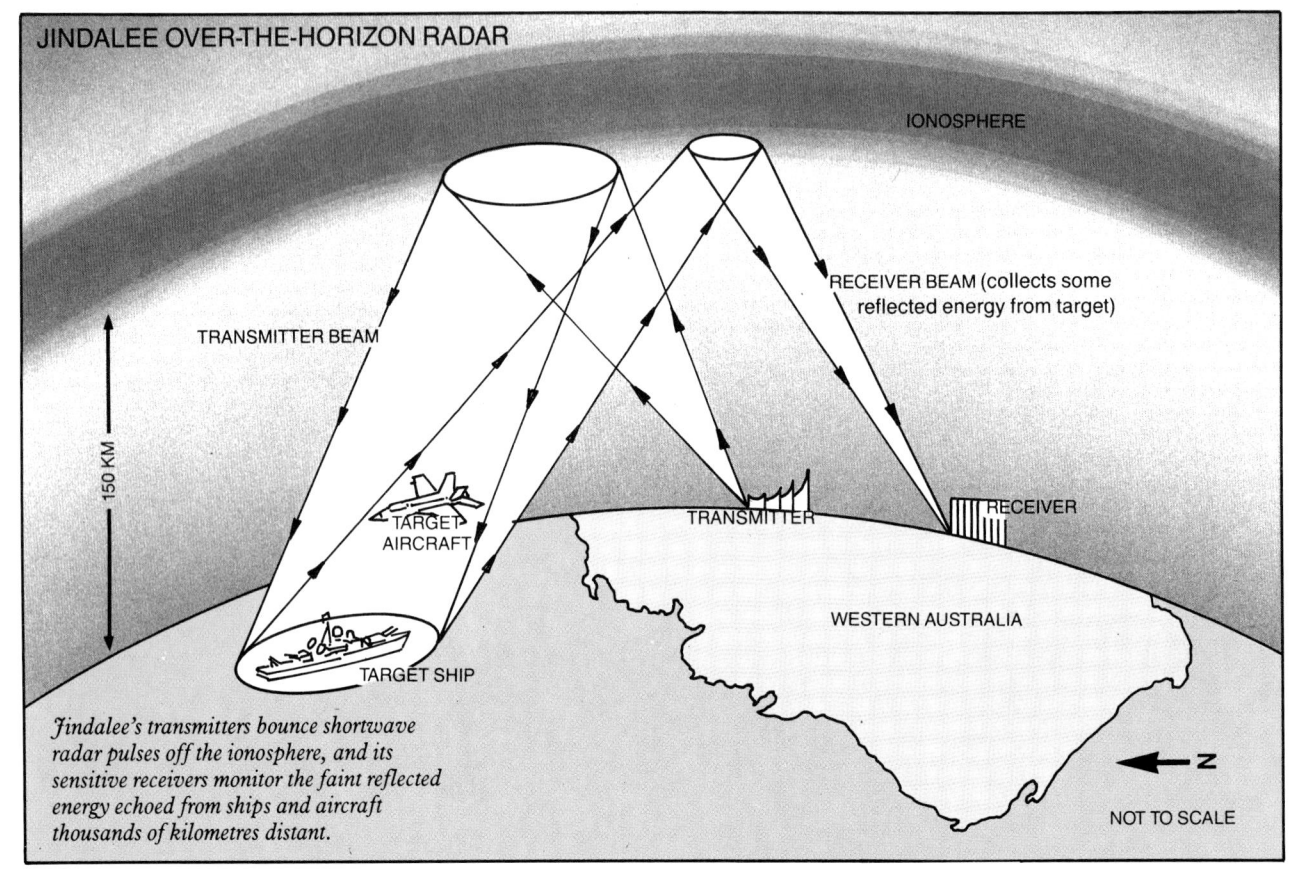

Jindalee's transmitters bounce shortwave radar pulses off the ionosphere, and its sensitive receivers monitor the faint reflected energy echoed from ships and aircraft thousands of kilometres distant.

larger region "illuminated" by the radar beam; to distinguish moving targets it uses a Doppler principle, monitoring a shift in the frequency of the reflected signal. Unlike microwave radars which curve slightly upwards allowing targets to move in under their range, Jindalee beams descend on their targets making them almost impossible to avoid.

At a projected total cost of $500 million, Jindalee will be fully operational by 1996 with two additional receiver/transmitter stations, one in the Charters Towers region of Queensland and another in the Merredin area of Western Australia, between Perth and Kalgoorlie. Directing data to a control centre at Tindal air base in the Northern Territory, the fully operational Jindalee stations will act as a sentry and surveillance system giving blanket radar coverage of the entire northern coastline to detect maritime and air threats.

Jindalee does have some weaknesses. It has a minimum range of 400 kilometres beneath which it cannot bounce waves off the ionosphere and receive them. It is heavily reliant on the stability of the ionosphere. And it cannot detect targets moving tangentially or perpendicularly to its transmission arc. But because Jindalee can give early warning of airborne threats, Australia will not have to depend on big planes carrying complex radars as, for instance, NATO forces in Europe must do. The RAAF will still need the precision of microwave radars to accurately locate incoming aircraft and to vector our F/A-18 fighters to intercept them. This places a greater emphasis on an airborne command and control role, linking in to the national air defence system. The RAAF has now developed a concept for a cheaper and smaller Airborne Warnings Control System (AWACS) that will use new technology, making obsolete the cumbersome radome on existing aircraft. The new system will electronically direct the radar beam through its sweeps using what is known as a phased array system. One advantage is that the antenna can be shaped to the fuselage of the plane used, probably a civilian airliner such as the Boeing 737-400, already in service with airlines in Australia.

Above: An American AWACS plane carries a huge dome. A similar early warning and control system favoured by the RAAF is designed for aircraft like Boeing 737s. Below: Jindalee's receiver station has an array of antennae almost two kilometres long.

With wings swept forward, two F-111s take off on a long-range maritime strike mission. On a pre-planned flight profile, the bombers will enter the threat area at a low level with wings swept back for maximum speed.

having fired from such a distance, Nelson needed to make a high-speed run to check out his flight's damage to the enemy force.

Intending to make every moment of the exercise count, Nelson screamed in at the ships with all his aircraft's defensive devices working overtime. In reality there was every chance that the enemy would still be able to attack. Nelson let go of the F-111's disposable chaff, thin strips of foil to create false returns on enemy radars. In the event of a heat-seeking missile being fired from a ship, his radar homing and warning system would detect such a weapon and he would fire out an infra-red flare to act as a decoy to the missile.

Despite the enemy's potential defence, Nelson's concentration returned instinctively to the job in hand. He was to get his own visuals on the ships; his navigator would use the F-111's new Pave Tack laser illumination and targetting system for a clear picture. With such sophisticated technology combined in any real combat with a selection of deadly weapons, the F-111s would indeed be an awesome opponent, remaining unchallenged in its role as the region's most potent long-range strike aircraft. The ships would have been sitting ducks if Nelson had planned, on this run, to attack again.

The exercise continued nearby. The P-3C moved quickly away from the F-111s' zone, and together with the *Adelaide*, *Derwent* and *Swan* hunted down the submarine. Their battle was soon to come. Down on the ground, the 1st Battalion group quickly surrounded the township of Weipa and burst through the perimeter established by the saboteurs. The enemy was greatly outnumbered and soon surrendered, their country's hopes of gaining a foothold there dashed. Meanwhile, to the west, the force of ships that had acted as a decoy for the Weipa raid now had to consider its options. Would it turn away from the MEZ, or would it proceed and recharge the conflict?

The RAAF and RAN were well equipped to cope with such an invasion, their combat aircraft, submarines and surface warships all capable of halting a conventional attack in mid-air or by sea. The Weipa scenario, however, was undertaken to practise for the kind of incursion that military strategists consider possible within

Australia's geographic and current political circumstances. The scenario was concocted essentially for the sake of establishing a military opponent, but the elements of the invasion were, indeed, indicative of the credible contingencies in Australia's defence environment. The enemy came from the north, through the Indonesian archipelago, and undertook low-intensity attacks upon remote coastal areas. The exercise was an essential part of the ADF's training to achieve a self-reliant defence policy to meet such eventualities.

That policy has evolved gradually since the Second World War. Up to and during the first two years of the war, Australia had traditionally based its defence policy on limited self-sufficiency within alliances based on the British Commonwealth. But after December 1941, the framework of cooperation shifted to the United States of America. In that month, the Japanese drove into the Pacific and South-East Asia and within 10 weeks Japanese forces had begun to attack the Northern Territory city of Darwin. For the first time since its European colonisation, the continent was threatened with invasion.

America, concerned with the security of the Pacific, presented Australia with a closer and more viable friendship in its time of need than could Britain. That relationship continued through the turbulent years after 1945, as the world divided into East and West political blocs, facing up to each other in a Cold War which threatened to boil over at any moment. Within this scenario, Australia still felt vulnerable, its geographic position below the teeming populations of Asia reinforcing the need for powerful allies. The perceived enemy of the time was expansionist Communism in South-East Asia — the enemy behind it, Red China and Russia.

During the 1950s and 1960s, Australian military policy was one of forward defence. Its stance was that if Australia had to fight another war in its region, it would do so as far from its own shores as possible. Strategic reserve forces were stationed throughout South-East Asia, and when crises occurred — in Korea, Malaysia and Vietnam — Australian military units were committed as part of that policy and to honour its role within the western alliance.

Since the withdrawal from Vietnam in 1972, Australian defence strategy has gradually turned inward. The policy of forward defence has been reined in, and now military strategists consider their priority to be the defence of the Australian continent, its territories and surrounds, coupled with the need to contribute to regional stability and prosperity.

Australia's northern neighbourhood is by far the most important strategically. The Indonesian archipelago acts as a buffer between Australia and Asia. As well, the security of passage through the islands is vital for trade, and for the movement of naval shipping between the Indian and Pacific Oceans. All indications are that the most likely direction of any military threat to the Australian continent would be from the north, through the archipelago. An invasion seems unlikely, as it would require massive forces that only major powers could call upon. But much smaller numbers of naval, air and land forces could cause regional instability, disruption of trade, and isolation of remote communities.

The Australian military must be prepared for both contingencies even if large-scale attack is considered improbable within the present political climate. The national defence policy is one of self-reliance within a framework of international alliances and agreements — the emphasis is on self-reliance, not self-sufficiency.

The dilemma in such a policy is that military strategy demands, as a precondition, identification of a threat and, in turn, a potential enemy. But within the region, such an enemy, the Australian Government maintains, does not exist at present. Thus defence strategies must develop a posture that does not offend Australia's neighbours, while at the same time preparing for action.

A top priority is knowledge of goings on in the region. Intelligence and surveillance have become a major component of the ADF's work, early warning of trouble or potential threats to Australia's sovereignty are an essential part of

Ready for a gruelling real-life exercise in northern Queensland, soldiers of Operational Deployment Force disembark from a Hercules. Full-scale wargames keep Australia's defence readiness at high pitch on land, at sea and in the air.

the military's strategy of defence in depth, in which layers of forces are placed out from the continent to meet a designated enemy.

To carry out such a policy, Australia's defence forces must have the ability to operate, either alone or with others, both across the broad continent and within the vast South Pacific and South Asian region. Regular exercises and joint operations are essential features of a small but high-tech military force's stance. Much of the activity now occurs in the north of the country, and there has been an increase in maritime and air-defence capability. Moves to place more equipment and men in the Top End serve as a natural defence mechanism. But they also take into consideration Australia's strategic role within the southeast Asian and southwest Pacific regions. Air bases at Tindal and Darwin in the Northern Territory, and at Derby in Western Australia mean that a range of RAAF aircraft can cover much of northern and western Australia's coast and approaches. They also provide a perfect base to launch those same aircraft, if need be, into South-East Asia. Likewise, the updated airbase at Townsville covers the northeastern approaches to the continent, but it is also within arm's length of Australia's Pacific neighbourhood. As well, the RAN now spends more time in the Pacific Ocean than ever in its recent past. And, all forces were placed on full alert several times in the late 1980s, as Fiji, the New Hebrides and Papua New Guinea faced domestic political flashpoints.

Such deployments are not considered necessarily to be the actions of a region's policeman, though this may be a concern to some of Australia's neighbours. Indonesia is perhaps the most sensitive issue. It is a hugely populated archipelago seen by some observers to have potential political and demographic problems, amongst them a volatile border with Papua New Guinea. Yet by increasing the ADF's northern deployments, does Australia directly threaten Indonesia? And likewise, what might be Indonesia's ambitions and capabilities in future years? The resolution of the question lies in the channels of diplomacy, but they cannot be ignored by Australian defence planners.

Other strategic problems lie waiting on the horizon. The build-up of India's defence capabilities, especially its navy, presages worrisome times ahead. It is not that India is a direct threat to anyone in the Indian Ocean region, but that the balance of power there is gradually moving into India's court, creating fears in Pakistan, Malaysia and Indonesia which in turn may be the catalyst for increased naval concentration by those countries. The concern for Australia about such shifts in the balance of power is that the stability of its approaches and surrounds may be upset.

Among Australia's many blessings of geography is the security that isolation affords. In a report to Australia's Department of Defence which has become the basis of the ADF's new regional stance, Dr Paul Dibb wrote in 1986 that "Australia is one of the most secure countries in the world. It is distant from the main centres of global military confrontation, and it is surrounded by large expanses of water which make it difficult to attack. Australia's neighbours possess only limited capabilities to project military power against it." And yet the world is growing ever smaller, and it remains imperfect and uncertain. If the stability of the region does break down, or if Australian territory is threatened, all three military forces have been equipped to meet the challenges.

VANGUARD OF THE SEAS

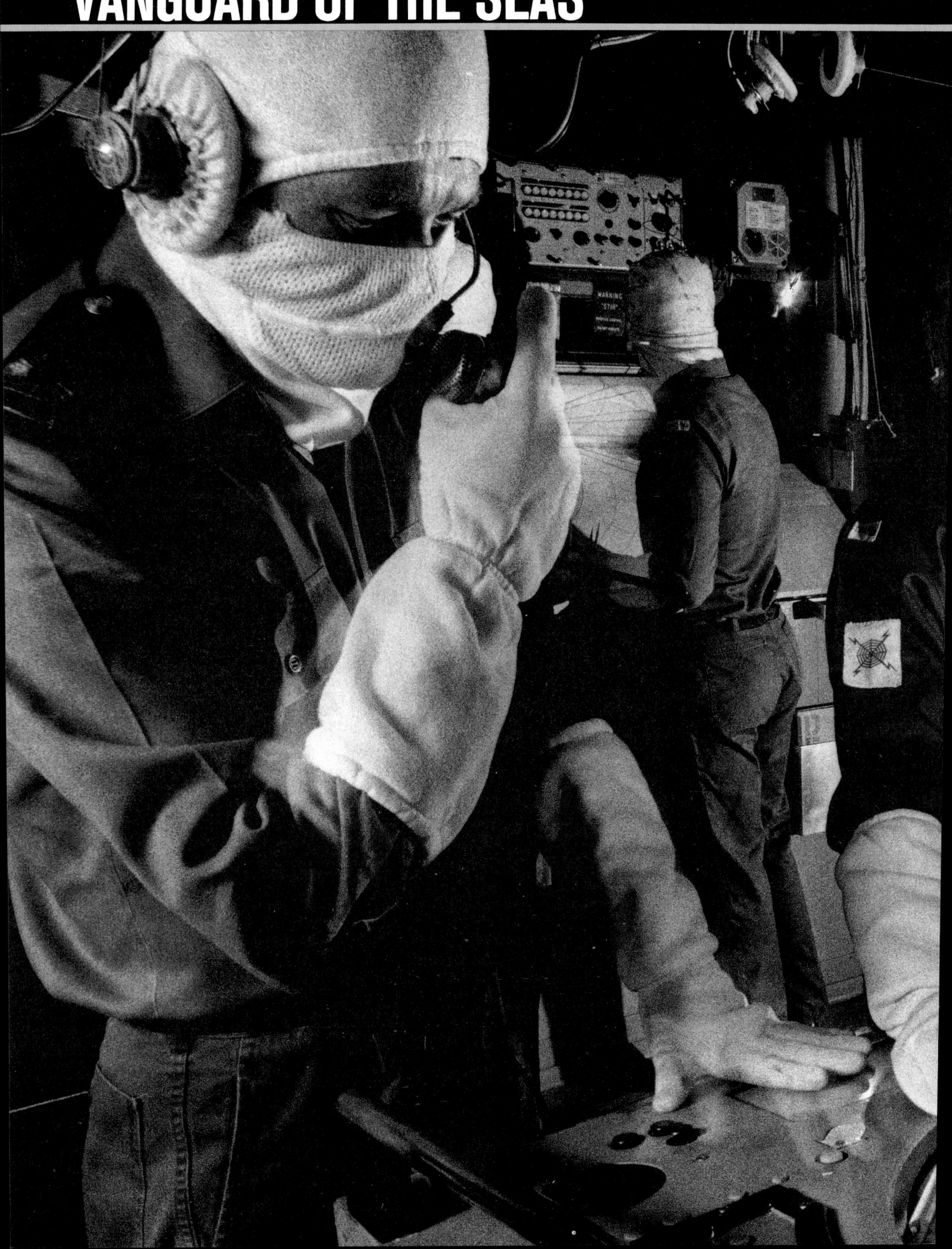

COMPUTERISED SEA WAR

The latest and most spectacular additions to the Australian Navy are four American built FFG-7 Oliver Hazard Perry class guided-missile frigates, HMAS *Adelaide, Canberra, Sydney* and *Darwin*. These vessels are veritable high-technology floating fortresses, well suited for prolonged independent patrol and surveillance operations and the multiple missions of fleet area air defence, surface combat and anti-submarine warfare. Two more such frigates are currently under construction in Australia. The $400 million HMAS *Melbourne*, was launched in May 1989 and will be fully fitted by 1991.

HMAS *Canberra* was commissioned for duty in March 1981. Displacing 3,600 tonnes in a length of 133.5 metres, she is larger than previous ships of her type to serve with the RAN, making accommodation for her 190 man crew less cramped. The high level of automation in all of the *Canberra*'s systems also allows her to be operated with a much reduced complement compared to older classes which cannot match her capability.

Powered by two computer controlled General Electric LM 2,500 gas turbines delivering 40,000 shaft horsepower and driven by a single controllable pitch propeller, the *Canberra* is capable of a maximum speed of 28 knots plus. Her sensor and weapons systems make the *Canberra* a state-of-the-art warship. Air and surface search radars allow her to scan to the horizon and beyond while separate fire control radars accurately lay her weapons on target. Mounted in a dome beneath the bow, the AN/SQS sonar provides passive underwater search and active attack capability against submarine threats.

On *Canberra*'s forward deck an Mk 13 dual purpose missile launcher fires both the Standard anti-air missile, with a 65 nautical mile range, and the over-the-horizon, self-guided, anti-shipping Harpoon missile which can reach out to about 100 kilometres. Amidships is a rapid-firing 76 mm medium range gun as a back-up for air and surface combat. On the rear top deck, the Vulcan Phalanx Close-In-Weapons-System is a six-barrelled gatling rapid-fire gun that fires a stream of 20 mm solid tungsten rounds at the fantastic rate of 3,000 a minute. Controlled by its own radar, the Phalanx provides point protection from air attack and counters low-level Harpoon attacks. Two triple-torpedo tubes, one each side of the ship, fire Mk 46 homing torpedos.

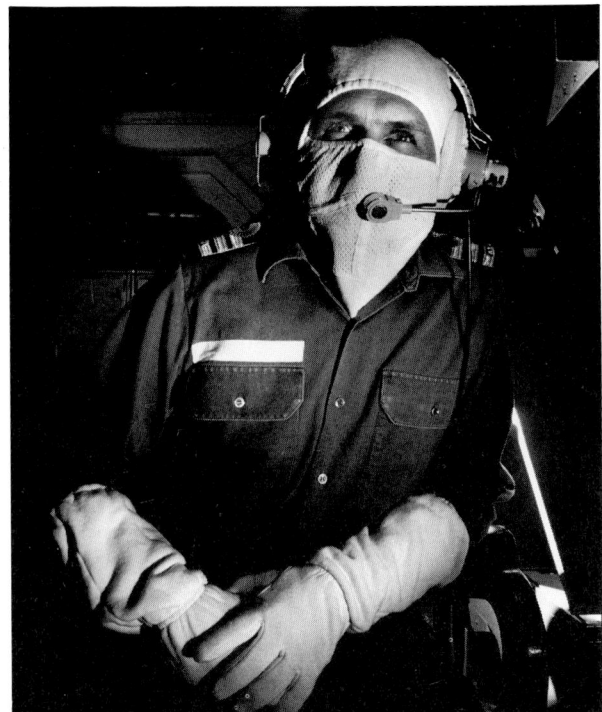

In anti-flash gear and wired to communicate on all tactical circuits, HMAS Canberra's captain, Commander Simon Harrington, commands all the ship's sensor and weapons systems from the operations room.

Right: The second of four FFG-7 guided-missile frigates commissioned in the early 1980s, HMAS Canberra shows her clean lines.

All the ship's weapons and sensor systems are controlled by a powerful digital Naval Combat Data System. At action stations, the *Canberra*'s captain conducts the battle from the operations or "war" room where computers display information from radars, sonars and electrical support systems and rapidly compute fire control solutions for all weapons.

The *Canberra*'s combat capability is expanded with the operation of two Sikorsky S70B Seahawk helicopters, accommodated on a rear flight deck and housed in an aft hangar. Fitted with its own combat computer system, the Seahawk can direct Harpoon weapons fire from its parent ship and other FFGs as well as co-ordinate long-range attacks by RAN destroyers. It can also locate and engage submarine targets at great distances from its parent ship. In this respect the Seahawk goes some way towards redressing the loss of fixed-wing aviation by the Australian Navy.

A Sikorsky Seahawk chopper hovers above Canberra's pitching aft deck, where handlers wait to grab a dropped line and winch the helicopter safely

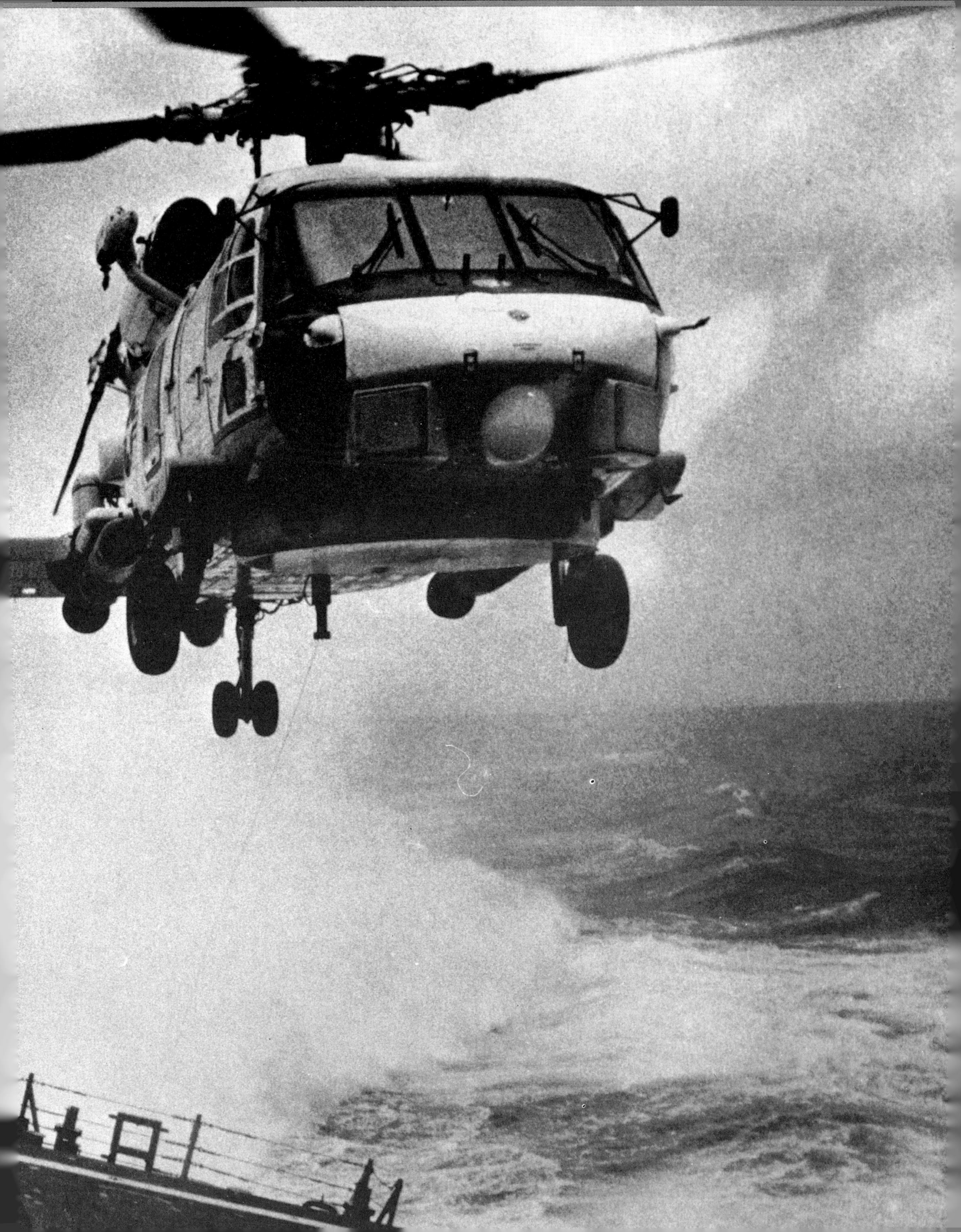

Above: As the last defence against a sea-skimming Harpoon missile attack, the Phalanx Close-In-Weapons System uses its radar (housed in the white dome) to detect missiles at a range of less than five kilometres and direct the six-barrelled Vulcan gun onto the target. The Vulcan gatling gun automatically throws up a barrage of 20 mm tungsten rounds to destroy the incoming missile. Right: A demountable 50 calibre machine-gun on Canberra's lower deck is used to track a hostile airborne target. For lower level contingencies such as policing Australian waters against illegal fishing boats, the machine-gun can fire a warning burst over the vessels' bows.

37

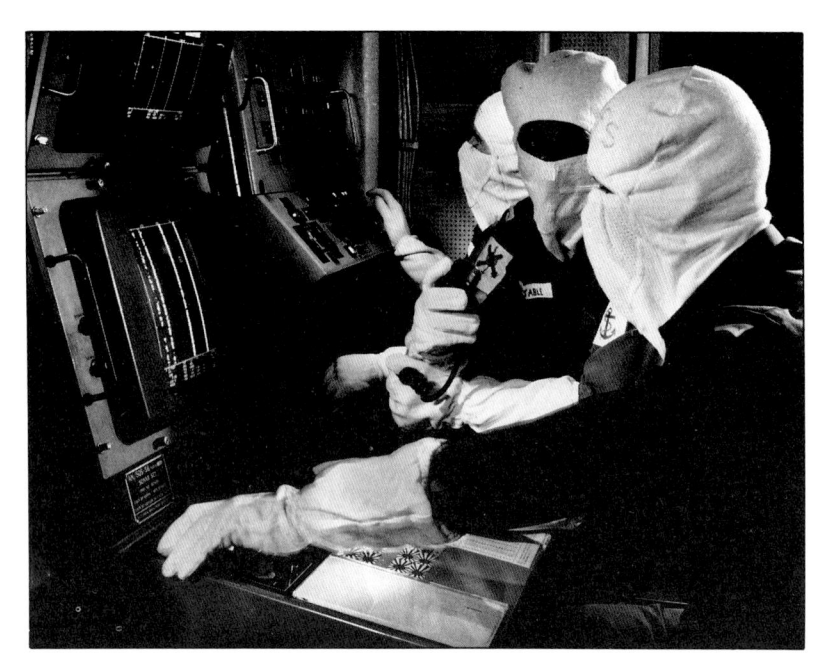

Right: At battle stations in Canberra's sonar room, sonar operators in anti-flash gear locate and track an enemy submarine, coordinating their attack with the weapons controller (background) who selects, launches and guides the torpedos.

A Harpoon anti-shipping cruise missile, whooshing from its launcher on Canberra's forward deck, begins its over-the-horizon trajectory. The missile makes its low-level attack run with its radar locked onto the distant target ship.

A Mark 46 torpedo belches from the triple-tube launcher on Canberra's portside. Remote-control guided through a thin, trailing wire it deploys during its underwater journey, the torpedo uses sonars to lock-on as it nears the target.

Fully automatic and relentlessly accurate in hitting air or surface targets, HMAS Canberra's midship 76mm gun hammers away with a maximum rate *of fire of about 80 rounds a minute. Ejected cartridge cases are still airborne as yet a third round exits the muzzle.*

2
BUILDING A MODERN NAVY

The Royal Australian Navy has grown with the times. Aircraft carriers fulfilled several roles, then guided-missile destroyers made their mark during the Vietnam era. Now, with powerful new frigates and high-tech submarines, the RAN is a major regional maritime force.

The Royal Australian Navy insignia has the Crown over an anchor and seven-point star, enclosed by marine cable.

A sharp warning prompted the cramped control room of HMAS *Oxley* into an urgent response. "Racket dangerous," called the submarine's electronic support measures operator. Three times. It was the message *Oxley*'s men had been trained to expect.

Above them, the dawn was being ushered in by a slight breeze ruffling the sea's surface, but the break of day had little effect upon the men encased below in one of the Royal Australian Navy's six Oberon class submarines. The dim red light of the control room was attended by a tense silence, and the call to action broke the quiet hum of anticipation.

The boat had been "snorting", running at periscope depth with her snort mast raised. The mast was a large air tube protruding into the atmosphere to provide air to her diesel engines and a precious charge to the two batteries which powered the *Oxley* when she was totally submerged. But the submarine's electronic listening device, known as Warner, had detected a strengthening incoming signal from an aircraft radar. It was of such magnitude that the aircraft was now a suspected "enemy". The *Oxley* risked detection of her snort mast above the sea's surface — it had to be taken in.

"Stop snorting. Down all masks."

The *Oxley*'s well-trained crew reacted instantly: the stop-snorting alarm toggle was pressed; the sailor at the mast controls flipped down the brass levers. Aft, in the engine room, the two huge diesels were brought to a crash stop. The sailor on the joystick which controlled the sub's hydroplanes and rudder, the so-called "one man control", pushed it forward in response to his captain's order to dive to a greater depth.

The boat was now quiet, her clamouring engines silent as their dying revolutions sucked a slight vacuum; ears popped as her bow dipped and she sank into the depths, seeking shelter in the thermal gradients and layers of the warm, tropical ocean.

So far the submarine had done well. Lying in wait for a force of approaching ships, she had taken up the strike role in a regular naval exercise designed to simulate combat operations. Both air and maritime elements were involved, so that combined forces could practise offensive and defensive action. The submarine's "enemy" consisted of a high-tech RAAF P-3C Orion surveillance aircraft, equipped with sensitive communication gear and capable of making its own interdiction and strike, and a group of two RAN ships led by a guided-missile frigate. Though carefully staged, the battle epitomised Australia's submarine and anti-submarine forces. Their job was to be trained to readiness in case any such contingencies become reality.

The Orion had first made a possible submarine detection when the boat was 13 kilometres from the aircraft. The pilot then reported the "sinker" to the frigate, 40 kilometres away, before closing in on the submarine to lay sonobuoys for more detailed bearings and to carry out an attack if he gained contact. But now, as the submarine's snort mast was retracted, the radar contact on the boat faded.

The submarine's captain, Lieutenant Commander Rick Shalders, was positioning himself well to attack the ships in the frigate's force which, Intelligence had informed him several hours before, would pass through his patrol area. As they closed, the submarine's long-range passive sonar, called Searcher, informed him that they were now approaching. Still, Shalders cursed mildly to himself as he ordered his boat to a depth of 200 feet and to a speed of eight knots. He had been harassed throughout the night by aircraft radar which had sent him deep several times when his Warner had told him the incoming signals were at dangerous levels. The new airborne threat of the P-3C was an extra hindrance he did not need right now as he planned to alter course to close his quarry. The ships, he knew, would have been warned by the Orion, and he expected them to turn away from the danger he posed.

Shalders was still some distance away from the projected track of the ships, and he had been snorting close to his optimum attack range of between three and five kilometres. Snorting would save using his battery before an attack, and after his weapons struck home he would be able to muster full power to evade the hounds that would certainly be set loose to counter him. Now, however, it seemed certain that the Orion had made a detection, and if so the submarine could be in trouble.

Two hundred feet below the surface, the crew of the now silent submarine listened as the P-3C laid its pattern of sonobuoys around his last known position. The pattern was designed to trap the evading boat within a fence of sound, each buoy probing different depths while the submarine used its bathythermograph, a device capable of measuring water temperature against depth, to find its most favourable level for disadvantaging the sonars.

Such a battle of detection and evasion was a very real contest involving the latest submarine warfare technology and tactics. The sonobuoys' beams of sound could be sent out of a straight line by temperature variations, and in extreme cases of sharp temperature changes at depth, a layer could even deflect such beams altogether.

Skulking below such layers was a proven tactic against ship-mounted sonars, but one not so easy against the pattern of sonobuoys set by the Orion at varying depths that were able to negate some of the distorting effect of different temperatures.

Shalders decided to break away from his position, making several radical course changes to leave sonar-confusing jinks in his wake. He also fired a decoy device that radiated noise similar to a submarine; the ruse most likely would confuse both sonars and their operators. If the *Oxley* could evade the aircraft's buoys, and the helicopter that would no doubt soon join the hunt from the frigate, there was every chance that the main body of ships might take up their previous course, bringing them back on line towards him. He could then resume his prime task — which had always been to sink his "enemy".

His boat, a conventional diesel submersible, was more than capable of doing the job. Although her performance has remained unchanged from the day she was built, she had been progressively updated in her weapons fit enabling her to fire long-range, wire-guided active/passive homing torpedos and a sea-skimming, anti-shipping missile. She was also fitted with six torpedo tubes in her fore-ends, with a mix of weapons up to a maximum of 20, and she was also capable of laying mines.

Like Australia's five other Oberon class submarines, the *Oxley* was a vital weapon in the RAN's arsenal, enabling the Navy to fulfil a vast range of given tasks. After more than 20 years' service, the boats have established themselves as long-term members of the country's fleet strength, and in fact were among the Australian Navy's most powerful units. With them, the RAN was ready and able to control the maritime approaches to Australia, to defend the continent's coastal waters, and, in the end, undertake sustained combat at sea.

Two British Oberon class ocean-going submarines, HMAS Otway and Oxley (top), comprise the RAN's underwater arm in 1927. One of the RAN's six current generation Oberons, HMAS Oxley (middle) was commissioned in 1967 and refitted by 1985 (right) with sonar dome, new attack sonar and weapons control systems and Harpoon missile capability.

The might of such vessels had clearly been established during the Second World War, but Australia was not equipped with submarine capability during that conflict, and after the end of hostilities in 1945, it was still at a loss to remain trained and ready against submarine forces. The gap was filled by the stationing of a Royal Navy submarine squadron at Balmoral in Sydney. However, the advent of the 1960s saw the start of Britain's withdrawal from east of Suez, and with the Royal Navy turning to nuclear propulsion in her submarine arm, the boats' days in Australian waters were numbered.

The RAN regarded a replacement for those ageing "T" and "A" class British boats as a necessity — the Navy was not about to be hampered in practising for what was now considered its prime role, anti-submarine warfare. It took until March 1967 for the first of the British designed and built Oberons to be commissioned for the RAN. They were then the most potent class of conventional submarines available in the world, and were a welcome addition to the Australian Navy's ongoing fleet update that had begun after the end of the Second World War.

Such a lengthy interim, however, did not affect the RAN's other major need after those hostilities. One of the great lessons for naval warfare arising from World War II had been how the use of aircraft had extended the application of sea power. The great battleships, around which fleets had previously been formed, had now been eclipsed by the carrier and its planes. The RAN did not allow the lesson to pass without notice.

Though battle-hardened, the Navy had come out of World War II a largely obsolescent force. It consisted of three ageing cruisers, several destroyer and frigate flotillas, and a myriad of special-purpose vessels constructed or converted to meet particular wartime contingencies. The RAN was simply not equipped to steam into the latter half of the century as a capable, stand-alone naval force.

In mid-1947, the Navy moved ahead with its plans to transfer two British light fleet carriers from the Admiralty to the RAN, accepting the recommendation that the ships be equipped with the aircraft currently operated by the Royal Navy, Hawker Sea Fury fighter bombers and Fairy Firefly ground attack and anti-submarine patrol aircraft.

Of the Majestic class, HMAS *Sydney* was the first to be delivered: she displaced just under 20,000 tonnes at full load, had a flight deck of 213 metres, and could steam at a maximum speed of 24.5 knots. When she arrived in Australia in May 1949, on board was the 20th Carrier Air Group consisting of 805 Squadron flying Sea Fury aircraft, and 816 Squadron flying Firefly aircraft. Each squadron operated 12 aircraft, although the ship was capable of working a maximum of 34 similar planes. Her ship's company was a mixture of Royal Navy and RAN personnel, time having militated against fully training sufficient numbers of Australian seamen — the first course of RAN aircrew had entered training at RAAF Point Cook, on Port Phillip Bay in Victoria, just two-and-a-half years before the *Sydney*'s arrival in home waters. And now, too, the intended force of two carriers and three air groups required the establishment of a major training and support base ashore, HMAS *Albatross* at Nowra on the south coast of NSW, and a secondary support base at Schofields in the outer west of Sydney.

The aircraft carrier returned to Britain to take on another two front-line squadrons, No. 808 Sea Furies, and No. 817 Fireflies, together constituting the 21st Carrier Air Group. Then in 1951, the *Sydney* commenced the first of her two tours of duty with the UN naval forces off Korea. She went on patrol, escorted by the destroyer HMAS *Tobruk*, in early October.

The call to action came on October 5 when she was steaming easily in the calm waters of the Yellow Sea. For many of the young Australian pilots, who had no doubt thrilled to the exploits of Spitfires over Britain in World War II, this would be their first taste of combat. The Sea Furies were about to go to war, joining US airforce ground-attack aircraft against enemy troop concentrations around the 38th

During trials off the coast of Scotland in 1949, aircraft are secured on the slippery, rain-washed flight deck of HMAS Sydney, the RAN's new aircraft carrier. On Sydney's first tour of duty in the Korean war in 1951, her aircraft flew 2,366 sorties against enemy supply lines and troop positions.

parallel, and the young Australian pilots were to fully experience this most difficult and demanding form of aviation.

The flight deck of a carrier operating aircraft was then, and still is, one of the most dangerous and most exciting places on earth. The Commonwealth naval flyers nervously readied themselves as their planes were marshalled onto the deck catapult. Armed with eight 60 lb explosive rockets, each of four 20 mm cannon loaded with 150 rounds, and carrying as well a 45-gallon fuel drop-tank slung below each wing, Sea Fury Fighter Bomber K141 was manoeuvred into takeoff position, the last of four in No. 52 Flight. Sub Lieutenant Ian Macdonald, in the pilot's seat, felt a slight jerk as the catapult and aircraft were tensioned, to prevent a premature exit, by a holdback wire connected below the tail of the aircraft. Kept secure by a frangible ring, the rig was strong enough to restrain K141 against the full power of its engine, but designed to fail against the thrust of the catapult.

All eyes turned to K141 as her 21-year-old pilot finally satisfied himself that his aircraft was ready: temperatures and pressures correct, control surfaces movement full and free. It was time to go. Macdonald settled himself into his seat, and advanced the throttle to full power, his right hand braced on the control column. With the throttle locked, and his head back firmly on the seat headrest, the young flyer took a final glance at the engine instruments then raised his left hand in salute to the Flight Deck Officer — all was well with K141.

The FDO looked straight ahead, choosing the right moment for a launch into the 30-knot relative wind tugging its way down the *Sydney's* flight deck; it was best on a rising bow. Suddenly the flag dropped, and the catapult officer, crouched in his howdah extending above the deck, stabbed a button. Thud!

No matter how many times Macdonald had experienced this moment in training, he was never really ready for the rush — the cat-shot from a carrier. The linked forces of the catapult and the 2,460 BHP Bristol Centaurus engine driving a five-bladed propeller hurled K141 down the track at an acceleration of 3.86 horizontal G, and after a mere 1.01 seconds on a takeoff run of less than 36 metres, K141 departed the ship at a speed faster than 100 knots. Wheels up, flaps up, jink to the right to clear the ship's deck of the aircraft's slipstream, eyes searching for the rest of 52 Flight; Ian Macdonald was airborne.

Not long after, 52 Flight rolled into a 60-degree dive at 350 knots, heading for its target in the Kojo region near the coast. Enemy troops, dug in along a ridge, were laying down fire on American-led guerillas attempting to evacuate the area. The Sea Furies blasted the enemy troops with rockets, fulfilling the navy's task, then returned safely to their carrier.

It had been a clean attack, but not all such raids came back unharmed. The enemy had strong anti-aircraft artillery and consistently peppered the air with heavy small-arms fire. Whether on ground attack or gunnery-spotting duties, the threat of being shot out of the air and captured on land was a new challenge for the men of the RAN.

The *Sydney*, like other carriers in the campaign, did not show its muscle without some loss. Three Australian pilots were killed from ground fire, while seven others were shot down but lived. Many planes were damaged, even so they were courageously returned to their carrier's deck. She served with great distinction, creating records for her class in the numbers of sorties flown in one day. But she was just one of nine Australian ships which gained a reputation there that was second to none for determined resourcefulness and efficiency in operations.

The naval air power Macdonald and his mates had exerted was the RAN's most significant development in its history since its official birth in 1911. In this post World War II era, rapid strides were taking place in the development of carrier-borne aircraft and the ships to operate them. The *Sydney*'s planes were piston-engine driven and she operated them from a straight deck fitted with aircraft barriers and a hydraulic catapult. A batsman was employed to provide advisory signals to each aircraft during its landing approach — damage to and even loss of planes was not uncommon.

Faster and heavier jet and prop-jet driven aircraft were about to come into service, and Britain's naval dockyards, currently working on Australia's other carrier, HMAS *Melbourne*, rose to the challenge. Angled decks, allowing an unimpeded operating area, the steam catapult, allowing for the launch of heavier aircraft, and mirror landing sights, making precise flight path information available to pilots on their approach to the deck, were all incorporated, together with larger aircraft lifts, into the new *Melbourne*. The lengthy modernisation meant that she missed the action off Korea, her commissioning not occurring until October 1955.

The *Melbourne* became the flagship of the Australian fleet — the cruel fate of progress had quickly caught up with the *Sydney*, who had shown her mettle on the Korean conflict but was now outmoded to the point that a proposal to update her to modern operational standards was cancelled in 1955 and she carried on in a training role until paid off temporarily in 1958. The *Melbourne*'s aircraft complement consisted of Sea Venom all-weather jet fighters of 808 Squadron and turbo-prop Gannet anti-submarine patrol and reconnaissance aircraft of 816 and 817 Squadrons. She also carried two Sycamore helicopters for search and rescue. Her aircraft complement was modernised in 1963 with the addition of Wessex anti-submarine helicopters, and later her fixed-wing elements were replaced by American Skyhawk fighter bombers and Tracker anti-submarine patrol planes. Finally, the Sea King helicopter replaced the Wessex.

Notwithstanding the great importance of its air arm, the RAN was not entirely preoccupied by it after the Second World War. Australia's

In 1977, the RAN's flagship HMAS Melbourne steams into Sydney Harbour, displaying her Skyhawk fighters, Tracker planes and Sea King helicopters. Despite tragic collisions with HMAS Voyager in February 1964 and USS Frank E Evans in June 1969, Melbourne served the Navy magnificently for 30 years until she was sold for scrap in 1985.

escort surface forces were also in great need of an update. Two destroyers of the British Battle class, the *Anzac* and *Tobruk*, had been laid down in 1946, to be followed three years later by two further British-origin destroyers, the Daring class ships *Voyager* and *Vendetta*. A third Daring destroyer, the *Vampire*, was completed in 1959. The Battles and Darings were powerful ships mounting six 4.5 inch guns as main armament, and they were progressively modernised in their anti-submarine capabilities.

The Australian fleet that was now emerging in the middle of the century was primarily a force dedicated to countering the threat of submarine attack. Both world wars had proved the stark vulnerability of maritime nations — and Australia is nothing if not a maritime nation — in the face of concerted submarine operations.

To further strengthen the RAN's capabilities in this role, four wartime destroyers of the "Q" class, HMAS *Quadrant*, *Queenborough*, *Quiberon* and *Quickmatch*, were taken in hand in the early to mid 1950s for conversion to a special new class of anti-submarine frigates. And a completely new class was also under consideration. These ships, once again based on a British design known as the River class, ran to a line of six vessels completed in three groups beginning in 1961.

It was a new era for the RAN, embracing missile technology, although the first two, the *Parramatta* and *Yarra*, were not immediately fitted but were later updated. The next two, the *Stuart* and the *Derwent*, entered service in 1963 and 1964 respectively, and were fitted with the Seacat anti-air point defence and an Australian designed anti-submarine missile system known as Ikara. In recognition of their additional capabilities, these two ships were reclassed destroyer escorts. The final two ships of the class, the *Swan* and the *Torrens*, were another departure again, constructed to a modified British Leander class design and additionally equipped as flotilla leaders. They had extra accommodation for a senior officer to embark with a small staff to provide greater command and control when the Navy's ships worked together as an organic group.

Progressive updates saw all these ships receive essentially the same weapons fit: one twin 4.5-inch gun mounting; the Seacat AA missile; the Ikara AS missile; one Limbo ahead-thrown AS mortar; type 177 and 170 sonars; a depth finder; and under-water telephone. The mortar was later replaced by six ship-launched torpedo tubes in five of the ships, while the *Yarra* was fitted with the Australian-designed medium range sonar, the Mulloka.

The 20 years after the end of World War II thus saw an almost complete replacement of old hull stock in the RAN with a progressive increase in its operational capability; it was a considerable investment to secure Australia's trade in its region, and to project military power elsewhere when necessary.

During that time, much had happened politically and strategically which affected how this new maritime force would be used. The Malayan Emergency had been declared in June 1948, and just two years later the Korean War broke out, devastating that peninsula for three years. On September 1, 1951, Australia joined with the United States and New Zealand in the ANZUS pact, and three years later the same three nations became signatories to the South-East Asian Treaty Organisation, SEATO, which also included Britain, France, Pakistan, Thailand and the Philippines. A further link to the southwestern extremity of South-East Asia was provided by another treaty, ANZAM, which saw the four British Commonwealth nations, Britain, Malaya, New Zealand and Australia, subscribe to an agreement to provide defence in the southwest Pacific including the volatile Malayan peninsula.

Australia's prevailing military philosophy was very much one of forward defence; the rim of the western Pacific was perceived by the Menzies Government throughout the 1950s as a series of stepping stones down which the communist monolith of China and her allies could advance to directly threaten the Commonwealth. Such a posture saw the establishment of the Strategic Reserve, a union of ships patrolling the Malayan region's waters.

Australia's contribution was two destroyers or frigates on permanent deployment, an annual visit by an aircraft carrier, the *Melbourne*, with other ships to be provided when and as required in emergencies. The sister destroyers *Arunta* and *Warramunga*, both of whom had seen service during World War II, were the first two RAN ships to take up duty with the Strategic Reserve in July 1955.

It was the height of the Malayan Emergency, and as communist insurgents threatened the stability of the Malayan peninsula, British Commonwealth units encompassing land, air and sea forces were brought into action to quell the uprisings. Australia was represented in all areas during the 12-year Emergency, and four RAN ships, the HMAS *Anzac, Tobruk, Quickmatch* and *Queenborough* were called on two occasions to bombard terrorist positions in 1956 and 1957.

A tour of duty for the destroyers and frigates committed to the Strategic Reserve saw them on station based upon Singapore for up to a year. Throughout their tour, the ships were on the move covering an area from Japan in the north, the Philippines in the east and the Indonesian archipelago in the south. Regular exercises were conducted with ships and aircraft from other nations of the ANZAM Treaty and SEATO, and continuous port visits throughout the region made Australia's sailors a familiar sight in the Asian nations of the Pacific rim.

The deployment of the aircraft carrier *Melbourne* normally coincided with large-scale maritime exercises held between all major members of SEATO. The countries involved committed major units to the operations and on average at least three aircraft carriers took part in concocted battles between "Blue" and "Orange" forces ranging through the waters of the Philippine and South China Seas and lasting between three weeks and a month. Ships sailed in mock combat against each other: carriers sent their fighters to neutralise other carriers; destroyer escorts pumped exercise artillery at designated "enemy"; while battle squadrons performed intricate manoeuvres to outwit each other in the militarily important South-East Asian waters.

The Strategic Reserve commitment was important for the RAN because it enabled the Australian ships to conduct exercises with larger concentrations of vessels than they could mount on their own. The exercises developed considerable skills in maritime warfare among the participants and undoubtedly gave pause to any nation considering overt military action against the pact members.

Stress within the South-East Asian region continued, and in 1962 Australia committed a small force of army instructors to aid South Vietnam, which had been declared a "protocol" state of SEATO. The following year, Malaysia proclaimed itself a newly federated state, but Indonesia interpreted the declaration as a "neo-colonialist plot" aimed directly as an aggravation to her interests. Indonesia's President, Dr Sukarno, announced a policy of "Confrontation" against the new state, and in turn Australia pledged military assistance in the event of Indonesia aiding communist insurgents within Malaysia.

The level of tension between the two nations remained high, and warships of the Strategic Reserve were engaged in patrol and escort duty in waters separating the countries. In April 1964, the Australian ships *Parramatta* and *Yarra* steamed the Straits of Malacca and close-by waters with orders to intercept both surface and sub-surface intruders. But the Indonesian Government was not deterred by the resolve of the ANZAM partners, and escalated its military activity throughout the year. The "Confrontation" rapidly became a major commitment for the RAN with a sharp increase in the tempo of maritime operations necessary to combat clandestine traffic in the area.

"The task became one of patrolling the Malaysian coastline to intercept a trickle of nervous and bewildered Indonesians in small boats, armed with rifles, a few hand grenades and a sackful of plastic explosive," recalled Lieutenant K. "Gus" Murray, who commanded

A Seacat anti-air missile screams from its launcher on destroyer escort HMAS Derwent. By the early 1970s, Derwent and her five sister frigates were armed with Seacats and Ikara torpedo-carrying anti-submarine missiles.

Two Vietnam war veterans still in service after major weapons and systems updates, guided-missile destroyers HMAS Brisbane (41) and HMAS Hobart (39) battle heavy weather in 1985.

During exercises in 1966, curious crew members of the RAN's new guided-missile destroyer HMAS Perth watch preparations for the launch of a Tartar anti-air missile.

the minesweeper *Teal*. "I formed a distinct impression that they had guns pointing at them at both ends of their short voyage."

The patrolling, however, became monotonous. The seas were mostly dead calm. Often radar contacts that led to action stations turned out to be floating debris. Mail, meals and movies became high priorities and extra time off duty when in harbour was always granted.

Operationally there was little of interest. But on December 13, 1964, HMAS *Teal* was fired upon by an unidentified vessel which then let slip for Indonesian waters. Lieutenant Murray responded without equivocation, returning the fire with light weapons and taking chase. The *Teal* successfully apprehended the boat and arrested its occupants. "The usual Indonesian reaction was immediate and, apparently, enthusiastic surrender," Murray recalled. He was later awarded the Distinguished Service Cross for his duty in the region.

While the *Teal* was busy dealing with such game smallfry, Australia's naval commanders were considering important new advances in technology for their fleet. The world's navies were fast entering the missile era, and it became apparent that the RAN's surface forces lacked area air-defence capability. Urgent steps were now taken to replace the ageing Australian gun-equipped Daring class destroyers.

Fortunately a fine class of guided-missile equipped destroyers was emerging from US dockyards at the time the RAN's search began. At 4,500 tonnes full load within a length of 437 feet, the Charles F. Adams class was much bigger than any previous destroyer in Australian service. And, equipped with two rapid-fire 5-inch guns, a Tartar anti-air missile system, the Ikara anti-submarine missile and six anti-submarine torpedo tubes, the Charles F. Adams ships represented a distinct leap in the RAN's firepower. Australia purchased three of the ships, HMASs *Brisbane*, *Hobart* and *Perth*. Importantly, they represented the first time that a source other than Britain had been considered to provide a major Australian naval unit.

Their commissioning between 1965 and 1967 was timely, as they were shortly to see active service alongside American vessels off the coast of Vietnam, and would easily be able to integrate within the US supply organisation.

The Vietnam conflict topped what had become a deep Australian involvement in the commitment to stabilise the Asian region. A battalion and SAS squadron were in Borneo, 11 RAN ships operated within the South-East Asian area, and now a major Australian involvement in Vietnam commenced with the announcement on April 29, 1965, that Australian ground forces would be used in battalion strength for the defence of South Vietnam.

HMAS *Sydney* sailed from the city of its own name on May 27, 1965, for Vung Tau, conveying the first Australian Army combat battalion to South Vietnam. Her first voyage was typical of the 23 trips she was to make as a fast transport. Loaded with personnel, military equipment, and cargo, the *Sydney* plied the 9,000-kilometre trip in 13 days. She was always accompanied by a destroyer escort and, when refuelling en route, the fleet tanker HMAS *Supply*. Affectionately known as the "Vung Tau Ferry", her duty was not necessarily a glamorous one, but vital nonetheless.

The logistical support given by the *Sydney* was just one of the roles played by the RAN in Vietnam. The Navy's clearance divers worked under very different circumstances, an RAN helicopter unit took part in intensive ground-support operations, and four destroyers forged a vital part in the US Navy's activities off the Vietnam coast.

The RAN's clearance divers were the first Australian naval men to become actively involved in Vietnam. Their initial job was in the port of Vung Tau where they were given the dirty and gruelling task of inspecting the hulls, rudders, anchors and cables of ships using the harbour to feed the land battle. The divers were looking for mines, and in almost 7,500 hull searches they came across and removed several sabotage devices. Later, the divers were also employed in riverine operations, often in Viet Cong held areas, clearing logs, blowing up enemy tunnels and bunkers, and supervising ordnance disposal and salvage.

While some Australians were active below the surface of Vietnam's waters, another naval unit, a helicopter flight and groundcrew, spent the war in the air, seconded to a US Army unit, the 135th Assault Helicopter Company, in late 1967. Known officially as the RAN Helicopter Flight, Vietnam, the Australian sailors cum soldiers sardonically termed their formation an Experimental Military Unit, and called themselves the "Emus". But far from being flightless birds, the naval aviators took part in many troop insertions, gunship supports, and medical evacuations in support of Australian, US, Thai and Vietnamese soldiers. Their job was always dangerous, and they suffered the heaviest casualties of any RAN unit in Vietnam, losing five flyers, and sustaining many injuries and damaged aircraft.

In a more traditional role, in the South China Sea and the Gulf of Tonkin the destroyers of the Australian Navy took part in hostilities against the Viet Cong and North Vietnamese regular army. Attached to the Naval Gunfire Support Unit of the US Seventh Fleet, the new destroyers *Hobart*, *Brisbane* and *Perth* spent their tours "on the gunline" supporting ground troops fighting close enough to the coast to call for artillery support from ships cruising nearby. Each vessel tracked in an oval-shaped course at least four kilometres offshore, and when fighting necessitated, a spotter on land would call in the ship's fire.

The RAN's first shot in anger in Vietnam came on March 31, 1967, when the *Hobart*, still fresh from its builders, bombarded Viet Cong concentrations in Quang Nai province. And from them on, during three, six-month tours of duty in four-and-a-half years, the *Hobart* saw gunline action both north and south of the Demilitarised Zone and took part in vital naval missions to interdict enemy maritime traffic.

Operations during the *Hobart*'s second deployment, from March to October 1968, were typical of gunline action. She bombarded oil depots, bridges, ammunition stores, and other strategic sites, and in return she faced fire from coastal defence batteries.

In late May, *Hobart* was on the gunline 25 kilo-

Loaded with army road transports, HMAS Sydney refuels from the fleet tanker HMAS Supply with destroyer HMAS Duchess as escort en route to Vietnam in 1965. Dubbed the "Vung Tau Ferry", Sydney completed 23 voyages to Vietnam carrying troops, vehicles, artillery pieces and aircraft.

metres southeast of Da Nang. On the afternoon of the 20th she destroyed 30 structures and 12 bunkers as well as sinking a sampan in a Viet Cong assembly area. Two days later she fired on enemy positions and flushed out 17 Viet Cong who were then captured. And on May 26 she moved north to Hue and from off Cap Lay she shelled and destroyed an active artillery site.

"*Hobart*'s accuracy was excellent and the reaction time was exceedingly rapid," the Commanding General of the American Division signalled later. "A troop commander stated that it was the best artillery support he had ever had. It was the best naval gunfire the air spotter had ever observed. Well done."

June 1968 was a busy month for the Australian destroyer. On the 14th, she and an American ship were given the task of blowing up three highway bridges northwest and inland of Cap Lay, but before she had a chance to turn into the firing course both ships came under bombardment from a six-gun coastal battery. As soon as the gun flashes were reported by spotter aircraft, the ships altered course just moments before the first five rounds splashed into the sea only 50 metres off *Hobart*'s port bow. Further rounds followed, but the destroyer left them behind. Then she turned and silenced at least one of the guns and marked the other sites with smoke shells for US Phantom aircraft to hit. It had been a close call — close enough to leave two pieces of shrapnel on *Hobart*'s upper deck.

Three days later the destroyer was on patrol when it suffered an unfortunate accidental night attack by an American jet fighter which fired three missiles into the Australian ship, killing two sailors, wounding several others and causing serious damage. The destroyer retired to Subic Bay in the Philippines, and her place was taken by the Daring class ship *Vendetta*, whose hasty departure for the war zone, complicated by the problem of supplying her with an odd range of main armament ammunition, demonstrated an admirable flexibility within a small navy operating diversely sourced ships.

The *Hobart* went on to serve another tour of

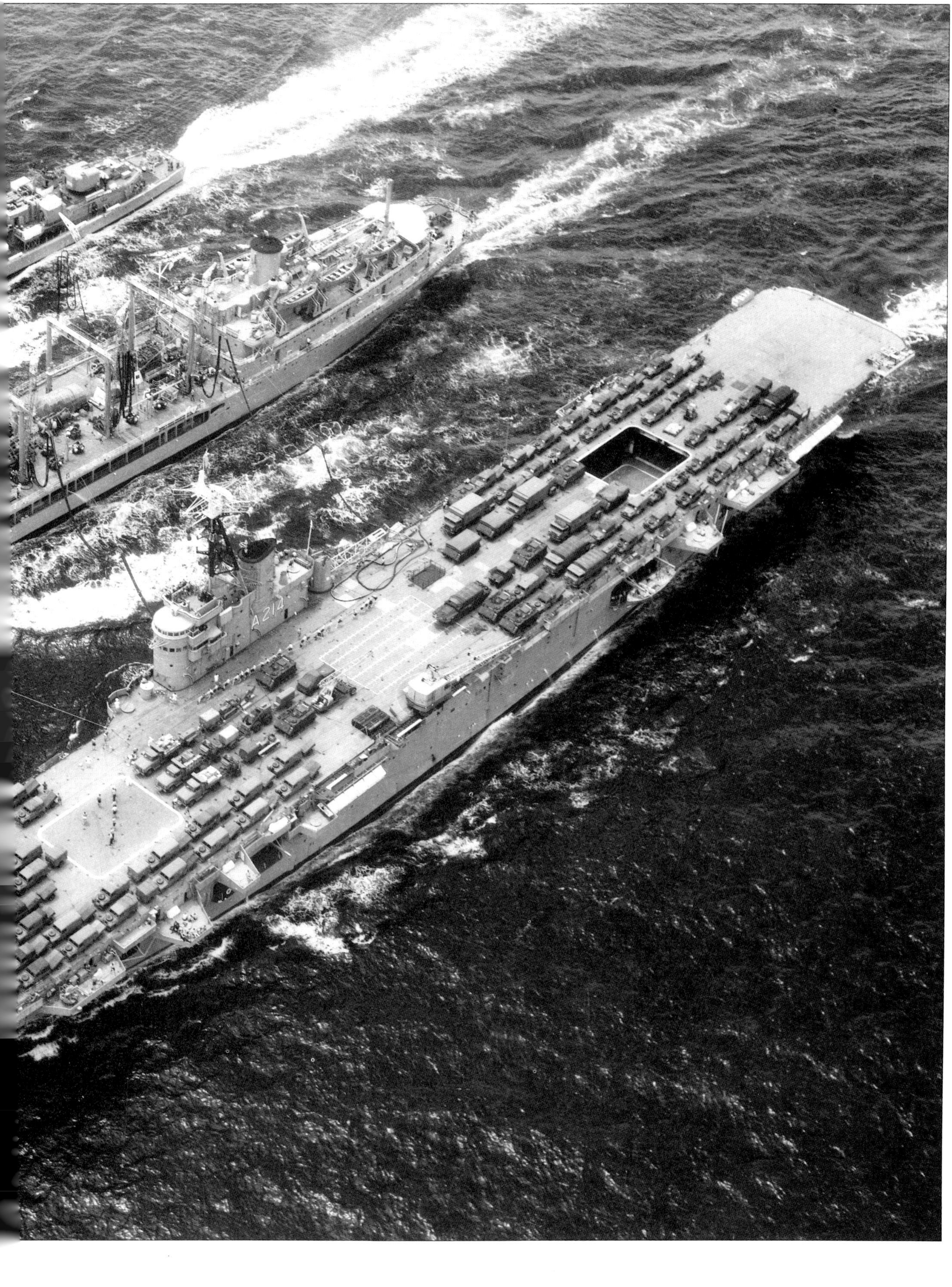
A214

Crew members examine the damage to HMAS Hobart, the accidental victim of a US jet fighter attack while she was patrolling off Vietnam on June 17, 1967.

duty, and like it HMAS *Perth* undertook three deployments while the *Brisbane* went twice. Apart from the missile attack, their war was much as *Hobart* saw it. All three ships distinguished themselves in the Vietnam war zone, and although that was the last combat they saw, the three guided-missile destroyers still remained vital and powerful units in the RAN. Their hulls were more than 20 years old, but they have been progressively provided with a weapon and combat system update that has maintained their value for many years to come.

Between 1974 and 1979, they received a new naval combat data system, updated 5-inch mountings and radars, and had their Tartar missile systems replaced by Standard missiles. A second modernisation began in 1985, which included the capability to fire Harpoon surface-to-surface missiles.

While these established forces of the RAN were heavily committed in the latter half of the 1960s, two other classes of vessels began to appear on Australia's fleet list: the submarines and the patrol boats. Both were of equal importance to the nation's sea defences.

Six Oberon class submarines were commissioned during an 11-year period from 1967: the *Oxley, Ovens, Onslow, Otway, Otama* and *Orion*. Although originally purchased mainly to provide training for the surface navy, as well as for the maritime wing of the RAAF, the boats have been progressively updated to become arguably the most powerful units in the RAN. Their hulls have remained by current standards outmoded, making for stringent living standards for crews, and a constant vigilance by engineers to maintain the level of quietness essential to modern submarine operations. But the boats are adapted to take a fearsome array of weapons. The Oberon's capability to fire the long-range, wire-guided Mark 48 torpedo and the sub Harpoon anti-ship, sea-skimming missile puts Australia at the forefront of conventional submarine operations.

Since the Oberons were first commissioned, many advances have been made in the design and operation of submarines. To maintain the RAN's capability in this most valuable arm of the fleet, six Swedish-designed and Australian-built conventional Kockums 471 class submarines are due to come into service from the mid-1990s. The 471s will feature a hydrodynamically efficient teardrop hull containing provision for the future fit of air-dependent propulsion. An American-designed combat data system will control all sensors, radio and weapons, which will remain the deadly mix of the Mark 48 torpedo, the sub Harpoon, and mines. They will be a powerful addition to the Australian Navy, vastly enhancing its conventional submarine fleet's capability to keep watch on the two major oceans east and west of the continent and the archipelagos of the northern approaches.

Australia has a coastline stretching for more than 36,000 kilometres, much of it remote and deserted, vulnerable to illegal entry and malevolent activities. The exclusive economic zone runs to millions of square kilometres of ocean. The patrolling of that area is an important part of the Navy's defence role, but even as late as the 1960s Australia had little in the way of maritime assets that could suitably do the job. Along with this gap in its fleet, the RAN found itself without any class of vessel capable of giving command experience to junior seamen officers. Accordingly, 20 Attack class boats were built between late 1967 and early 1969, five of them later becoming part of the Papua New Guinea military services.

The 149-tonne patrol boats were 32.6 metres long, and powered by two 16-cylinder diesels they could make more than 20 knots. But they were small and uncomfortable in any kind of seaway, and were severely limited by weather. They were only lightly armed, carrying a 40 mm Bofors, two 50 mm calibre machine-guns, and a launcher for illuminating flares. Still, they were sufficient for their patrolling tasks, watching out for illegal entrants and fishermen, and contributing an extended search and rescue capability without tying up other more expensive naval units in such domestic duties.

The Attack boats were popular with their crews and did sterling service throughout their careers, but a heavier and faster craft was needed to fulfil the Navy's expanding patrol duties. And so, a class based upon a Brooke Marine design was progressively commissioned from March 1980. The first, HMAS *Fremantle*, was built in England and gave its name to the class, but the remaining 14 were constructed in Cairns in North Queensland. At 30 knots they were much faster than their predecessors, they

Fremantle class patrol boat HMAS Dubbo slices through the water at top speed in an exercise off the Queensland patrol-boat base HMAS Cairns. The RAN's 16 Fremantle vessels are faster and bigger than the previous Attack class.

were also 80 tonnes heavier, and offered a much higher standard of habitability and considerably extended time on patrol, thus they were able to secure Australia's frontiers more effectively.

By necessity that service, as any navy presuming a blue-water capability, must be able to keep its combat vessels in action, and therefore operate fleet support and auxiliary craft. Over the years the RAN has had several such vessels, and amongst the most enduring was the fleet oiler, *Supply*. For almost 25 years she was practically a fixture on the horizon for all the RAN's ships, offering fuel, limited supplies of other stores and water, and giving them a largely unsung service. The *Supply* went out of commission in 1985 and was replaced by the *Success*, which was constructed at Cockatoo dockyard in Sydney to a French design modified to meet Australian conditions. The *Success* was able to provide both marine and aviation fuels, dry and victualling stores, as well as limited ammunition replenishment.

Two other ships round out the heavy auxiliaries to the fleet, the *Stalwart* and the *Jervis Bay*. The *Stalwart*, currently the RAN's flagship, is a destroyer tender capable of offering full engineering to destroyers and frigates at remote anchorages. She is virtually a floating workshop offering support in all the black trades, electronics and electrics. The *Jervis Bay*, originally a vehicular passenger ferry, serves as the Navy's training ship, particularly in regard to junior officer training. However, in times of stress or disaster, her capacious vehicular deck and good speed make her a valuable army support and relief vessel.

The need to provide a heavy lift capability in support of the army is met by a landing ship, the *Tobruk*, and six heavy landing craft, two of which are employed in survey work, with three in reserve and one active. The *Tobruk*, a modified British Sir Bedivere class built at Newcastle, NSW, and commissioned in 1981, is an unpretty vessel but probably the most versatile ship in the RAN. Her task is primarily to support the army in forward areas. To do so she has the capability to operate helicopters, landing craft and amphibians, and she can also carry two ship-side mounted pontoons for ship-to-shore movement of troops, vehicles, and other stores. She is also capable of beaching and discharging cargo directly onto shore through

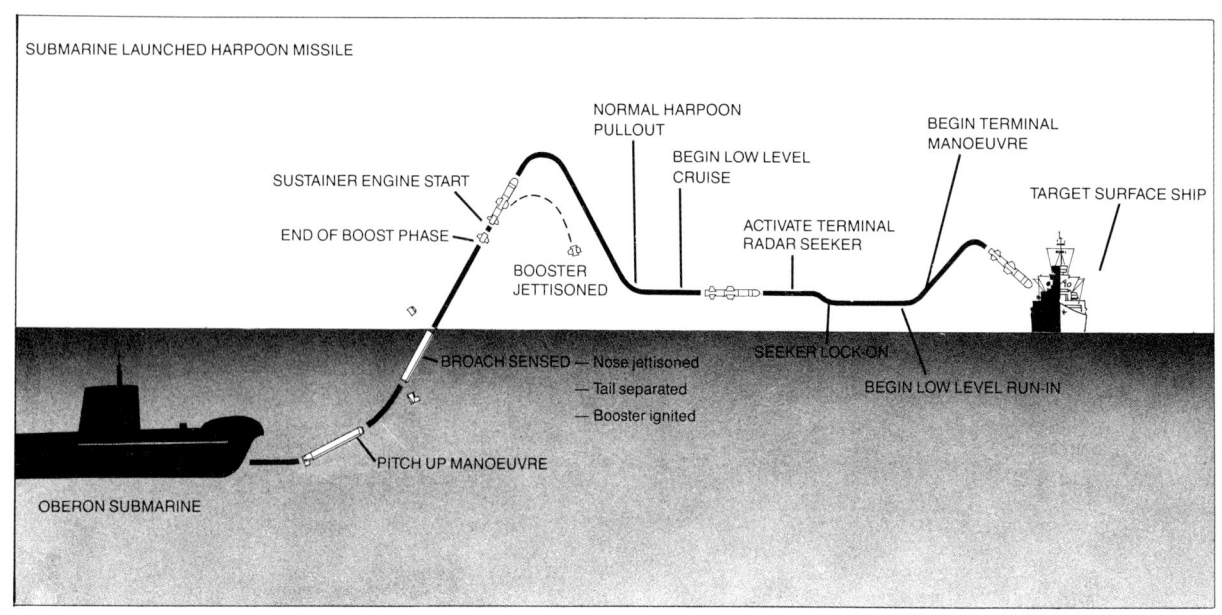

A McDonnell Douglas Harpoon anti-shipping cruise missile is launched from an Oberon submarine. Powered by a jet engine, it flies low into the target area, seeks the target with its own radar and in the final attack, pulls up and dives on the target, exploding a warhead and remaining fuel.

UNDERWATER STRIKE FORCE

Modernised with new weapons and sensor systems, the RAN's Oberon submarines are a sleek fleet of silent killers.

Australia is one of the world's oldest proponents of submarine warfare. As early as 1914, the infant Royal Australian Navy acquired two British 'E' class boats, the AE1 and AE2, both lost on active service during World War I. In 1919, six Royal Navy 'J' class submarines were transferred to the RAN but by 1922, were scrapped. In 1927, two RN boats of the first Oberon class, the *Otway* and *Oxley*, served with the RAN for four years. The RAN did not operate submarines in World War II and did not get back into submarines until the 1960s. Six boats of the current generation Oberon class were commissioned between 1967 and 1968 largely to replace a Royal Navy submarine squadron based in Australia to serve as "targets" for anti-submarine warfare exercises. Completed by 1978, the fleet now consists of HMAS ships *Oxley, Otway, Ovens, Onslow, Orion* and *Otama*. They give the RAN an effective strike and deterrent weapon.

The RAN's Submarine Weapons Update Programme (SWUP) completed between 1978 and 1985 means the RAN's modernised Oberons rank among the most formidable non-nuclear submarines in the world today.

As an electric-diesel driven submarine, the Oberon, displacing 2,417 tons submerged, has a top speed of 16 knots surfaced and 19 knots submerged. When running on its batteries the submarine is ultra-quiet but has to spend considerable time at air-breathing snorkel depth for the diesel engines to recharge its batteries.

With major refits of a new computer-controlled combat data and weapons fire control system, the Oberon can now employ the Mark 48 torpedo and the Harpoon missile. The Mark 48 is an active-passive wire-guided high speed torpedo with a range of about 18 kilometres. Directed by remote control to the target it automatically locks on in active mode as it nears its victim. The low level Harpoon anti-shipping cruise missile has an over-the-horizon range of up to 100 kilometres with a high hit probability in all weathers. The RAN's Oberons were the first submarines in the world fitted to fire and guide Harpoon missiles.

Such weaponry places the Oberons among the most potent conventional submarines today. With six new boats on order — the Kockums Type 471, the RAN plans to base its submarine squadron at Stirling, Western Australia, in line with the increased importance of the Indian Ocean in Australia's naval strategic planning. From there, the Oberons will continue their regular anti-shipping and anti-submarine patrols. When needed they can be called on for minelaying, landing special forces and photographic surveillance. As the Navy's long-range strike force, the submarines have become a vital component in the most forward line of Australia's defence.

OBERON CLASS SUBMARINE

The Oberon carries a full crew of seven officers and 57 sailors. On board are 19 marine technical sailors, 13 electrical technical sailors, 15 underwater controllers/weapons experts manning sonar, radar and weapons systems, 4 "sparkers" or radio operators and six supply branch sailors. The bow of the updated Oberon is distinguished by the large passive sonar dome used to listen for moving vessels in its vicinity; with a tape library of sound signatures, it identifies specific types of vessel and determines their course and speed. Active sonar bounces a sound pulse off a potential target giving a direct range when the Oberon is about to attack.

1.
2.

JNR. SAILORS' BATHROOM (Portside)
SNR. SAILORS' BATHROOM (Starboard)

ACCOM. FOR ENGINEERING SAILORS
AFTER ESCAPE HATCH

MAIN DIESEL: Two V16 4-stroke supercharged 1900 BHP
ADMIRALTY STANDARD RANGE ENGINES

THE FIN

TWO MAIN MOTORS

AFTER HYDROPLANES
RUDDER
WATERTIGHT BULKHEAD
KEEL

TWO DC ELECTRICAL GENERATORS
(1280 kilowatts each)

CAPTAIN'S CABIN (Starboard)
W/T OFFICE (Starboard)

WATERTIGHT BULKHEAD

Engineers check the diesels. These drive generators to charge the batteries, used for propulsion when submerged.

In the control room, the attack periscope is up while the officer-of-the-watch and an underwater controller manoeuvre the sub.

1. SNORT EXHAUST
2. W.T. MAST
3. SNORT INDUCTION MAST
4. ESM MAST
5. RADAR MAST
6. SEARCH PERISCOPE
7. ATTACK PERISCOPE

CONTROL ROOM
Including:
— ONE MAN CONTROL STATION (Steerage and depth control)
— MAIN VENT-CONTROL PANEL (For diving)
— HIGH-PRESSURE AIR BLOWING PANEL (For surfacing)
— PERISCOPE-CONTROL HYDRAULIC BLOCKS
— OFFICER-OF-WATCH-PANEL (Motor telegraphs,
— Revolution indicators, Trimming control station)
— SEARCH PERISCOPE
— ATTACK PERISCOPE

LOOKOUT'S POSITION (Port and starboard)

CONNING POSITION

ACTIVE SONAR TRANSDUCER

FORWARD HYDROPLANES

FORWARD ESCAPE HATCH

PASSIVE SONAR BOW ARRAY

SOUND ROOM (Sonar systems)

ACCOM. SPACE

No. 2 MAIN BATTERY

No. 1 MAIN BATTERY

6 BOW TORPEDO TUBES

ROL ROOM

WATERTIGHT BULKHEAD

WATERTIGHT BULKHEAD

TORPEDO AND WEAPONS STOWAGE COMPARTMENT

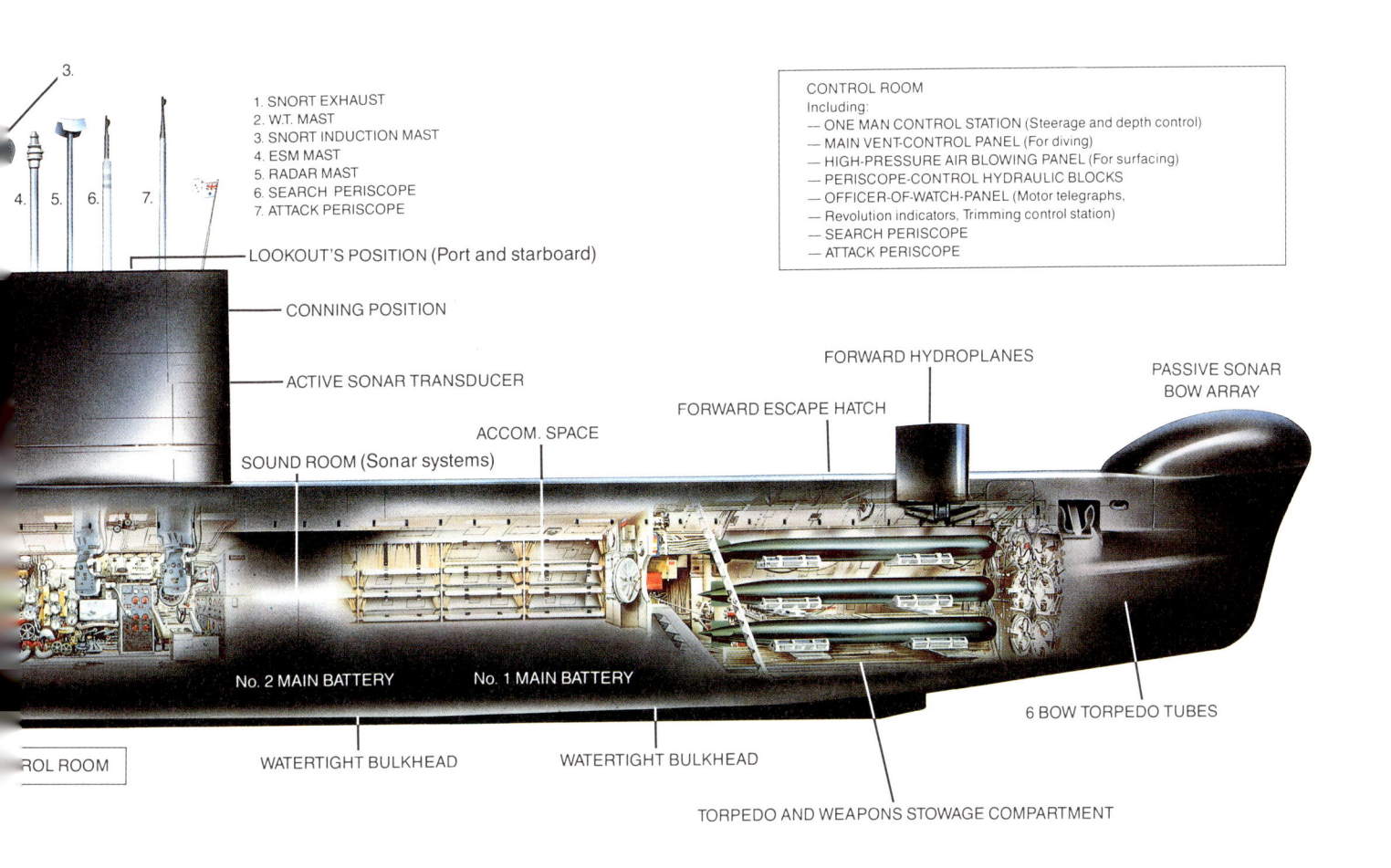

Weapons racks in the torpedo stowage compartment carry up to 20 green deadly torpedos, loaded through six tube doors.

SWIFT AND SILENT

Recognising the limitations of the Oberons and the need for a faster, quieter class of submarine with greater endurance and operational availability, the RAN ordered six Swedish design submarines in 1987 to be built in Adelaide dockyards. The first submarine will be launched in 1994 and commissioned about 18 months later; others will follow at yearly intervals with an option to order two more submarines.

Outfitted for RAN requirements, the Kockums Type 471 is adapted from the A-17 Vaster-Gotland class submarine currently in production at the Kockums Shipyards in Sweden and designed to take advantage of Swedish experience in the world's toughest submarine operating environment — the Baltic Sea. Though shorter than the Oberon (about 75 metres compared to 90 metres), the Type 471 is an overall larger submarine with a hydrodynamically efficient non-keeled tear-drop hull, about nine metres in diameter. The X-shaped control surfaces at the rear allow the submarine to "fly" through the water, banking like an aircraft when it turns. The 471 will dive deeper and travel quieter than the Oberon. It requires a crew of only 42 men and with more internal space should prove more habitable than its predecessor.

Rapidly recharging batteries means the 471 will spend less time "snorting" at snorkel depth to run its diesels. There is also an option for retrofitting the new submarines with a supplementary air-independent propulsion system consisting of a Stirling external combustion engine running off oxygen cylinders, allowing extended time underwater in tight tactical situations.

Fitted with the latest generation of combat systems, the submarine will carry Mark 48 torpedos and underwater-launched anti-ship missiles; an optional minelaying saddle system can carry mines without reducing torpedo load. Apart from a hull-mounted passive sonar, the 471 will have a towed array sonar, a kilometre long cable with multiple transducers, which will precisely locate targets over long distances.

With its new fleet of 471 submarines, borrowing the best of nuclear submarine technology but using conventional propulsion, the RAN have taken the next step forward in meeting the challenge of submarine warfare of the future.

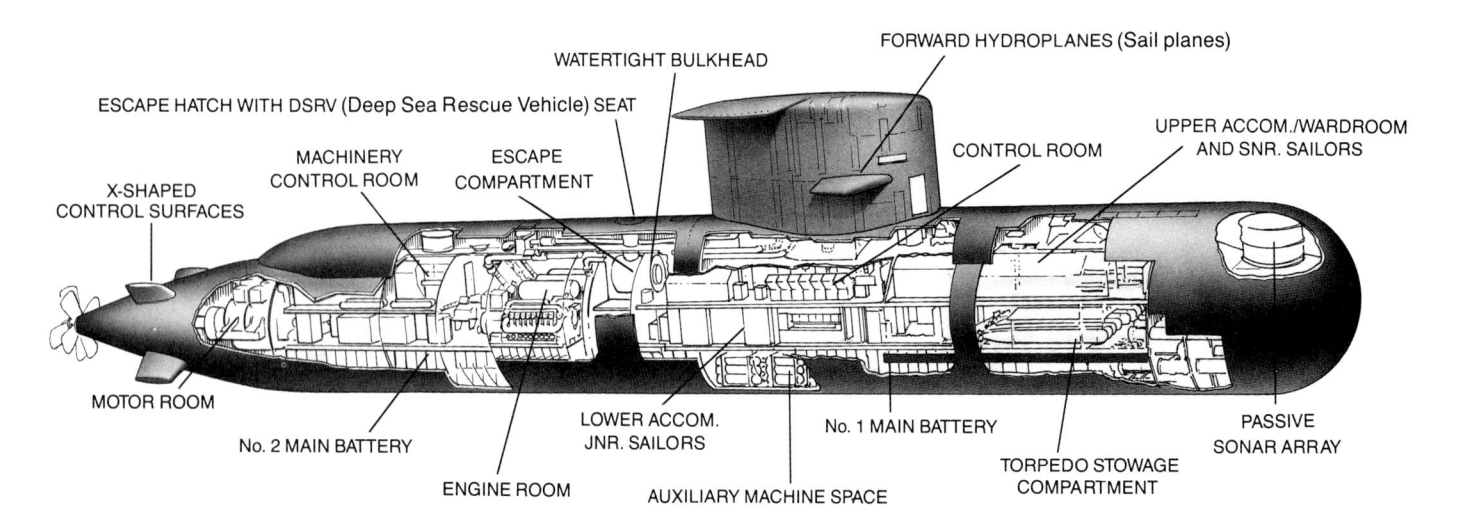

An A-17 Vaster-Gotland class submarine being built in Kockums shipyards in Sweden is the almost identical model for the RAN's new Type 471. The Australian submarine will be larger and fitted out to RAN specifications.

Most information on the 471 remains classified but a simple cutaway shows general internal layout and important features. Without keel or rudder, the 471 is trimmed and steered using hydroplanes and X-shaped control surfaces.

bow doors. The *Tobruk* can carry a considerable military load, comprising 18 Leopard tanks or 35 armoured personnel carriers or 27 five-tonne vehicles on a tank deck, and 46 APCs or 35 five-tonners on a vehicle deck. Her troop decks can take up to 550 men, and she can also stow 500 tonnes of cargo and 30 tonnes of ammunition.

The *Tobruk* and its crew is typical of the hard-working support vessels of the RAN. They serve loyally but with little glamour or notice. But they indicate most clearly that in maritime warfare no single offensive or defensive capability can operate in isolation, and that Australia's three services have to be complementary and interdependent. Although the Navy's specific role is to organise, train and equip maritime forces for sustained combat operations at sea, vessels such as *Tobruk* are closely tied to the army's operations. On the other hand, the RAAF's Orion aircraft are a vital part of the success of the Navy's strike forces.

The RAN must therefore embrace a huge variety of tasks: surveillance and reconnaissance; patrol; the protection of coastal shipping against submarines, ships and aircraft; mining and mine countermeasures; maritime strike and interdiction; and amphibious operations. Each demands purpose-built ships and equipment, and the Navy must have a comprehensive range of hardware to pursue its maritime doctrine of sea control. Currently at its disposal is a surface combatant force of four guided missile frigates, three guided missile destroyers and five destroyer escorts, and a sub-surface force of six modified Oberon class submarines, all supported by a replenishment ship and a destroyer tender. These represent the Navy's deep field capability, and are backed by 15 patrol boats, two inshore minehunters, an amphibious landing ship and LCHs, two hydrographic survey vessels supported by two LCHs in an interim role, an oceanographic research ship and a major training vessel.

Although the RAN lost its front-line fixed-wing aviation capability in 1983 when the *Melbourne* went out of service, it still operates a force of helicopters to provide for various fleet needs, and as well it flies two land-based HS 748 electronic warfare training aircraft. Of the helicopters, the most potent is the Sikorsky Seahawk which entered service in early 1989. It is a powerful aircraft and an integral part of the total weapons system of the guided-missile patrol frigates, the US designed and built FFGs, which partly filled the gap exposed in the RAN's beyond the horizon patrol and attack capability after the demise of the fixed-wing component.

The first four FFGs, *Adelaide, Canberra, Sydney* and *Darwin* were delivered in four years starting in late 1980, and two more under construction in Australia are to be added. The FFGs are long-range escort vessels with the primary roles of interdiction, reconnaissance, surveillance, area air defence and anti-submarine warfare. They are the Navy's most capable surface fighters, gas-turbine powered to 30 knots and capable of delivering both Standard anti-air and Harpoon anti-ship missiles. They also have a 76 mm rapid-fire gun, the Phalanx close-in weapon system and torpedo tubes to launch the Mark 46 anti-submarine torpedo; all are controlled by a computerised naval combat data system.

Perhaps their most potent punch comes from the ability to carry two Seahawk helicopters, which carry their own combat systems fully integrated with those of their parent ships. The Seahawks, like the RAAF Orion P-3C, carry sonobuoys and they also carry a brace of Mark 46 homing torpedos, enabling the helicopters to attack submarines at a much greater range than that of a surface ship alone. Their special attribute is their ability to provide automatic data to their parent vessel, thus extending the frigate's range of visual, radar and sonar influence to well beyond the horizon.

The marriage of frigate and helicopter greatly stretches the range of the ship's systems, and undoubtedly points the way to the future for the RAN. It is a future based on the high-technology naval hardware already in service, as well as the ability to update the current fleet with improved and enhanced weapons systems. It is also a future that requires the Australian Navy

GUARDIANS OF THE COASTS

As experience in World War II demonstrated, the island continent and maritime trading nation of Australia is extremely vulnerable to mine warfare, demanding constant vigilance to keep ports and waterways safe for shipping. In the 1980s Australia's sea mine countermeasures capability has dangerously declined and steps are being taken to upgrade it.

Mine warfare has become far more sophisticated since the days when a moored or floating mine, bristling with horns, awaited a lethal chance encounter with a passing vessel. Modern mines, often adapted from cheap mass-produced aircraft bombs, can be fitted with long-term timers and lie on the bottom of a harbour or channel for months before being activated. Other versions are programmed to recognise the sound and pressure signature of a specific type of ship, such as a tanker or carrier, in order to select their victims. Deepwater, anti-submarine mines, having identified their target's signature, launch a torpedo to hunt the submarine. Minehunting and minesweeping have entered a new era of menace and complexity. Australia must meet this challenge.

For minesweeping, the RAN plan to equip "craft-of-opportunity" such as fishing boats, cruisers or tenders, with towed cutting wires and devices for simulating the signatures of larger ships to trigger off hidden mines. But for intensive searches of the seabed, and remote-controlled detonation of mines, the RAN have two prototypes of Australian-designed and built Bay class Minehunters, HMAS *Shoalhaven* and HMAS *Rushcutter*.

These catamaran-hulled, non-magnetic fibreglass ships are designed to operate in shallow waters for close inshore work and to withstand the effect of nearby underwater explosions. The engines and other machinery are shock-mounted high above the twin hulls to reduce noise levels in the water, magnetic influence and sensitivity to pressure mines. The Krupp Atlas MWS 80 Minehunting system, built into a modular operations room, has computer controlled navigation and sonar systems for detecting and identifying mines. Data banks store sonar maps of the seabed. When an unusual object is encountered a small remote-controlled submarine, called a Mine Disposal Vehicle (MDV), is sent down to investigate with a TV camera; if it finds a mine, the robotic sub attaches a charge, retreats and the mine is exploded by remote control. Each minehunter carries two MDVs on the rear deck.

HMAS *Shoalhaven* and HMAS *Rushcutter* form the core of a new fleet of minehunters, whose naval reserve crews will have a full-time job guarding the nation's ports and harbours against the daunting threat of modern mine warfare.

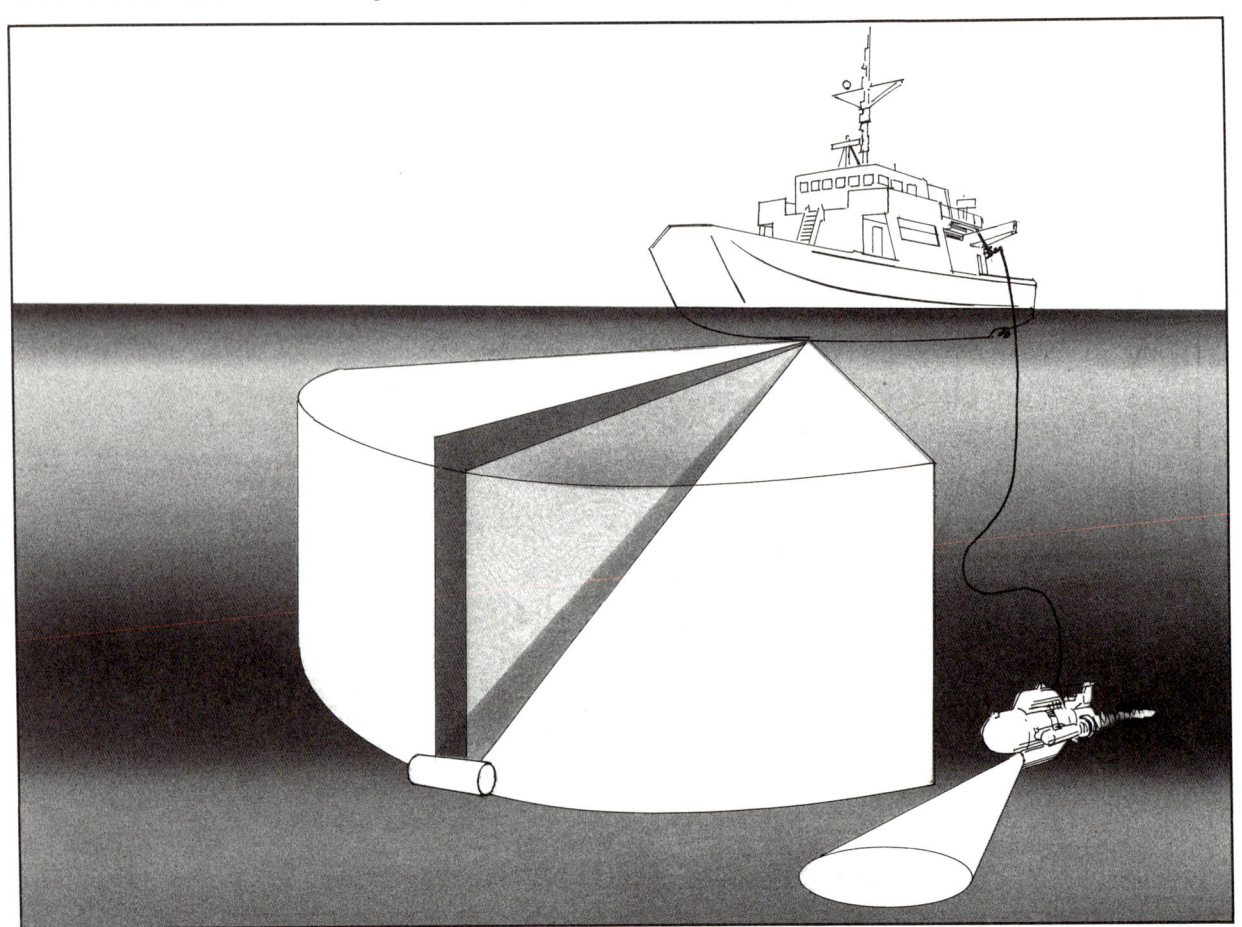

The RAN's minehunter detects a possible mine on the seabed using high-definition sonar. A remote-controlled robot sub dives to investigate with searchlight and TV camera, then lays a charge, retreats and the mine is detonated.

The RAN's first Bay class Minehunter, HMAS Rushcutter lowers one of its two Mine Disposal Vehicles (MDVs) for an underwater probe of the seabed.

A double-hulled fibre-glass minehunter designed, tested and built in Australia, undergoes shock trials to simulate the explosion of a mine close to the craft. Such blasts are an operational hazard for minehunters.

to be always at the ready for combat operations in near and distant seas, and to be supremely capable of discharging its responsibilities in all three levels, above, upon and below the surface of the world's oceans.

The dawn was now rapidly coming on as the pilot raised the collective lever in the cockpit of his Seahawk helicopter and departed the flight deck of his parent frigate, HMAS *Canberra*. He selected the course setting given him by his tactical operator beside him, and as they swooped from the deck they called the P-3C Orion, which was already hunting the suspected submarine. The datum, however, was now "cold", and it seemed that the suspect may have given the Orion the slip.

Back on board the *Canberra*, Lieutenant Mark Shelvey, the principal warfare officer standing the morning watch in the frigate's operations room had digested all the information from the Orion. He now reduced the surface attack unit's speed to allow both the frigate's and consort *Torrens*'s sonars an optimum chance to detect the submarine — the flow noise past the sonar dome seriously degraded its performance. He also took over from the Orion as scene of action commander, thereby taking control of all the forces committed to the search. He faced the threat of the submarine drawing a bead on him, so he planned a short-leg zig zag and chose the optimum speed of 18 knots to hamper the submarine's fire control without degrading his own sonar readings.

Below, the submarine's commander weighed up his attack options as well. He had some 100 minutes of battery power in hand to make a good firing position, and his long-range torpedo allowed for a considerable addition to that flexibility, as it could be launched many kilometres away from its target. The CO had dismissed the use of the Harpoon missile, as its steep climb to 300 metres above the sea before diving towards the ocean to commence its run was a huge advertisement of the submarine's presence. The Harpoon was best used against non-military targets. Instead he would manoeuvre closer, choosing his direction and speed to optimise an interception. His torpedo would be the best selection of weapon.

The light of day was breaking when the submarine commander Lieutenant Commander Shalders decided to have a look at what was going on. His own passive sonar had indicated that the ships which were closing him at high speed had now slowed and activated their sonars and noisemakers. As well, the field of sonobuoys appeared to have had additions laid toward his present position. He ordered periscope depth, gliding up at only four knots so as not to show too great a feather in the water, especially with aircraft in the vicinity. As well, he ordered that *Oxley*'s weapons be brought to action state.

In his mind's eye he conjured up what he might see — and it was as he expected. The mastheads and radars of two ships appeared about five kilometres apart and almost due east of him. His inclination was fine on their bows, and their intentions quite plain, even though they were some distance off.

"Standby, the bearing is that," Shalders called.

"Cut. Zero nine three."

"The range is that."

"Cut. Fifteen thousand yards."

"Yes. Put me five degrees to port FFG."

"Roger, target designated ID3." The battle had begun.

Both aircraft had failed to see the slight swirl caused by the brief appearance of the periscope just five kilometres south of them — the breeze was still luckily about, and they were preoccupied with laying the extension to the buoy field. But the confrontation now swung in the balance. The ships, well aware that a killer submarine was lurking below, were now undertaking protective measures, zig zagging and making noise.

The submarine was definitely under threat from two well-equipped anti-submarine ships. If by chance the aircraft gained contact and were able to supply an accurate position of the submarine, the *Torrens* would be able to launch

The RAN's latest warship, the Australian-built guided missile FFG-7 frigate HMAS Melbourne slides down the slipway at Williamstown dockyards, Melbourne on May 5, 1989; fully fitted, it will join the fleet in 1991. The RAN also plans the construction in Australia of 12 new ANZAC light frigates for the Australian and New Zealand navies.

a long-range attack using her Ikara anti-sub missile. The Orion and Seahawk themselves could strike at the boat, using a vectored attack, called a "vectac", with the helicopter using its own sonar receivers and radar to direct the Orion to drop one of the Mark 46 torpedoes in its bomb bay.

Back in the *Canberra* and *Torrens* operations rooms, the new information from the Orion and the Seahawk was appearing on the tactical plots. In the sonar control rooms the operators watched and listened. Suddenly the aircraft went "hot" on one of the southern most sonobuoys, and reported their contact back to the *Canberra*. At the same time they began to cooperate for a vectored attack. The frigate's captain Commander Simon Harrington and his warfare officer considered their next step: consent for the vectac was given and the ships turned away to stay clear of the torpedo area.

The battle, however, was still not all one-sided. Although the submarine's sonars were indicating a dangerously high transmission level from a nearby buoy, and Shalders had spotted through his small attack periscope a helicopter in the hover to the northeast and the P-3C rolling into a turn towards him, the *Oxley* was itself preparing to hit the frigate. If he could get his range and bearing right before his opponents struck him, a Mark 48 torpedo would soon be heading out on its deadly path. It could destroy the frigate in minutes.

"Put me 70 degrees to starboard," ordered the CO. "Load the after submerged signal ejector with a green grenade."

The submarine's multi-functional signal flare ejector, situated on the starboard side of the boat, was now prepared, ready to fire a green grenade which for exercise purposes indicated a torpedo fired at the surface ship it had targetted.

"Standby. Three, two, one. Fire!" As compressed air forced a slug of water from the torpedo tube, a slight thud was felt within the boat. "Fire the after submerged signal ejector."

In the meantime, the two aircraft had coordinated their strike upon the submarine. Just as the boat let go its weapon, the Orion dropped two of its own grenades. The *Oxley*'s sonars reported the explosions — it had been pinpointed and comprehensively attacked.

"Green one zero zero, green grenade. Far," the starboard lookout aboard the *Canberra* shouted as he sighted the green pyrotechnic leaving the water. The operation room's response was virtually automatic, and without further orders the crew began to carry out torpedo countermeasures. However, against a true weapon under initial wire guidance until it itself gained active or passive contact and homed faster than 45 knots, however, evasion would be no easy task. The ship manoeuvred violently, creating "knuckles" in the water that would confuse an incoming weapon's picture. As well, the *Canberra* employed noisemakers suited to the particular active-passive homing torpedo. And with the two aircraft having made their kill, the ships did not have to worry about re-establishing a position to fire at the submarine; their job now was to get out of the expected path of the torpedo as soon as possible. Despite the fact that in real combat there would be little chance of survival, the captain wanted full value from the exercise.

The mock battle had climaxed in a flurry of attack and counter attack, pushing all the players to fight to the finish. Each of the components fulfilled their capabilities, proving to the RAN that in real combat its ships and crews could master the seas surrounding the Australian continent. This, and many other roles it must undertake with all kinds of craft, was a demanding bill of fare for the Australian Navy, but it has taken up the responsibility and shown that it can ably do the job.

THE ULTIMATE AIRCRAFT

A No. 77 Squadron figher pilot, Flying Officer John Lonergan shows off his F/A-18 Hornet's performance with a dizzying vertical climb over RAAF Base Williamtown. Hornets are the basis of the RAAF's air-strike power.

FIGHTING FIT

When Australia's fighter pilots climb into their aircraft they have at their fingertips the high technology systems of one of the most potent jet fighters in the world today — the McDonnell Douglas F/A-18 Hornet. These twin-jet, swept-wing combat planes form into three RAAF squadrons; Nos. 3 and 77 at Williamtown in NSW and No. 75 at Tindal in the Northern Territory. Their strategic aim is to control the continent's northern airspace, a big job for a fleet of 75 but possible because the Hornet is a very versatile multi-role aircraft.

The F/A-18 is equally at home with air-to-air combat and interception, close ground support, air-to-ground attack and maritime strike. With a maximum speed of Mach 1.8, the Hornet is marginally slower than interceptors like the F-14 Tomcat and the Soviet MiG-23; however, most aerial combat takes place at subsonic speeds and at heights where a capability of Mach 2+ top speed is not relevant. The Hornet has a ferry range, without refuelling, of 3,700 kilometres but can carry extra fuel pods on wings and fuselage. Mid-air refuelling from Boeing 707s, modified as tankers, can extend a Hornet's range with optimum weapon load.

The crucial factor remains manoeuvrability. The Hornet's acceleration is four times that of the now outmoded Mirage and its exceptional turn rate and turn radius give full command of any tactical situation. With this manoeuvring capability and its high survivability the Hornet has a distinct edge in air combat roles. The experience and skill of the pilot decides the rest.

With a maximum ordnance load of 8,550 kilograms, the Hornet can carry a deadly mixture of weapons: long range, radar guided AIM-7 Sparrow missiles; close range, infra-red, heat seeking AIM-9 Sidewinder missiles; Harpoon anti-ship cruise missiles; air-to-ground HARM missiles and conventional and laser-guided bombs. The plane is also armed with a 20 mm multi-barrelled 100-rounds-per-second cannon for close-quarter fighting.

The Hornet's avionics are state-of-the-art. Advanced digital computer systems and sophisticated electronics in the cockpit allow the pilot to call up a mass of information for all-weather, day or night navigation and precision target acquisition and weapons delivery. Two mission computers share navigation and weapons systems processing so that if one fails the other takes over as a back-up. A quadruple redundant digital flight control system has manual override if all four computers fail or are damaged.

The heart of the Hornet's combat information centre is the Hughes APG-65 multi-mode pulse Doppler radar system able to detect, track and lock onto hostile airborne and ground targets, day or night and in all weathers. By flicking a throttle switch, the pilot selects either air-to-air or air-to-ground radar; toggle switches then select more specific modes. Once a target is acquired the plane's computers automatically lock onto it and launch missiles or drop bombs cleared by the pilot.

With its impressive and deadly accurate strikepower, its exceptional manoeuvrability and its multi-role flexibility, the Hornet is regarded by its RAAF pilots as the ultimate fighter-bomber aircraft, easily upgraded for the future with new software and additional avionics and weapons systems. The F/A-18 force gives the RAAF a combat capability that will ably carry it into the next century.

Kitted up with his helmet, G-suit and flying gloves, Hornet pilot Lonergan dresses for a day's work.

The layout of the Hornet's cockpit was designed by McDonnell Douglas after more than 5,000 hours of simulator (left) time with many pilots. Using the HOTAS or "Hands on Throttle and Stick" system, the pilot keeps both hands on the throttle and control column while operating finger-tip controls to clear weapons for launch, switch radar modes and trigger other in-flight functions. The three cathode ray tube screens (DDIs) can be selected for radar scans and maps, moving map and navigation displays, simulated flight instruments and various systems information. The upfront control panel between the two top screens is for computer systems data entry and menu selection. The pilot is able to read out displays without looking down at his instrument panel by using the "Head Up Display". HUD is a set of symbols, projected onto a screen in front of the windshield, that show flight information, time and distance to destination and way points, weapons status and target lock-on.

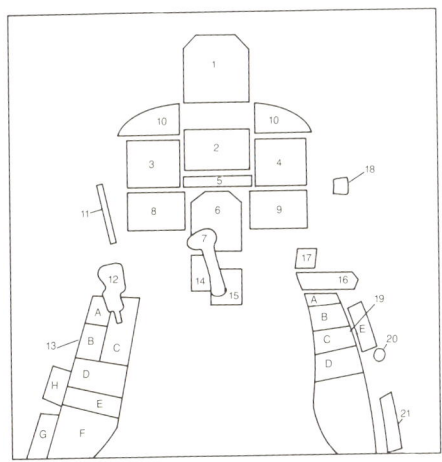

F/A-18 COCKPIT LAYOUT
1. Head-up-display (HUD) **2.** Upfront control panel **3.** Left digital display indicator (DDI) **4.** Right DDI **5.** HUD control **6.** Horizontal indicator **7.** Control column **8.** Fuel gauge; Engine monitor indicators; Landing gear and flap position lights; Heading and course set switches **9.** Standby analogue flight instruments: Attitude indicator; Airspeed; Altimeter; Rate of climb **10.** Fire warning/extinguishing lights **11.** Canopy internal jettison handle **12.** Throttle **13.** Left console: a) Ground power panel b) Exterior lights c) Throttle quadrant d) Fuel panel e) Flight control system panel f) Communication panel (Radio) g) Antenna select panel h) Auxiliary power panel **14.** Chaff and flare dispenser panel **15.** Clock and cockpit altimeter **16.** Hydraulic pressure gauge; Caution lights; Flight computer cool switch **17.** Radar altimeter **18.** Standby magnetic compass **19.** Right console: a) Electrical power panel b) Environmental control system panel c) Interior lights panel d) Sensor panel — FLIR and radar switches e) Defog panel **20.** Utility light. **21.** Map and data case.

McDONNELL DOUGLAS F/A-18 HORNET

Role: *Air interception and combat, ground attack, maritime strike, enemy supply line interdiction*
Engines: *Two low bypass General Electric F404 engines, each 16,000 lbs thrust*
Airframe: *Length — 17.1 metres*
Height — 4.7 metres
Wingspan: *12.3 metres*
Weight: *9,900 kilograms basic*
23,500 kilograms maximum
Speed: *Mach 1.8*
Ceiling: *Above 45,000 feet*
Range: *Ferry range — 3,700 kilometres*
Combat radius — 740 kilometres
Interdiction — more than 1,000 kilometres
Crew: *One pilot*

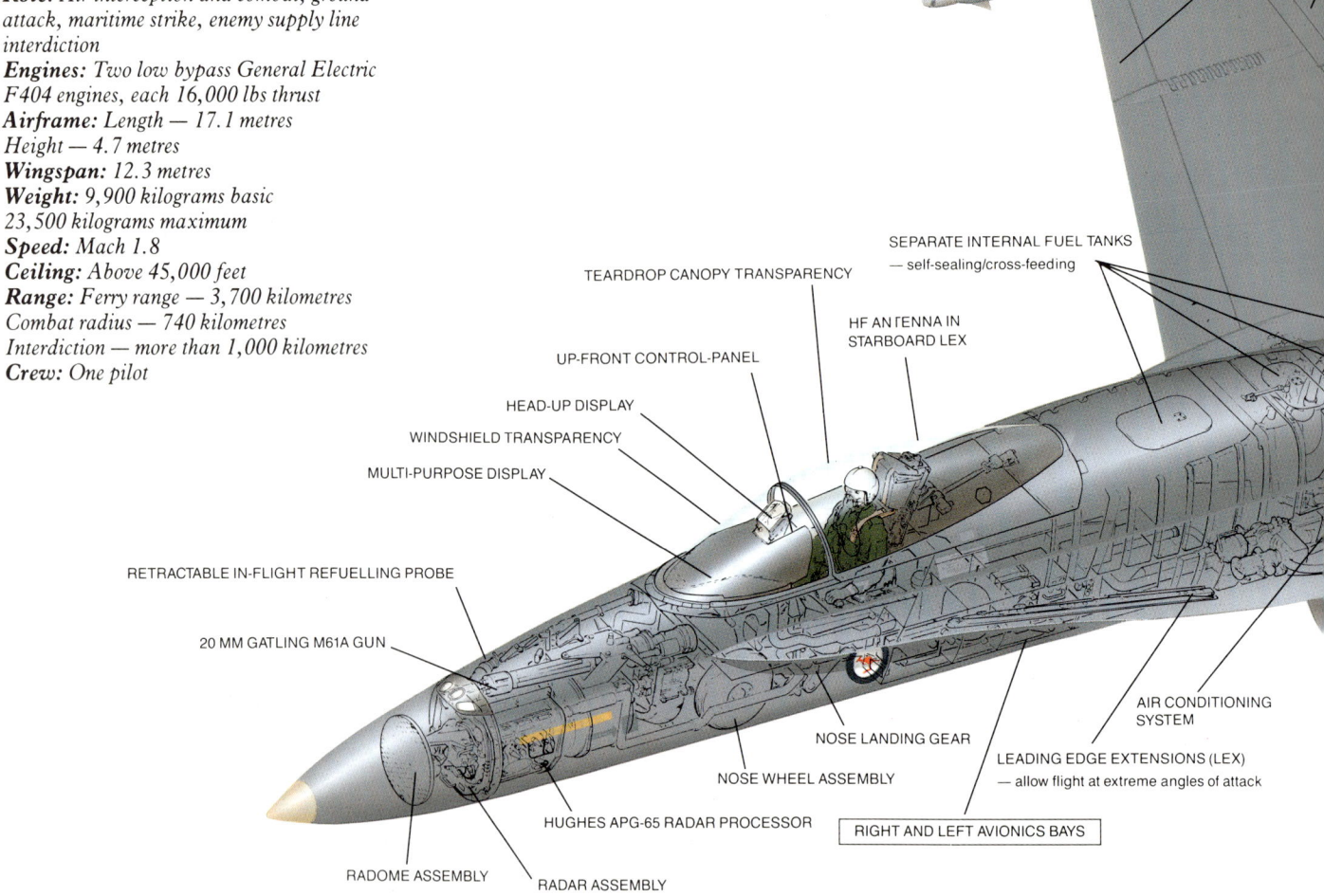

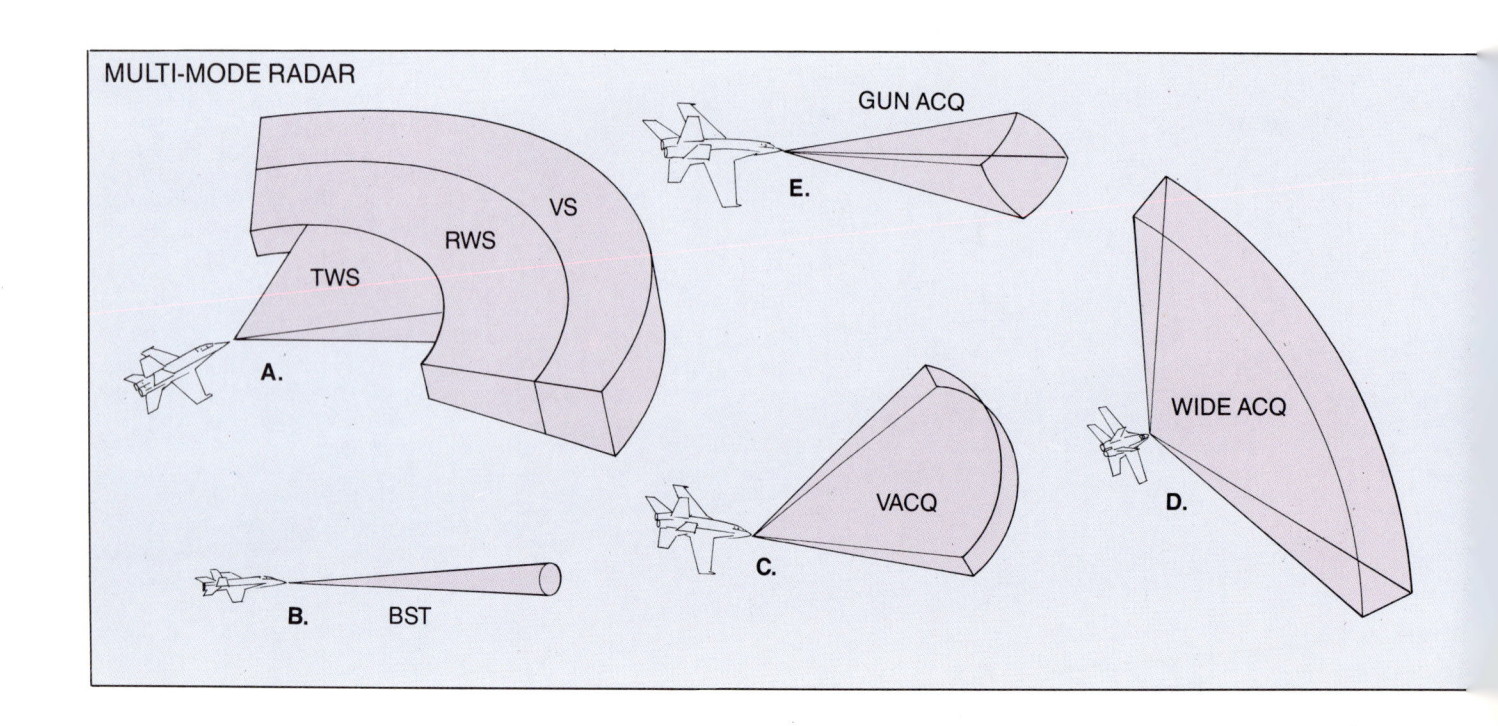

TEARDROP CANOPY TRANSPARENCY
SEPARATE INTERNAL FUEL TANKS — self-sealing/cross-feeding
HF ANTENNA IN STARBOARD LEX
UP-FRONT CONTROL-PANEL
HEAD-UP DISPLAY
WINDSHIELD TRANSPARENCY
MULTI-PURPOSE DISPLAY
RETRACTABLE IN-FLIGHT REFUELLING PROBE
20 MM GATLING M61A GUN
AIR CONDITIONING SYSTEM
NOSE LANDING GEAR
NOSE WHEEL ASSEMBLY
LEADING EDGE EXTENSIONS (LEX) — allow flight at extreme angles of attack
HUGHES APG-65 RADAR PROCESSOR
RIGHT AND LEFT AVIONICS BAYS
RADOME ASSEMBLY
RADAR ASSEMBLY

MULTI-MODE RADAR

A. TWS / RWS / VS
B. BST
C. VACQ
D. WIDE ACQ
E. GUN ACQ

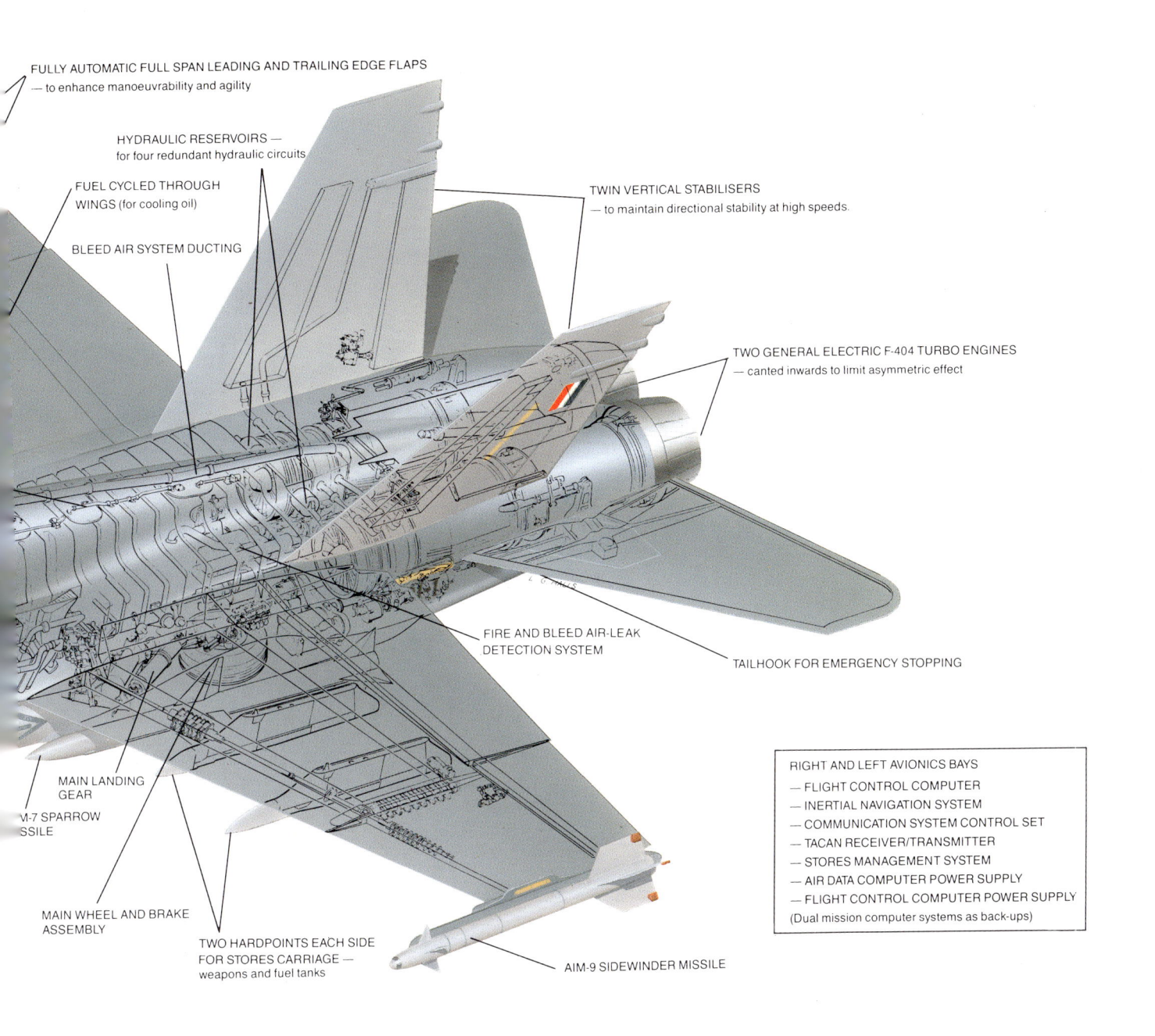

- FULLY AUTOMATIC FULL SPAN LEADING AND TRAILING EDGE FLAPS
  — to enhance manoeuvrability and agility
- HYDRAULIC RESERVOIRS —
  for four redundant hydraulic circuits
- FUEL CYCLED THROUGH WINGS (for cooling oil)
- BLEED AIR SYSTEM DUCTING
- TWIN VERTICAL STABILISERS
  — to maintain directional stability at high speeds.
- TWO GENERAL ELECTRIC F-404 TURBO ENGINES
  — canted inwards to limit asymmetric effect
- FIRE AND BLEED AIR-LEAK DETECTION SYSTEM
- TAILHOOK FOR EMERGENCY STOPPING
- MAIN LANDING GEAR
- M-7 SPARROW SSILE
- MAIN WHEEL AND BRAKE ASSEMBLY
- TWO HARDPOINTS EACH SIDE FOR STORES CARRIAGE —
  weapons and fuel tanks
- AIM-9 SIDEWINDER MISSILE

RIGHT AND LEFT AVIONICS BAYS
— FLIGHT CONTROL COMPUTER
— INERTIAL NAVIGATION SYSTEM
— COMMUNICATION SYSTEM CONTROL SET
— TACAN RECEIVER/TRANSMITTER
— STORES MANAGEMENT SYSTEM
— AIR DATA COMPUTER POWER SUPPLY
— FLIGHT CONTROL COMPUTER POWER SUPPLY
(Dual mission computer systems as back-ups)

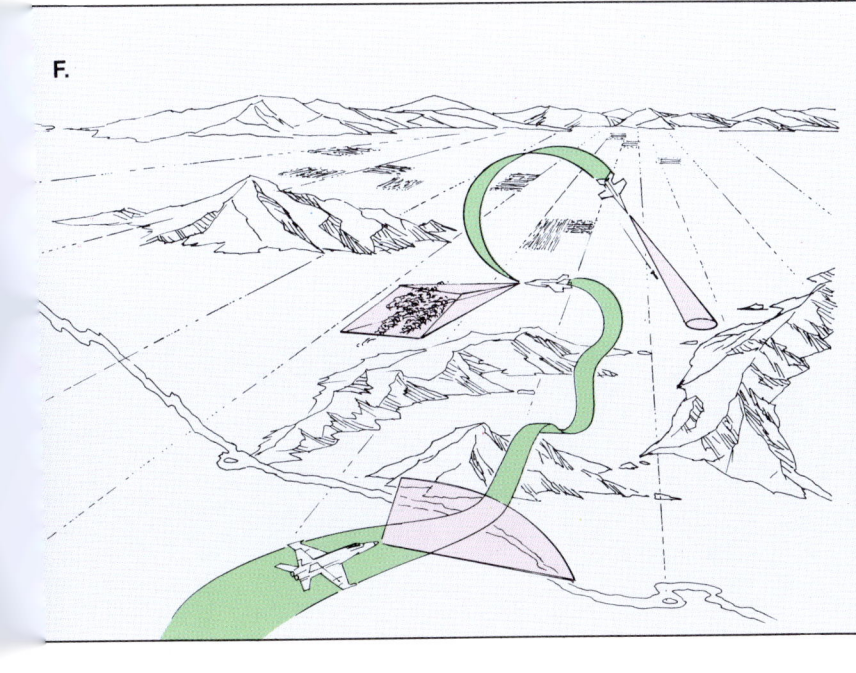

The Hornet's APG-65 multi-mode radar system offers many choices of air-to-air and air-to-surface radar beam sweeps for navigation, target detection and acquisition, and precision weapons delivery. A: In air-to-air function, a long-range, wide-angle scan "Velocity Search" (VS) eliminates "clutter" from ground and weather and gives a bearing on any fast-approaching target. "Range While Search" (RWS) mode broadens the search area for other targets and tracks and fixes a range on an approaching target. "Track While Scan" (TWS) can track up to 10 targets and analyses threats, displaying targets in order of priority. B, C, D: Three short-range "Aerial Combat Manoeuvring" (ACM) modes automatically acquire airborne targets ranging from 500 feet to five nautical miles in Boresight (BST) and Vertical Acquisition (VACQ) and out to 10 nautical miles in Wide Acquisition mode (WACQ). E: When the pilot uses his guns, a radar sweep in the HUD field of view gives an excellent director gunsight in Gun Acquisition mode (GUN ACQ). F: Air-to-ground and air-to-sea radar sweeps give surface mapping and terrain avoidance modes for navigation and for detection and tracking of surface targets.

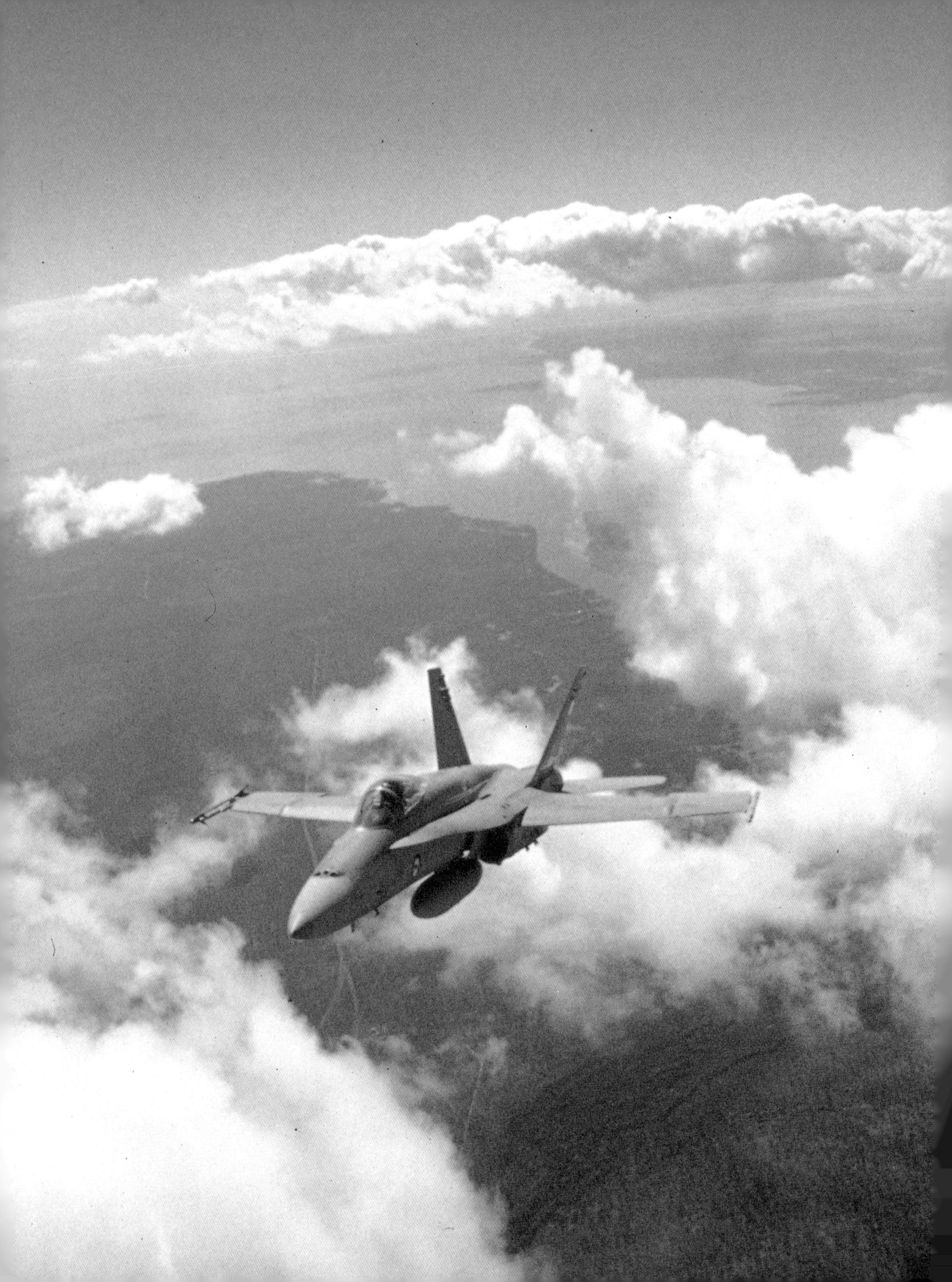

Two Hornets on combat air patrol, armed with Sidewinder missiles and carrying long-range fuel tanks, fly in classic fighter formation of flight leader and wingman.

During the US-Australian exercise Pitch Black, a Hornet, ready for a scramble, is given its end-of-day check and refuelled by ground crew at RAAF Base Darwin.

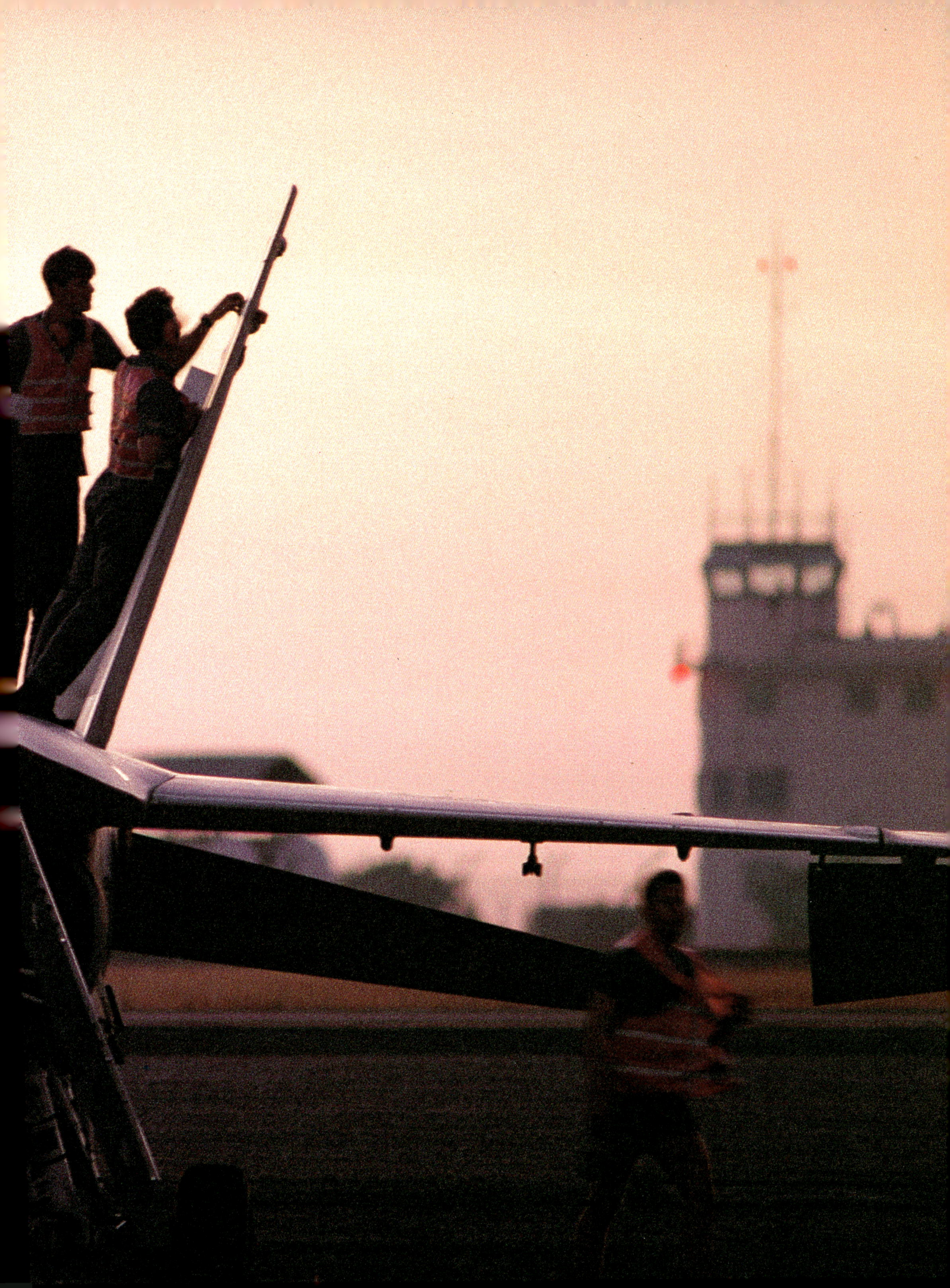

3
FROM MUSTANG TO HORNET

Australia's airforce has flown in the forefront of modern aircraft advances, operating a range of jet fighters and bombers, helicopters and transports, and establishing a triumvirate of sharp-eyed Orions, devastating F-111s, and the new fighter, the F/A-18 Hornet.

The RAAF insignia with Crown, Australian wedge-tailed eagle and wattle, bears the motto "Through Struggle to the Stars".

Flight Lieutenant "Bert" Foster tightened the shoulder harness that secured him into the cockpit of his F/A-18 Hornet fighter. The job ahead of him was of supreme importance — to protect the city of Darwin from an expected dawn air attack. Foster settled into his seat, but as the darkness of the early morning hours surrounded him, his thoughts turned fleetingly inward, to his own safety and comfort. The rocket-powered ejection seat that he was now fastened into had saved many lives over the years; the latest version fitted into the Hornets allowed safe ejection from a stationary position at ground level. Unlike earlier hard seats, these new models were even comfortable.

Foster refocussed his attention. He quickly completed from left to right the checks that ensured his aircraft's switch positions were ready for start-up. And beyond his aircraft, he glanced out, again from left to right. The three other members of his formation were also completing the same routine.

The pilots had been up and at work for two hours already, completing pre-flight briefings with the "met", the local meteorological forecaster, and the "spy", the squadron Intelligence officer. Weather in and around Darwin was typical for winter: cool and crisp in the early morning with the sky clear all the way to the moon. Contrails were expected above Angels 39. The spy's brief was similar to that of the last few days: the "enemy" was expected to carry out air raids upon the Darwin area.

The attacks, however, were staged. The city and its military installations, and the Tindal airfield to the south near Katherine, where the RAAF No.75 Squadron was based, were all on a war exercise alert. It was the annual Pitch Black air defence manoeuvres which Australia hosted in the Top End. American and Australian airforces were flying both as allies and enemy, practising to maintain the expertise needed in the north in case any such contingency proved to be real. Today the enemy's order of battle were US Marine Corps A-6 Intruder bombers and US Air Force F-15 Eagle fighters.

Their briefing over, the four pilots were ready for their combat air patrol. First, they had kitted up into their safety equipment, a G-suit fitting tightly around the legs and abdomen. Under the pressure of G-forces, it would inflate, stopping the blood pooling in the lower body and thus delaying the onset of blackout and ultimately the loss of consciousness. Next, on went the life-preserver jacket, which not only contained "water wings" that automatically inflated when wet, but also a two-way radio and other communications equipment for emergency uses. As well, in remote areas such as this, the pilots wore a shoulder harness carrying a 9 mm automatic pistol for survival purposes.

Foster now gave the wind-up signal to the other pilots as well as the troop assisting in the start of his own aircraft. All four auxiliary power units began in unison, followed shortly afterwards by the whine of the General Electric F-404 engines. The aircraft inertial navigation systems had been fully aligned, and the all-the-way point data to get them automatically to their destination entered.

Ten minutes later the Hornets taxied out towards the runway — as the base was operating under radio silence, no transmissions were made. Taxi clearance was communicated by using aircraft landing lights and a green light from the tower. With millions of dollars worth of high-tech hardware ready to go to war, they still used the same procedures practised since before basic radio was first put into aircraft. Likewise, takeoff clearance was obtained.

The aircraft lined up on the runway in Battle-four formation, two staggered pairs in echelon, so that the first two Hornets could run up to takeoff power without blowing foreign objects down the intakes of the jets behind. Foster and his wingman released their brakes and engaged afterburners; and as 32,000 pounds of thrust per aircraft propelled them down the strip, the pilots were pushed back in their seats. The Hornets accelerated rapidly to touch 300 knots over the far end of the runway, then less than half a minute later, the second element released their brakes and followed the leader. The crackle and thunder of the jets' exhausts ensured that no one within three kilometres would remain asleep for long.

And the noise would continue for most of the morning — soon after the first flight had left the airfield, other Hornet formations repeated the procedure. The sky above the north of Darwin would be busy today.

The plan now was to rendezvous 80 kilometres up the track with a USMC KC-130 tanker, which would top up the fighters' fuel tanks before they entered the conflict zone, allowing the flight maximum time on combat air patrol some 150 kilometres out to sea from Darwin.

They climbed quickly, Foster concentrating on the sky ahead. The Hornet's integrated systems meant that he did not have to glance down into his cockpit, allowing him to devote full attention to lookout — as well as the plane's all-seeing APG-65 radar, the pilot still flew with well-trained, eagle-like eyes. He was able to manipulate the aircraft's systems to best advantage using its "hands on throttle and stick", or HOTAS; both the throttle and joystick were covered with a myriad of buttons and switches so that the aircraft's vital operations could be selected without moving his hands away. All the switch selections were shown on the HUD, the head-up display which provided the pilot with flight and weapons data.

Foster levelled out on heading to meet the mid-air tanker, his hand and eye movements second nature after 16 years in the air. He had come a long way from his first training days at Point Cook in Victoria, where basic handling and aerodynamics had been learned on a little piston-engined CT-4, a bright yellow aircraft lovingly referred to by the trainee pilots as the "plastic parrot". Then followed advanced flying training at Pearce base in Western Australia, and his conversion onto the Italian Macchi jet trainer — that had been the beginning of Foster's addiction to high-powered flight. From there he went to Williamtown in NSW for his introductory fighter course, where he learned the basics of fighter flying on the now familiar Macchis, and graduated onto the exhilarating Mirage, the aircraft the men called their beautiful French lady.

The F/A-18 was a whole new world, the most recent measure of Australia's military progress. The Hornet had computing power that the makers of the Mirage would never have dreamed of. The pilots not only flew the aircraft, but managed its extremely complex weapons platform as well, and depending on its mission, the Hornet could undertake air defence, ground attack or maritime strike duties. Its multi-role capability was the key to its position in the RAAF — the F/A-18 could only be replaced by a large number of more specialised, and undoubtedly more costly, aircraft.

The key to the aircraft's flexibility was its state-of-the art technology. The Hornet was typical of the best modern combat aircraft. Its engines produced more power more efficiently than fighters of previous generations, and it had impressive acceleration and speed. Coupled with these qualities were a manoeuvrability and unsurpassed agility that could only be achieved with the relaxed stability of fly-by-wire aircraft. All that, and a rugged airframe, have made the Hornet a powerful weapon in Australia's remote Top End. How well the aircraft has been adapted, and how effectively its pilots have learned their lessons, would soon be seen.

The Pitch Black exercise was a high-pressure scenario not normally available to either the US airforce or the RAAF. It enabled both forces to validate doctrine and tactics between different aircraft — if shown to be necessary, changes in either would be made. The mock combat also allowed battle commanders to get hands-on experience with the dynamic situation being thrown at them by exercise controllers. Today's mission could likely unfold into a major mid-air conflict. It was now up to the men in the air to come up with the goods.

Bert Foster and the rest of his formation had adapted well to the RAAF's new technology and the demanding environment of northern Australia. They were at the leading edge of the airforce's history, the origins of which had been firmly established with the flyers and aircraft of the First and Second World Wars. When the Axis powers surrendered in 1945, the RAAF was the fourth largest airforce in the world after the USA, Britain and Russia. But the RAAF scaled down its strength in the post-war years, retaining a vast number of its wartime aircraft, many of which were on occupation duties in Japan. When tensions in Korea exploded in mid-1950, No. 77 Squadron RAAF joined with United Nations forces and entered the conflict, flying their P51 Mustangs which were famous for a top speed of more than 700 kph and a 2,700 kilometre range.

But six months after the Korean War began, the fast and manoeuvrable Russian-made MiG 15 jet fighter entered the fray, rendering the Australian Mustangs obsolete. The RAAF sought a replacement fighter; it wanted America's new F86 Sabre jets which had a swept-wing design like the MiG. But none of America's Sabres were available, so Australia entered the jet age with British-built Gloster Meteor Mark VIII fighters powered by Rolls Royce Derwent engines. They were capable of

Requiring great concentration and flying skill, a two-man Hornet slows for mid-air refuelling from an American KC-130 tanker, linked to a probe in the fighter's nose by a 24 metre fuel-line. For extended range missions, RAAF Hornets will refuel in-flight from a fleet of modified Boeing 707 tankers.

Like two winged silver bullets, Meteor jets of No. 77 Squadron RAAF skim over village rooftops, watched by Australian airmen near their South Korean base at Kimpo in 1952. Outclassed and outnumbered by the deadly enemy MiGs, RAAF Mustangs and Meteors still flew almost 19,000 escort and ground-attack missions over Korea.

800 kph and able to operate at 40,000 feet.

It was soon obvious, however, that the Meteors were no match for the more agile and faster MiGs. The Meteors were reliable and strong, and the safety of two jet engines meant they often got home even after a mid-air battering. But patrolling and ground attack duties suited the hardy jet better than mismatched dog-fights. Even so, air combat could not always be avoided and by the end of the war in 1953, with a score of three MiGs and three other fighters downed, No. 77 Squadron had lost 42 pilots. It had been a rugged baptism of fire for Australia's first combat jet pilots.

It was clear that a modern swept-wing aircraft like the F86 Sabre was needed in the RAAF, but it was not until the mid-1950s that Australian production began. The F86 had shown its mettle against the MiGs, and the Australian version benefited from several years' combat experience. The airframe was thus modified to take Rolls Royce Avon axial-flow, turbo-jet engines, making the RAAF's new fighter the most powerful Sabre in the world.

The Avon Sabre was a complete success, and became an integral part of Australia's front-line fighter squadrons from 1954 until 1971, a period when the stability of South-East Asia was of major political concern in Australia.

Malaya had also entered Australia's defence sphere of influence, when, in the late 1940s, armed terrorists had attacked police stations, rubber plantations, tin mines and communications networks, forcing the Malayan Government to declare a state of emergency. Worried by the prospect of a communist power build-up in the region, and pressured by Britain to contribute forces to the area. Australia responded; RAAF units and equipment were quickly sent.

First to go was No. 38 Transport Squadron flying Second World War vintage C47 Dakotas in support of British Commonwealth ground forces in mountainous jungle country. The Dakotas fulfilled their role well, and were further utilised when, to the north, the Korean conflict expanded and several of the Australian transports were brought in to ferry wounded soldiers between Korea and Japan and to provide other medical support services.

Malaya also saw the RAAF's No. 1 Squadron in action, tirelessly flying four-engined Lincoln bombers day and night in bombing missions on insurgent hideouts. The Lincolns were a derivative of the World War II Lancaster, and were fitted with V-12 Merlin engines. In a constant effort to uproot the jungle-based terrorists and to drive them into ambushes, the Lincolns dropped more than 80 per cent of all the Commonwealth forces' bombs in Malaya until, in 1958, they returned to Australia.

Meanwhile, although Australia's defence interests were concentrated in Asia, as an active participant of the British Commonwealth other parts of the globe attracted the strategic notice of the Australian Government. During the post-war period, Britain was concerned about the Middle East, particularly its oil supplies and its route to the east, the Suez Canal. As a result, No. 78 Wing, with two squadrons of Vampire jet fighters purchased from the British for the task, was based at Malta in the second half of 1952 for garrison duties in support of the Royal Air Force. The Vampire was yet another World War II period aircraft, with twin booms, a single engine, a top speed of more than 850 kph, and the ability to climb higher than 40,000 feet. No. 78 Wing, however, did not see combat in the region, and with tensions rising further in Asia, it was withdrawn after only two years service — the Meteor and Sabres were in the meantime chosen as the RAAF's combat fighters.

Australia was increasingly concerned by the instability of its northern neighbourhood, and became a member of the South East Asia Treaty Organisation, SEATO. Also, with Britain and New Zealand, Australia established a Far Eastern Strategic Reserve Force in the region, which kept both airforce and naval units on exercise and patrol, and maintained a military presence that could act both as a deterrent and in immediate response if needed. At the time, the Australia Government espoused a policy of "forward defence", based essentially on the premise that it preferred to fight any new conflicts a long way from home. The Prime Minister, R.G. Menzies, stated quite clearly: "If

At Williamtown in October 1958, Avon-Sabre jet fighters of No. 3 Squadron RAAF prepare for service with the Commonwealth Strategic Reserve at Australia's Malayan airbase, Butterworth.

there is to be a war for our existence it should be carried on as far from our soil as possible."

Australia provided one bomber and two fighter squadrons for the reserve force, and to accommodate these aircraft a strategically placed wartime airfield at Butterworth, on the Malayan mainland opposite Penang Island, was rebuilt by the RAAF into a modern jet airbase. A new generation of jet-powered bombers, the Canberras, now replaced the Lincolns, and two squadrons of Sabres based themselves there.

The Malayan Emergency gradually petered out as the terrorists were scattered and reduced to small bands, and on September 16, 1963, the Federation of Malaysia was declared as an independent, self-governing country. Instead of a return to stability, however, the region immediately exploded. Indonesia's President Sukarno reacted angrily to the new nation's announcement, declaring it a "neo-colonialist plot". He called for "Confrontation" and hostilities soon began between Indonesia and Malaysia and her British Commonwealth allies. Indonesia was armed mainly with Russian equipment, particularly aircraft, and thought by many defence observers to have been gathered into the communist's Asian gambit.

During the next two years, Indonesia posed a potentially dangerous air threat, and to counter it, fully armed Sabres flew from Butterworth, Singapore and Labuan, in nothern Borneo, with briefings to attack on sight intruding Indonesian combat aircraft. The Sabres flew many missions, including dawn patrols, in defence of Penang and Butterworth, as well as low-level sweeps over the jungle of Sabah and Sarawak. However, despite continual tension, no combat between the RAAF and Indonesian aircraft occurred. Then, on October 1, 1965, Indonesia's position changed dramatically when a communist coup attempt was defeated by anti-communist elements of the Indonesian Armed Forces; the confrontation position rapidly abated and Indonesia adopted an anti-communist stance in the region.

Meanwhile, to the north, during 1962 Thailand had become fearful of troop movements in neighbouring Laos and North Vietnam. As members of SEATO, the US, Britain, Australia and New Zealand decided to set up a holding force able to take any strain, if necessary, until reinforcements could be sent. Australia sent No. 79 Squadron and its Sabres, which were integrated with the Thai air-defence system from June 1962 until August 1969, and flew out of Ubon in the east of the country. A key consideration of the establishment of RAAF aircraft so far from home as well as the closest major base at Butterworth was the capability of another newcomer into the airforce, the Hercules C-130 transport aircraft, which came into service in 1958, making Butterworth a viable proposition so far from Australian soil. These large aircraft weighed more than 70,000 kilograms fully loaded, cruised at 550-600 kph, and could carry close to 23,000 kilos up to 4,000 kilometres. The range, reliability and capacity of the C-130s made them ideal for long-distance courier flights, heavy supply services and, later, medical transport home for wounded soldiers.

In the early 1960s, the Vietnam region was fast becoming a problem area, and after a letter of appeal from South Vietnam, as well as pressure from the United States, Australia responded by sending in a small group of army jungle warfare instructors. The threat to South Vietnam worsened and the SEATO conference of April 1964, expressing grave concern at the situation, requested that those nations already assisting South Vietnam increase their aid. The Australian Government responded, committing six Caribou transport aircraft for airlift support to South Vietnamese forces in the field. Such support was badly needed, as airlift capability meant that the South Vietnamese could respond quickly to both enemy guerilla operations and the dispersed conventional engagements that were now dominating the fighting.

There were no defined fronts in much of the Vietnam War, and the enemy's style of operations often dictated when and where the conflict was to be fought. The Caribou was an ideal choice for airlift in South Vietnam. Designed for short take-off and landing (STOL) operations out of unsealed airstrips, with a rear-opening ramp door allowing rapid loading and discharge, the Caribou was able to carry 32 troops or 26 paratroops, or around 3,000 kilos of cargo, in and out of most airfields in the region. They became a common sight from Khe Sahn in the north, Dalat in the mountains, to the numerous small strips in the Mekong Delta.

Officially called the RAAF Transport Flight before being upgraded to No. 35 Squadron in mid-1966, they were soon known throughout the country as "Wallaby Airlines". The fleet numbered never more than seven Caribous, and flew almost 80,000 sorties in Vietnam in more than seven years of service. Losses were minimal; the only Caribou casualty in Vietnam was early on, in November 1964, when at A Ro in the mountains one went down in heavy ground fire during a supply mission to a Special Forces camp.

The fighting in Vietnam intensified, with both sides undertaking a large build-up of forces. In response, in mid-1966 Australia sent a combined Army/RAAF task force which included

On a remote airstrip in the central highlands of Vietnam in 1966, an RAAF Caribou crew are warmly greeted by Montagnard youths. As all-purpose troop and cargo transports from 1964 to 1973, Caribous of No. 35 Squadron RAAF, carried more than 41,000 tonnes of freight and 700,000 passengers with no loss of life.

No. 9 Squadron with eight Iroquois UH1B helicopters. The squadron had been formed in 1961, and had since become seasoned operators of their Bell choppers, but now they were to go to a war where the helicopter was one of the allied nations' major front-line weapons. Its ability to hover and to land and take-off vertically meant it could operate almost anywhere without prepared airstrips, making it invaluable in spread-out, reactive fighting like that in Vietnam. As well, the lack of any enemy air threat also favoured helicopters, despite their slow speed making them especially vulnerable to ground fire.

The RAAF's helicopters fulfilled three main duties in Vietnam. The main role was manpower carriage, known by the flyers as "slicks"; then there were medical evacuations, called "dust-offs"; and finally, gunships. The RAAF's helicopters were used to support the Australian ground forces, the flyers backing-up both Special Air Services teams and regular army operations operating out of Nui Dat in South Vietnam's Phuoc Tuy province in the Mekong Delta area. The Australians saw intensive fighting near their base as North Vietnamese regulars and guerillas swept into nearby villages, building bunker systems and establishing local control. SAS patrols would venture out into enemy territory — inserted and extracted when necessary by No. 9 Squadron's choppers — to locate and dispose of Viet Cong concentrations, while the Australian regulars operated in a more controlled environment within artillery coverage. Enemy contact and ambushes occurred continually as the opposing forces dominated then lost pockets of the province. The helicopters became invaluable in the scattered fighting, offering reinforcement, resupply and dustoff missions and, when patrols became "hot", critical extractions.

They showed their worth in the battle of Long Tan in August 1966, when two Viet Cong units had ambushed an Australian company which was running dangerously low in ammunition and faced destruction. Two RAAF helicopters raced in to the rescue, in very poor weather skimming the trees at night and dropping vitally

In May 1968, one of No. 9 Squadron's new heavily armed UH1H Iroquois gunships, nicknamed "Bushrangers", hovers low over Australian Army Centurion tanks in South Vietnam.

needed ammunition to the ground forces which were then able to fight their way out. As the battle turned in the Australians' favour, more helicopters flew quickly to the area to remove 21 wounded Diggers; despite their brave exploits, 18 soldiers had been killed.

During 1968, when the Vietnam conflict escalated rapidly after the Viet Cong forces launched their Tet offensive early in the year, the RAAF No. 9 Squadron strength was increased to 16 aircraft, and was re-equipped with a more powerful Iroquois, the UH1H, allowing for extra carrying capacity and the addition of a dozen rockets, two 7.62 mm mini-guns for the pilots, and side-firing M60 machine-guns with two gunners per aircraft. The Australians could now fly gunships in full support of the Australian Task Force soldiers on the ground; they christened their new machines "bushrangers".

They were soon in the thick of the fray, as Viet Cong activity in Phuoc Tuy remained busy during the following year and most SAS insertions went in "hot". Although enemy aggression slowed by the turn of the decade, heavy engagements continued close to the Australians' base. The gunships ran racetrack patterns of fire at about 200 feet around troop insertions and extractions. The Bushrangers' mini-guns ran a one-in-five tracer, easily pointing out the direction of fire for the pilots controlling them. Also on board were 14 rockets, two of which were white phosphorus markers, the other 12 genuine 2.75 mm weapons, which were fired at enemy concentrations on the ground. In the back, two gunners on either side trained their M60s on Viet Cong forces when they threatened operations.

The Iroquois fulfilled all their roles admirably. "They were a very strong aircraft," recalled Pilot Officer Garry Dunbar, who flew choppers in 1971. "There were a lot of people severely shot up, but few went down from gunfire damage alone." More feared than the heavy ground fire was a rocket-propelled grenade that the Viet Cong began to use — it was responsible for the loss of an RAAF chopper

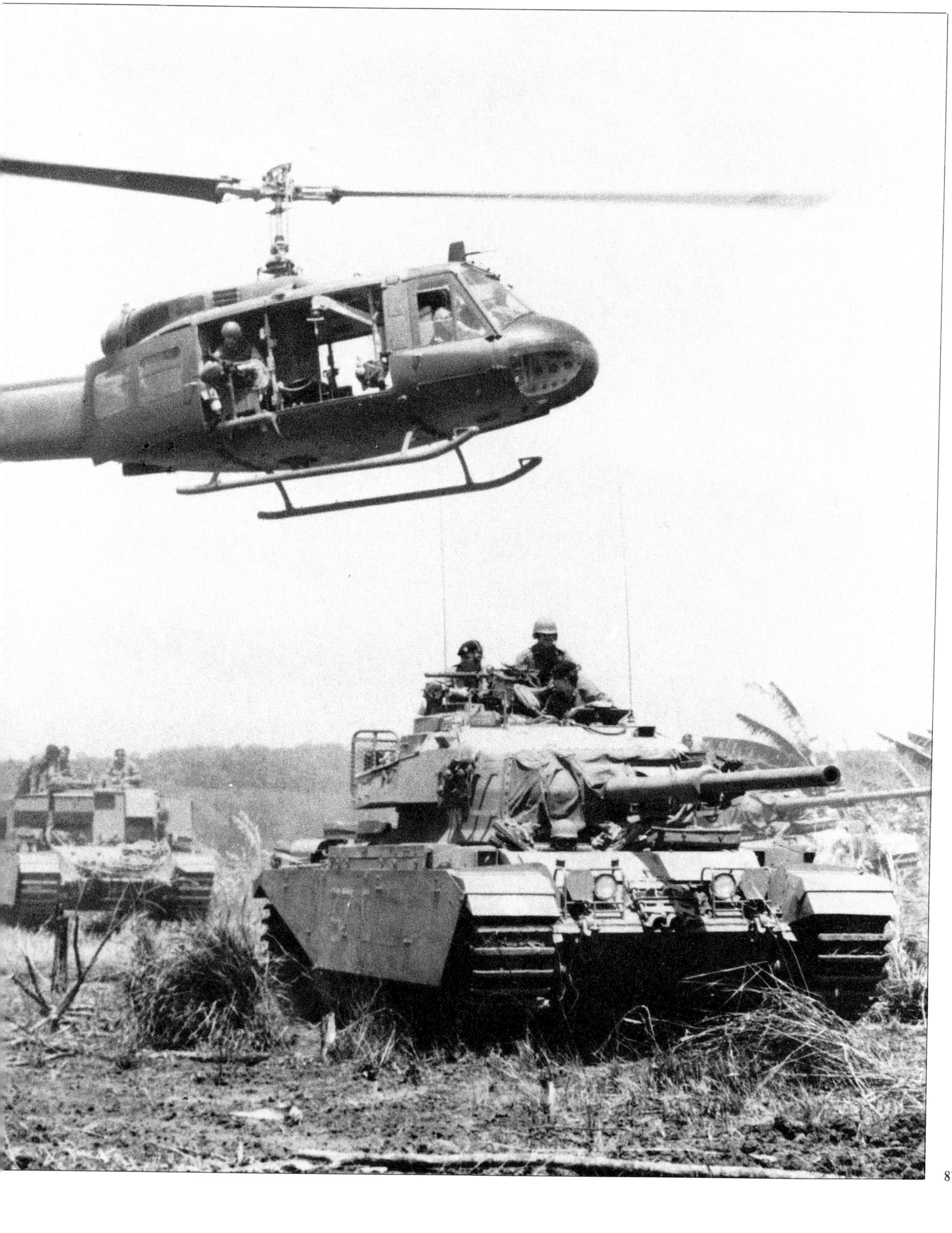

during a medivac in the Long Hai ranges.

Gunship duties had added to the danger of helicopter operations in Vietnam. As the war progressed, the enemy became more knowledgeable on how to fire at choppers; many aircraft were damaged, some serious crashes occurred, and by the time the Iroquois were withdrawn from Vietnam in November 1971, four helicopter aircrew had been killed. Their loss was to be weighed up against the lessons learned about helicopters in Vietnam. Away from excessively dangerous battlezones near the borders, the RAAF's choppers were not to see heavy-calibre machine-guns or anti-air missiles that packed enough punch to physically knock a helicopter out of the sky. Above the jungle canopy, and in an era of relatively ineffective surface-to-air weapons, the helicopters were successful, but in a different environment, such as an open desert, and in a time of increased firepower against such slow-moving targets as helicopters, the Iroquois, without infra-red masking, would be a sitting duck.

Since Vietnam, the Iroquois squadrons of the RAAF have in fact been deployed twice in such country, contributing to Middle East peacekeeping forces but only as transport aircraft. With new weapons commanding the world's modern war zones, the front-line role of the Iroquois has diminished. In their place now, and under the auspices of the army, Australia flies a modern force of twin-engine Sikorsky Black Hawk helicopters that incorporates the latest battlefield technology.

Vietnam's skies were full of aircraft — transport and choppers flying missions constantly — and from April 1967 until May 1971, eight Canberra jet bombers of No. 2 Squadron joined the crowded airspace, operating out of Phan Rang in South Vietnam. The Canberras were Australia's major offensive bomber since 1957, making up No. 2 Squadron in Malaya from the following year.

Now, as one of the units of the US Air Force's 35th Tactical Fighter Wing, No. 2 Squadron RAAF began flying night missions, called "Combat Sky Spots", which were pre-planned bomb strikes under the direction of high-definition ground radar, often on supply routes or reinforcing areas and similar tactical objectives. The squadron flew eight missions every night, seven days a week, but the role was a clinical exercise for the Australian crews: the flying was closely directed; the dropping points were indicated automatically by radar controllers then passed on to the Canberras; and the bombs let go after a calculated countdown. All the RAAF Canberra navigators had to do was push their drop buttons and return to base.

"It was a poor man's introduction to Vietnam," recalled Flight Lieutenant John Tyrrell. "It was the easy way to do it. Combat Night Spot required us only to fly straight and level, at a constant speed, and to drop bombs on cue. Our flights were uncomplicated, we were up high, there was basically no threat to speak of, and we got used to operations."

Such missions were, however, not always safe. The RAAF lost its first Canberra in a Combat Night Spot in early November 1970. After dropping a load in support of South Vietnamese soldiers, a Canberra was blown out of the dangerous sky near the Cambodian border, most likely by a surface-to-air missile. With such weapons, the era of high-flying bombing missions where aircraft presented good SAM targets was fast coming to a close.

The Australian Canberras were also operating day missions by this time, and most of the RAAF bombers were flying visual low-level sorties. The Canberra, though originally conceived as a high-altitude, long-distance, bomber-stream aircraft, now went on missions for which it had never been designed. "Though the Canberra was used entirely out of role," recalled Tyrrell, "it still proved to be a great asset. It was strong, with an incredible range, up to 4,000 kilometres, and it had great endurance."

In a war where most aircraft dive-bombed, the RAAF Canberras would come over target zones at between 1,000 and 3,000 feet at 300 to 500 knots, flying straight and level and giving no sign of hostile intent until they dropped their load. Hence the Australian bombers attracted little ground fire — in fact, at low level, their own bomb fragments often posed the biggest threat, especially to bomb-aimers lying flat in the perspex nose cones of the aircraft.

The delivery method of the Canberra's eight bombs was indicative of how the aircraft was fast becoming an anachronism. The ballistics were taken care of by a gyro-stabilised bomb sight which reacted in response to the aircraft's pitch, heading, attitude and ground speed; still the bomb-aimer was left to judge the drop, and the pilot had a major input with his flying skill determining speed and attitude. The ballistic "computer", however, had been designed for high-level bombing, but a reduction gearing was developed by Australian flyers to factor the bomb sight down to low-level operations.

"It was World War II stuff that we had modified," said Tyrrell. "It did fairly well, but it

Top: Strapped into a cockpit that appears primitive by modern standards, a Canberra bomber pilot gives a "thumbs up" signal before take-off. Above: After 13 years of magnificent service with the RAAF in Malaya and Vietnam, three Canberra bombers perform a farewell fly-past over their Queensland base at Amberley.

was still like playing golf — you could never guarantee a good shot. If you had a bad day you could be a couple of hundred yards off, but on a good day you could get a direct hit. There was a lot of human input, from the pilot and the bomb-aimer. There was a lot of skill, but also a lot of guesswork and a lot of hope. Still, it was the best aircraft available at the time."

No. 2 Squadron returned to Australia in May 1971. In four years in Vietnam it had flown close to 12,000 bombing sorties and had lost two aircraft, one with its crew. The Canberras continued to fly as photo-reconnaissance aircraft — however, rapidly advancing post-Vietnam war technology had caused Australia to review its bomber needs.

While the Canberras were flying in Vietnam, Australia had ordered a new aircraft made by General Dynamics in America. It was originally designated the TFX, Tactical Fighter Experimental, and the previously untried aircraft flew solo night missions out of Thailand during the Vietnam conflict, although these were fraught with technical problems. Even so, it had the capabilities the RAAF were looking for in a tactical bomber needed for regional operations in the coming 25 years.

The threat then was, and largely still is, detection by ground-based radars controlling fighters or missiles. In most cases, aircraft flying high can be detected at enough range to provide an enemy with the time to scramble or vector fighters or to organise a missile attack. Very few radars can detect aircraft that fly below the horizon, and thus the answer for attack aircraft was to get down among the weeds — to fly close to the ground — and in all weather. The TFX, later known as the F-111, could do exactly that.

The F-111 was designed for survivability in the modern anti-aircraft world. Its electronics were mind-boggling for the period. It had a terrain-following radar, TFR, allowing it to fly supersonically close to the ground. Its radar homing and warning system was able to detect and warn of hostile radars and missiles, and its active radar jammers, its disposables such as radar-confusing chaff, and infra-red flares could block enemy radars and decoy missiles. Furthermore, its wings could be swept forward and backward in flight, effectively redesigning the aircraft for speed and economy and thus increasing its range, endurance and bomb-load capacity for specific missions.

Australia ordered 24 of the F-111s in 1965, but production was delayed by technical problems with the swing-wing, and the aircraft was eventually bought in 1973. In the interim, the RAAF lived with a reduced concentration on bombers, although it operated a leased force of US Phantom F4E fast-strike fighters that were utilised in a compromise role. During the delay the price of the F-111s soared, but so too did the knowledge of its flying and attack capacities. The RAAF took it on as a bomber and operated it as a bomber, with no pretence of its fighter capacity. Its technological advances were a revolution in Australia's skies.

"The old Canberra bomber was very basic, very strong, very rugged and quite simple," recalled John Tyrrell, who went on to fly the new aircraft. "The F-111 was like going from a Mini Minor car to a Mustang. It was a complex machine and especially so for the crews. When we first began training in them, the stress of flying such an aircraft was at times physically nauseating. I could barely pull myself out of the cockpit at the end of an early training flight."

The F-111 was a phenomenal aircraft for its time, with integrated navigation, radar and weapons systems that represented a two-generation step in technology for the RAAF. "In all respects it was a great leap forward," said Tyrrell. "Its avionics, the simulators for aircrew training, the restructuring of squadrons, even the management of stores all involved a massive upgrading."

It is still an impressive performer today, and among its most important features is a ferry range of more than 6,000 kilometres. This is a key factor in its role as a tactical bomber, and points to its best possible use. With a dry weight of 25 tonnes, it can be loaded with fuel and weapons to more than double that, up to 57 tonnes. Then fully loaded, it can take off on a

The long "aardvark" noses of F-111 bombers on the flightline at RAAF Base Amberley house the navigation/attack antenna and the twin terrain-following radars. The aardvark, or ground-pig, gives the F-111 its nickname "The Pig".

REVOLUTION IN THE SKIES

Designed and built by General Dynamics in the 1960s, the F-111 strike bomber remains an impressive performer in the 1980s with several special features that set it apart from other aircraft in its class. Most famous is the F-111's swing-wing. On the left side of the cockpit, just above the throttles, an F-111 pilot has a control lever to alter the sweep angle of the F-111's wings.

The swing-wing effectively allows the aircraft to be re-designed in flight, giving the optimum aerodynamic shape for different speeds. The wings can be set fully forward to 16 degrees of sweep for slow flight, part way back for economical cruising speed or fully back at 72 degrees sweep for a top speed of Mach 1.2 at sea level and Mach 2.5 at an altitude of 50,000 feet. Part of the complex problem of designing the swing-wing for a bomber was keeping the bombs, carried under the wings, aligned in the straight-ahead position as the wings swept backwards and forwards.

Another revolutionary aspect of this aircraft is its Terrain Following Radar (TFR) which provides a remarkable all-weather low-level strike capability. The TFR computer, integrated with other excellent radar, navigation and weapons systems, rapidly processes data from vertical-looking and forward-looking radar antennae and checks it against data from other sensors on the aircraft. Collating this data, the computer feeds a contour map of the terrain into the flight control system so that the F-111 can hug the ground as close as 200 feet at full speed even over mountainous terrain at night or in heavy cloud cover. The TFR display in the middle of the instrument panel shows a profile of the terrain ahead and the "ski-shaped" flight path the aircraft will follow. The F-111's TFR can direct the plane under the detection envelope of most ground-based radars and minimise time spent in the engagement zone of enemy missile systems.

The recent fit of the Pave Tack pod, an all-weather infra-red target acquisition and laser-guided bomb system, will further enhance the F-111's ability to find a target and hit it with pinpoint accuracy while reducing exposure to hostile radar and surface-to-air missile systems. For added protection, the F-111 carries the Radar Homing and Warning System (RHAWS), to detect and warn of enemy radars and missiles, as well as systems to electronically jam missile radars and to fire off chaff and flares to confuse incoming missiles.

All 22 F-111s of the RAAF's bomber squadrons, Nos. 1 and 6, based at Amberley in Queensland, are capable of carrying a wide range of weapons. Even with maximum weapons load of 10,800 kilograms, the F-111 can manage a radius of action of 600 nautical miles. With a typical mission flight profile of high-low-high (high for economical flight to the threat area, low for survivability to and from the target and high again on the way home), the F-111's operational radius of action is up to 1,000 nautical miles.

The F-111 may be a veteran of the RAAF but its unique abilities remain unmatched in Australia's region and these extraordinary bombers will keep flying well into the next century.

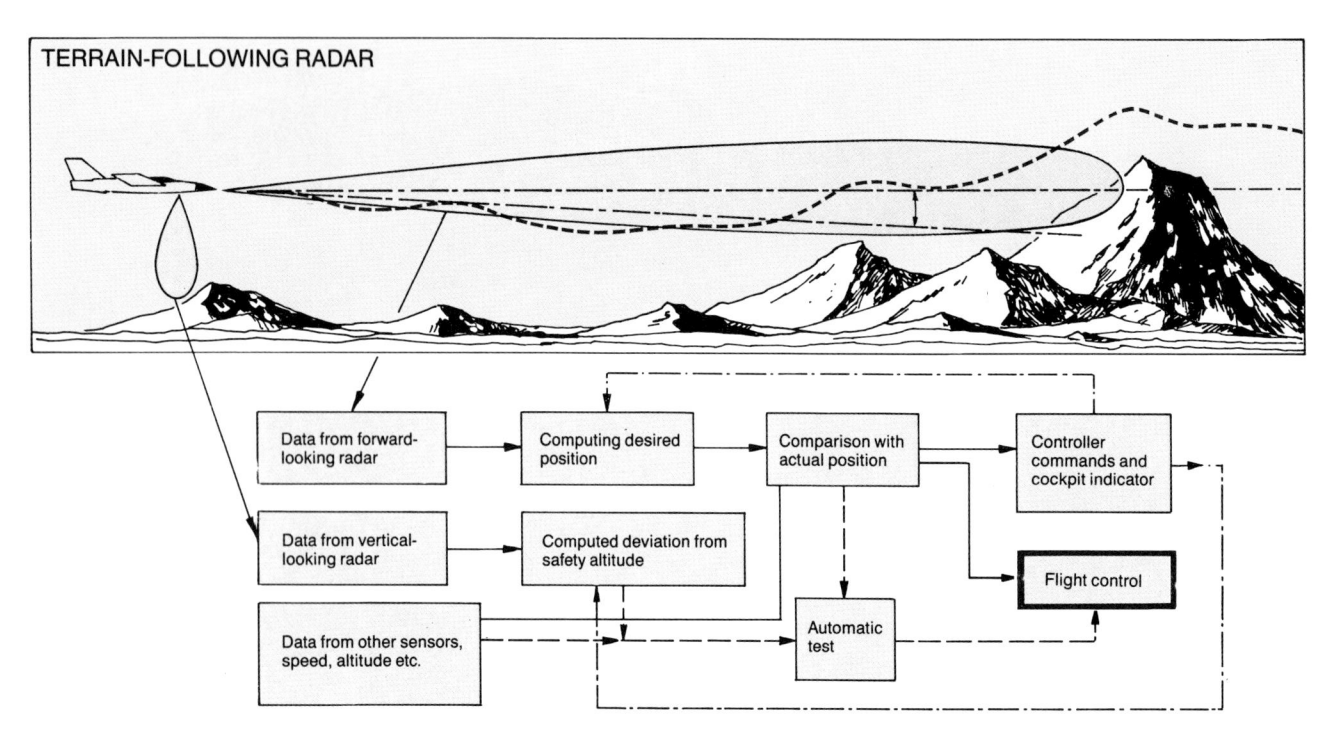

Using its remarkable swing-wing feature, the F-111 can change its wing angle mid-flight. With wings swept back (above) the plane flies supersonically into a target area. Wings swept fully forward (below) reduce approach and landing speeds and give fighter manoeuvrability, while intermediate angles give economic cruising speeds.

The F-111's terrain-following radar uses two sets of radar, looking forward and looking down, to map the terrain. Computers keep the jet at a set distance above the ground.

The versatile F-111 strike bomber has a range of weapons including (from nearest the aircraft to foreground): GBU-15 TV guided bombs, Harpoon anti-shipping missiles, GBU-10 laser-guided bombs, 200 lb free-fall bombs, cluster bombs, practice bombs, laser-guided and free-fall 500 lb bombs, Sidewinder air-to-air missiles and 20 mm cannon ammunitions.

2,500 metre airstrip in very hot conditions, it can do Mach 2.5 at altitude, and land empty in about 760 metres. It can take off from Amberley in southeast Queensland loaded with ten 2,000lb bombs, fly to Darwin and refuel, then go on to conduct a mission from there. Its long-range strike capability is extraordinary.

"Essentially too big and heavy to manoeuvre tightly in battlefield situations," said Tyrrell, "the F-111 is designed to go a long way, penetrate an enemy's defences at low level, and thump the hell out of a major target."

Such capabilities were seen in their fullest when American F-111s attacked Libyan targets in 1986. It was the first time that anyone had been to war in an aircraft after sitting for 18 hours in the cockpit. The F-111s had to fly over international waters all the way from England, steering around the west of Spain and through the Straits of Gibraltar. They refuelled many times in mid-air from KC 10 tanker versions of DC 10 airliners, swiftly delivered their bombs, then returned by the same route. The durability of the equipment was proved, the planning cycle and flight tactics were flexible enough to cope with the mission's changing circumstances, and the pilots gained incalculable experience from the action.

Flying and tactical information gained from that action was passed on to the RAAF, and as the only other operator of F-111s it has proved invaluable, adding to the store of experience gathered from regular exercises over the Australian mainland and with allied navies and airforces operating in the region. The F-111s fly practice bombing missions from Edinburgh in South Australia over the old rocket base of Woomera and they do the same from Darwin and Townsville, as well as in the Philippines and over Malaysia. Mock war scenarios are developed with visiting navies, involving the RAAF's major players such as the F-111s, the F/A-18s, and the Orion P-3Cs in action against missile-equipped ships practising their anti-air capability. From these the F-111s hone all their skills. They fly typical high-low-high flight profiles of high to the edge of the attack or threat zone, low to and from the target utilising the TFR, and high back to home. The pilots learn to fly confidently at high speeds close to the ground, in cloud, at night, and to find and hit small targets. And they learn to use the F-111's excellent navigation and weapons systems. Four of the RAAF's current force of 22 are fitted with a comprehensive reconnaissance package with visual, infra-red and electronic sensors in addition to their normal bombing fit, so extra techniques are also garnered with these.

Already the F-111 is the most capable bomber and reconnaissance aircraft and the most powerful long-range strike weapon in Australia's region. It acts as the RAAF's big deterrent to any potential threat, and with updated technology its capabilities will be enhanced. It is now fitted with the US-designed Pave Tack, an infra-red aquisition and laser-designator system which improves the aircraft's target identification and gives pin-point accuracy with laser-guided bombing. Along with a planned digital update of the aircraft's avionics, Pave Tack enables the F-111 to continue to act as a key element in Australia's defence in depth into the next century.

To keep a complex machine like the F-111 and its fellow RAAF aircraft continually ready to perform any of their roles is not just a matter of superbly trained aircrew and high-tech hardware. It is also a great feat of teamwork requiring top calibre engineering, maintenance, supply and other support resources. Indeed, almost 8,000 RAAF engineers and technicians work on Australia's military aircraft — all 16 types. Considerable maintenance support is also provided by civilian contractors, and the supply of parts alone — from air traffic radars to uniforms — is a major business involving 3,000 people, 650,000 items, and more than $1.5 billion worth of stock. Modern defence is neither simple nor cheap.

The task of patrolling the vast areas surrounding the Australian continent faces similar intricacies. This role is undertaken by the P-3C Orion, a converted Electra turbo-prop airliner with a modified airframe and engine combin-

ORION THE HUNTER

A No. 10 Squadron RAAF P-3C Orion maritime patrol plane exercises as a submarine hunter with HMAS Oxley.

The voice of the radar operator crackles over the intercom: "Radar contact zero-four-two, five zero miles. Contact is about 20 miles north of the main stream of ships. Recommend we investigate". The Tactical Co-ordinator replies: " Agreed. Track zero-four-two, please, pilot." The RAAF Orion, with her 12 man crew, banks gently left and levels out over the Indian Ocean. "Two zero miles dead ahead" reports the radar operator after a few minutes. "Seems to be all alone."

The Tactical Coordinator requests Electronic Support Measures (ESM) contact to detect and analyse the lone ship's radar emissions and give a bearing. The Orion descends for closer inspection and a photographic run. The pilot watches keenly through binoculars, gyro-stabilised to damp out vibrations of the aircraft and the human hand to give more stable magnified images. "Its a KASHIN, either Soviet or Indian." He can clearly see the SAN-1 anti-aircraft missiles fore and aft and the Peel Group missile radar on the masts. The warship turns out to be Indian, probably headed east for the Nicobar Islands. The Orion climbs to 2,000 feet to continue its patrol, cruising at 230 knots with one engine shut down to save fuel for the long trek.

This is a typical friendly encounter for an RAAF P-3C crew on a military surveillance flight along the "Iron Highway", a heavily trafficked shipping route running from below Sri Lanka to the northern tip of Sumatra. In its peacetime role, the RAAF's fleet of 20 P-3C Orions regularly patrol the Pacific and Indian oceans to monitor shipping activities in Australia's strategic region.

Named appropriately after the mythical Greek hunter, the Orion is a modified Lockheed Electra airliner with enough fuel and engine power for a range of more than 8,000 kilometres, over 12 hours endurance and 400 knots speed. The P-3C has powerful digital computers onboard to analyse and display the mass of data received by the aircraft's varied sensor arrays, used to hunt submarines and surface ships.

In wartime, the Orion relies on its sensors to track hostile targets while staying out of missile range and relaying the information to other airborne and maritime units. Its excellent communications can give strike direction for other Harpoon-fitted aircraft or ships.

The Orion's radar employs synchronised fore and aft antennae to sweep through 360 degrees for surface targets out to 100 nautical miles. Special ESM receivers, detecting and analysing other vessels' radar emissions, are used for intelligence gathering and threat warning of hostile radars. To enhance viewing at night or in hazy conditions, the Infra-Red Detecting System (IRDS), using a steerable detector mounted on the Orion's chin, gives a high resolution contrasting temperature TV image of a target. The Orion's tail has the long Magnetic Anomaly Detector (MAD) boom to pick up variations in the earth's magnetic field such as those caused by submarines even when submerged.

For more refined detection and tracking the Orion uses sonobuoys. Launched or dropped free-fall from the aircraft, sonobuoys consist of a surface buoy with a suspended submerged array of underwater microphones. They transmit all acoustic signals to the AQS-901 receiver-processor unit onboard which extracts the signature of a ship or submarine and gives a precise bearing.

For coordinating maritime defence, conducting surveillance patrols and armed to hunt and sink enemy warships and submarines, the P-3C Orion is a truly multi-role asset for Australia's defence in depth.

LOCKHEED P-3C ORION

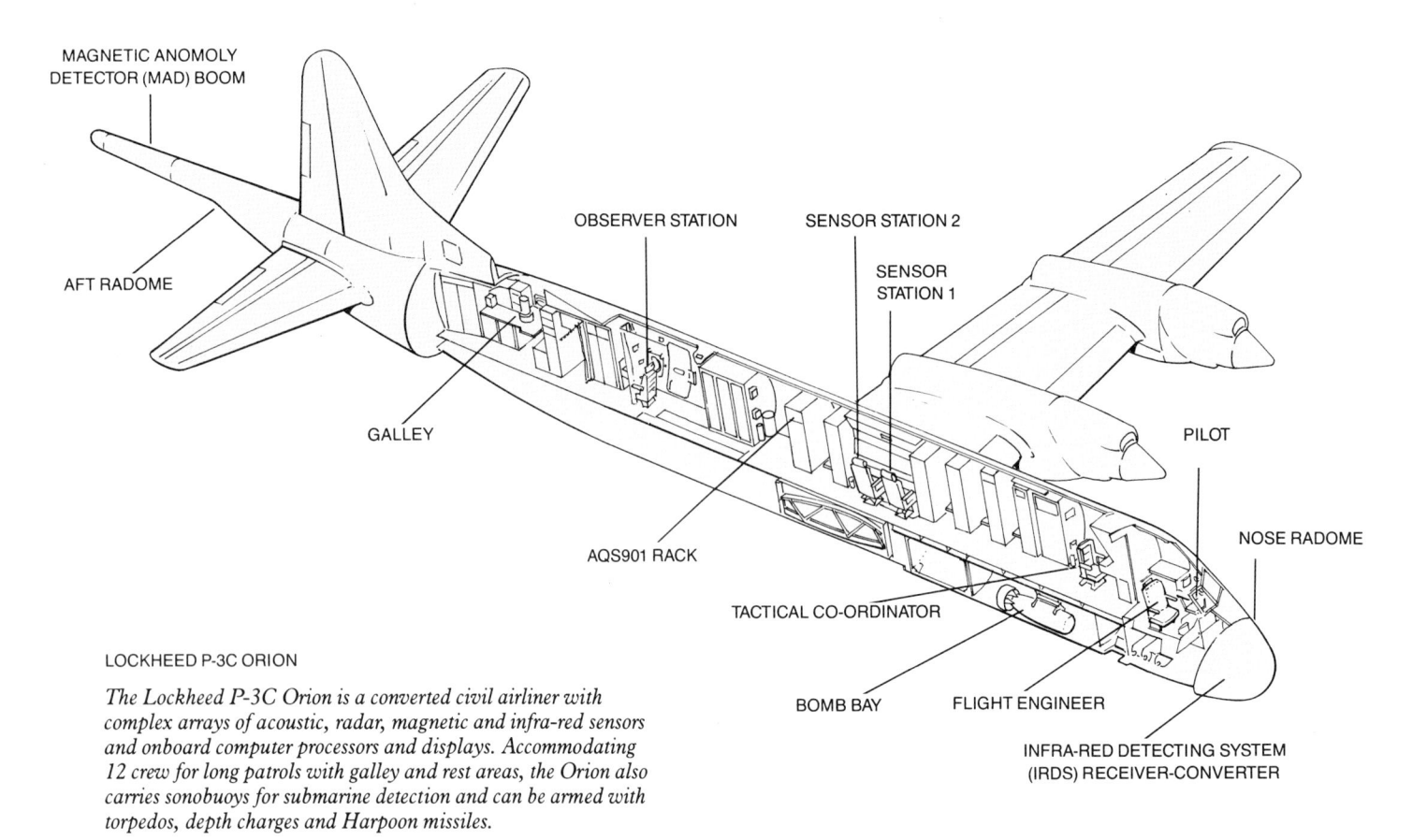

The Lockheed P-3C Orion is a converted civil airliner with complex arrays of acoustic, radar, magnetic and infra-red sensors and onboard computer processors and displays. Accommodating 12 crew for long patrols with galley and rest areas, the Orion also carries sonobuoys for submarine detection and can be armed with torpedos, depth charges and Harpoon missiles.

An Orion's Air Electronics Analyst officer feeds a sonobuoy tube into a chute in the Orion's launch bay. Most sonobuoys are loaded before flight from outside the aircraft.

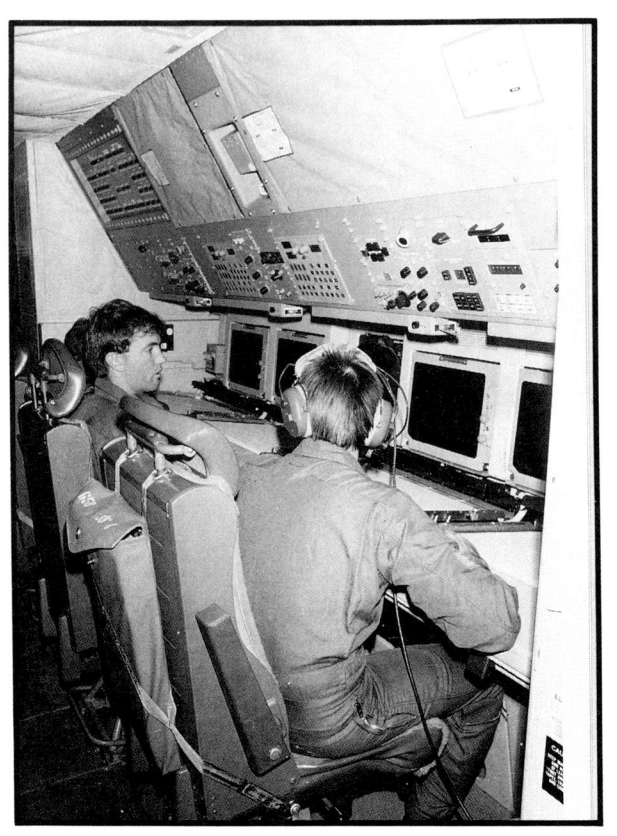

Orion electronics operators at Sensor Stations 1 and 2 monitor up to 16 sonobuoys simultaneously through the AQS901 acoustic processor to detect, classify and locate targets.

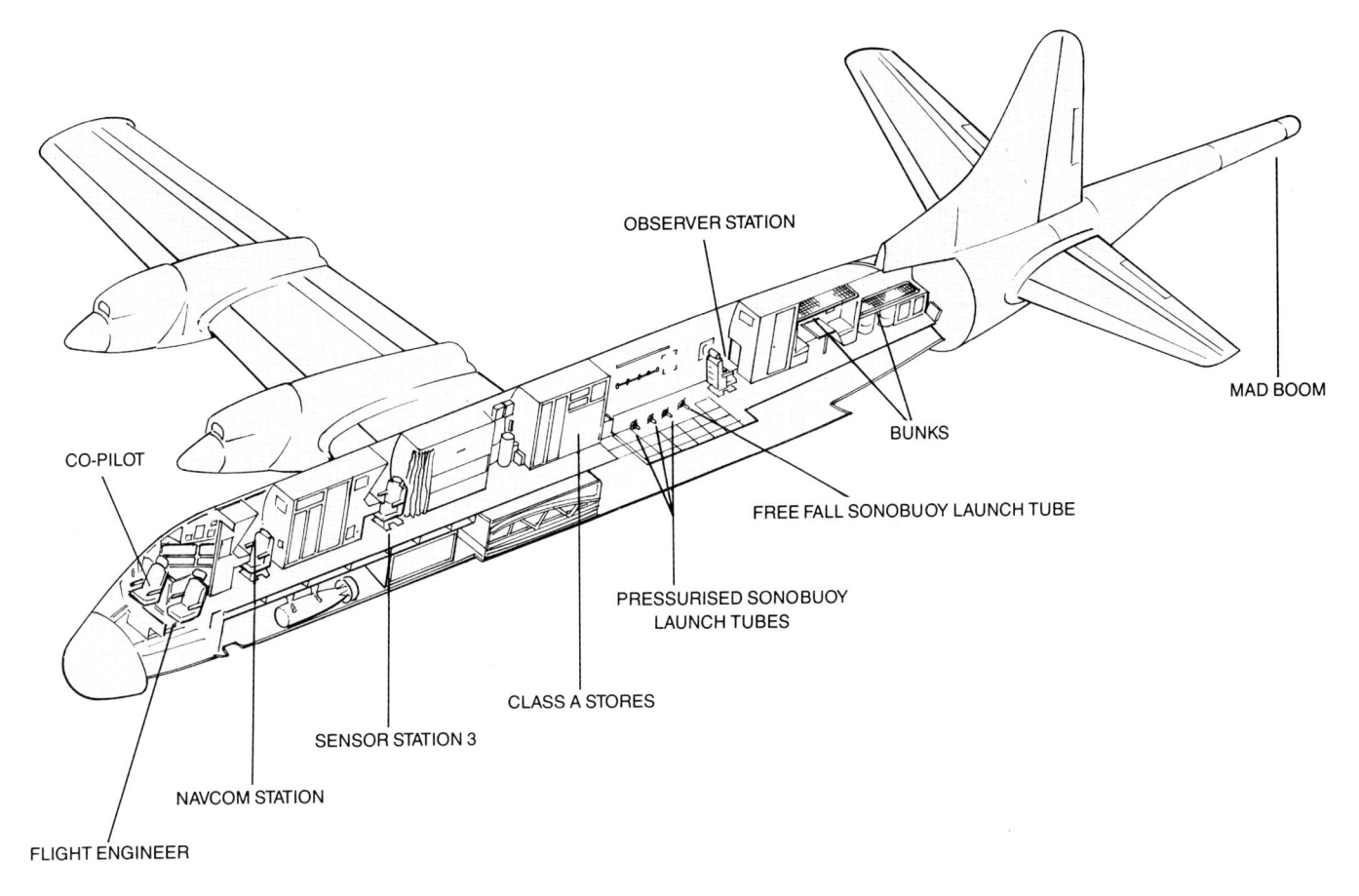

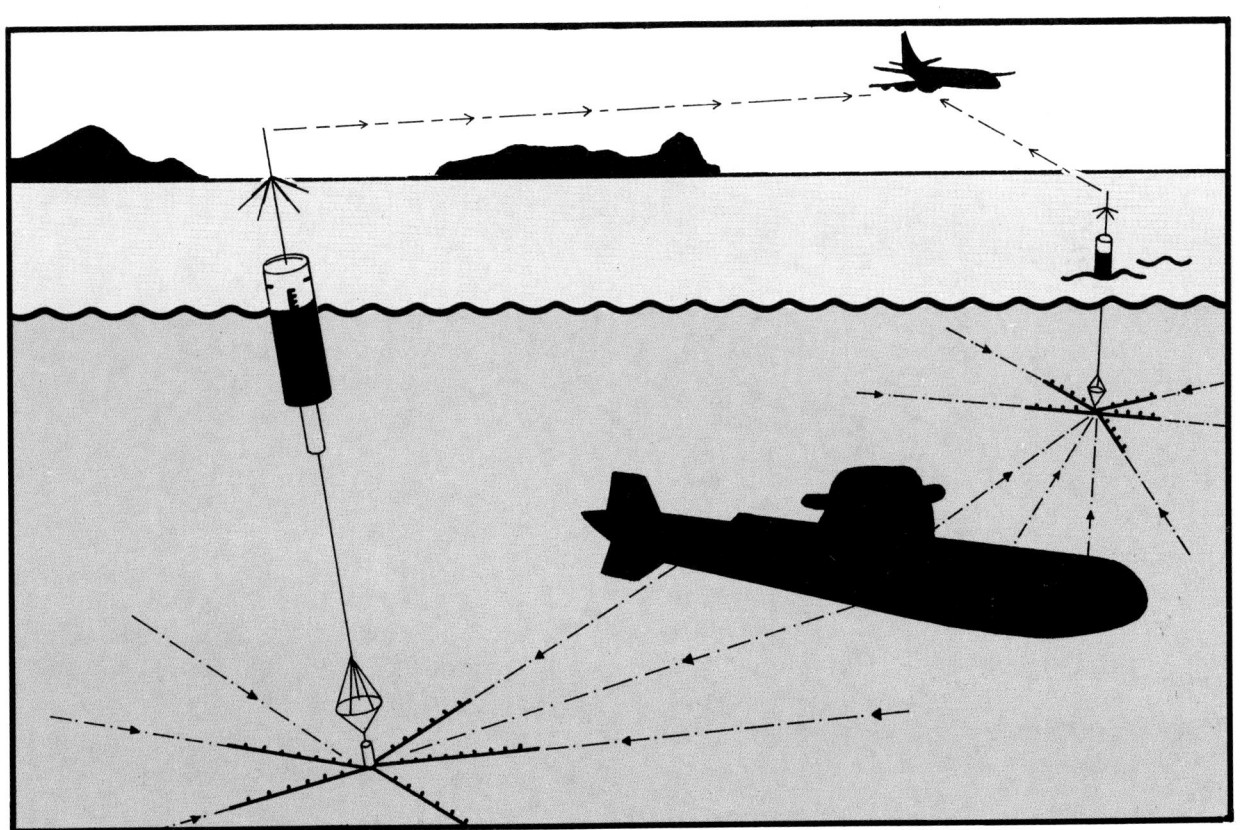

Launched from an Orion aircraft or a Sikorsky Seahawk chopper, Australian-designed Barra sonobuoys deploy a suspended array of hydrophones, operated at selected depths. Either singly or laid in patterns, sonobuoys can detect the quietest submarines in noisy waters and relay bearing and speed information to the Orion to plot the target's position.

Against the dramatic Sunrise Mountains in Nevada, F-111s of No. 1 Squadron RAAF await their young pilots in the daring biennial Red Flag exercise in April 1989. Since its inception in 1975, Red Flag has claimed 33 pilots' lives.

ation. The Orion's capabilities are not based on any revolutionary design, like the F-111, but instead on the equipment it carries. Its roomy airliner fuselage provides the space for a large range of sensors and computers which enable the crew of 12 to perform surveillance, interdiction and strike, anti-submarine warfare and fishery patrols throughout the Pacific and Indian Ocean regions and neighbouring South-East Asian areas.

The need for such duties has been a defence priority since World War II. Firstly a squadron of purpose-built Neptune P2V5s and another of converted Lincoln bombers undertook the role, then in 1961 the Lincolns were replaced by more advanced Neptunes, which contained modern acoustic and electronic detection gear. But the added equipment weighed down the planes, reducing their range, and in the late 1960s the Neptunes began to be replaced by Orions, which had good speed, habitability for the tropics, and above all, excellent range capability. The current crop of 20 P-3Cs can trek more than 8,000 kilometres with a transit cruising speed of more than 700 kph.

In peacetime, their main occupation is to keep track of shipping activities in Australia's surrounds. Regular patrols fly over both the Pacific and Indian Oceans, and under agreement with the Malaysian Government the Orions also gather for both countries information from the South China Sea and the northeast corner of the Indian Ocean. As well, the P-3Cs are often called upon to assist in search and rescue activities in the whole region.

In wartime, the Orion has an important role of coordinating the RAAF's air elements during maritime strikes. Or it can carry out an action unaided by firing its own anti-ship Harpoon missiles. Given Australia's military defence priority emphasising surveillance and operating in the north, the Orions, along with the F-111s, form a major part of the country's triad of combat airpower.

The final link is made up by the fighters. Dramatic advances in aircraft design during the

Carrying long-range fuel tanks, an RAAF Mirage lifts its nose for take-off at Butterworth base in Malaysia. Four Mirage squadrons, Nos. 3, 75, 77 and 79, did tours of duty at RAAF Butterworth from 1969 until 1988.

jet age have reshaped all the world's airforces, and from the mid-1950s supersonic fighters quickly began to replace their slower ancestors. Just two years after the first Australian-built Sabre was airborne, a superb new fighter flew in France, while the US, Britain and the Soviet Union had made rapid leaps in supersonic fighter production. Australia's defence planners knew that they would have to catch up; the Sabres were day fighters only, with an advanced gunsight but no search radar. In a world where major developments had occurred in airborne intercept radar combined with improved ground defences, the F-86 was now an easy kill.

A number of new aircraft were considered, the two main contenders being the Lockheed F-104 Starfighter and the French Mirage. But the Mirage's handling was far superior, and while the F-104 carried only a Sidewinder missile, the early Mirage was similarly equipped but had the additional benefit of an all-hemisphere weapon which gave it the ability to attack from all quarters. Later the Mirages' Sidewinders were replaced with Matra missiles.

It was the era of tail shoots and incredibly fast fighters with top speeds of more than Mach 2. The Mirage represented the full development in that direction, and performed its interceptor role easily. Unlike other fighters of the time, it could get quickly to a high Mach number and manoeuvre once there, enabling it to get to attacking aircraft faster and further away.

During production testing of a prototype Mirage IIIA in France, the RAAF's Squadron Leader Bill Collings, who was a test pilot with the Aircraft Research and Development Unit, stretched the new fighter to its limits. In his first flight, he took off, climbed and accelerated to Mach 2, before turning back towards the base and landing. "That was 19 minutes," Collings recalled, "and I didn't have much fuel left. It was very fast."

The first 30 of an eventual 116 RAAF Mirage 1110s were ordered in 1960, and all but the initial two aircraft were made in Australia.

ON TARGET

Even with the most modern weapons, a miss is still as good as a mile. For an aircraft bomb to inflict any decisive damage on an enemy bridge foundation or hardened shelter, it must hit within five metres of the bulls-eye. Aircraft fitted with the best optical or radar bombing systems can usually achieve five metre accuracy under favourable circumstances. But conditions are rarely perfect and factors such as bad weather, aircraft reliability and the pressure of combat all contribute to aircrew stress and reduce bombing accuracy.

The solution is weapons that can be guided to or independently home in on a target using the heat, radar, sound or laser energy emitted by the target or reflected from it. These guided weapons have been developed for air, surface and underwater use, and in most cases can be fired from a far greater distance than conventional bombs, shells or torpedos.

For anti-submarine attacks, the RAAF's P-3C Orion launches either Mk 44 or Mk 46 torpedos, which home in on their target using the reflected sound from their own active sonars or noise emitted from the target itself. For air-to-air combat, the RAAF's F/A-18 Hornets use "Sidewinder" and "Sparrow" missiles. The "Sidewinder" is a short-range heat-seeking missile which employs infra-red emissions from the enemy aircraft's engines to "lock-on" and home in. The "Sparrow", on the other hand, uses return echoes bounced off the enemy by the Hornet's radars to home in on aircraft within a radius of 30 nautical miles.

For precision bombing of ground targets, the RAAF has Guided Bomb Units. These are conventional 2,000 lb and 500 lb bombs fitted with laser detectors and steerable fins to make them "smart" bombs. Called GBU-10s and GBU-12s respectively, they can be guided to home in on targets illuminated by laser energy. The United States Air Force and Navy pioneered laser-guided "smart" bombs during the attacks on North Vietnam in 1972. The technique required two aircraft, one to illuminate the target with a laser beam and a second to drop the bomb, which homed in on the beam.

The RAAF's F-111s are presently being equipped with Pave Tack pods. The Pave Tack pod has a revolving head with a turret on which are mounted two laser-designators and a forward-looking infra-red window (FLIR). The FLIR system uses infrared energy to form a detailed picture of the ground ahead to guide the pilot in all weathers, day or night, while the advanced laser-designators make it possible for a single aircraft to laser-guide its own weapon.

Using Pave Tack for a bomb run, the two-man crew of an F-111 can identify the target with FLIR. They then make a low-level approach, climb swiftly to release or "throw-off" their bomb while still some distance from the target, switch on their laser-designators and then quickly dive and turn away, keeping under the enemy radars and avoiding over-flying the heavily defended target area. Gyro-stabilised systems hold the laser beam on target throughout the bomber's flight even as the aircraft makes its quick escape. The ability of laser-guided weapons to be released out of range of enemy radars and missiles and still hit home with pinpoint accuracy enhances the aircraft's survivability.

Guided weapons give their user increased, and often decisive, range and accuracy. And just as importantly for the RAAF with its relatively small number of bombers, it improves the chances of the aircraft returning from a successful mission.

Using Pave Tack (above), the F-111's navigator/weapons controller, seated right in the cockpit (below), uses a hood for infra-red and laser viewing.

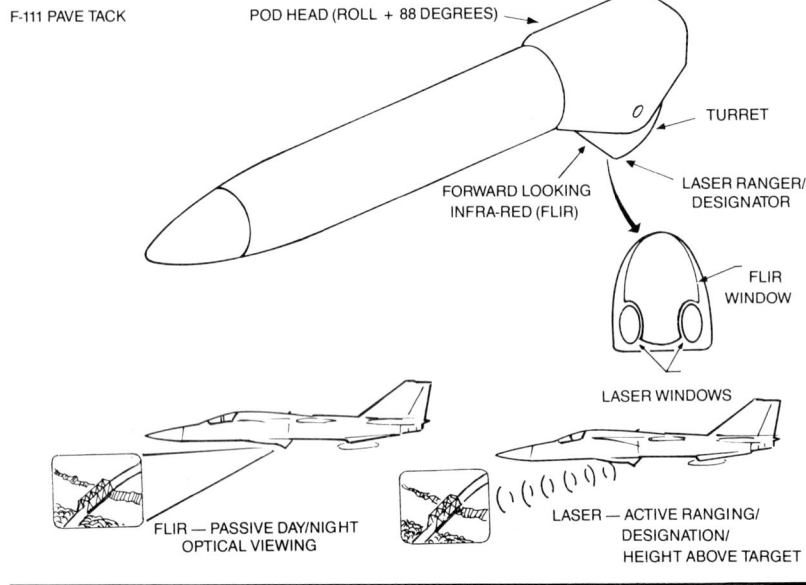

Left: From the weapons controller's point of view, an infra-red image of Sydney's Centrepoint Tower has the target designator locked on the revolving restaurant, photographed during an F-111's night exercise bombing run over the city. Pave Tack can give "through-the-window" pinpoint accuracy. Below: An F-111 has its Pave Tack pod lowered beneath the centre fuselage.

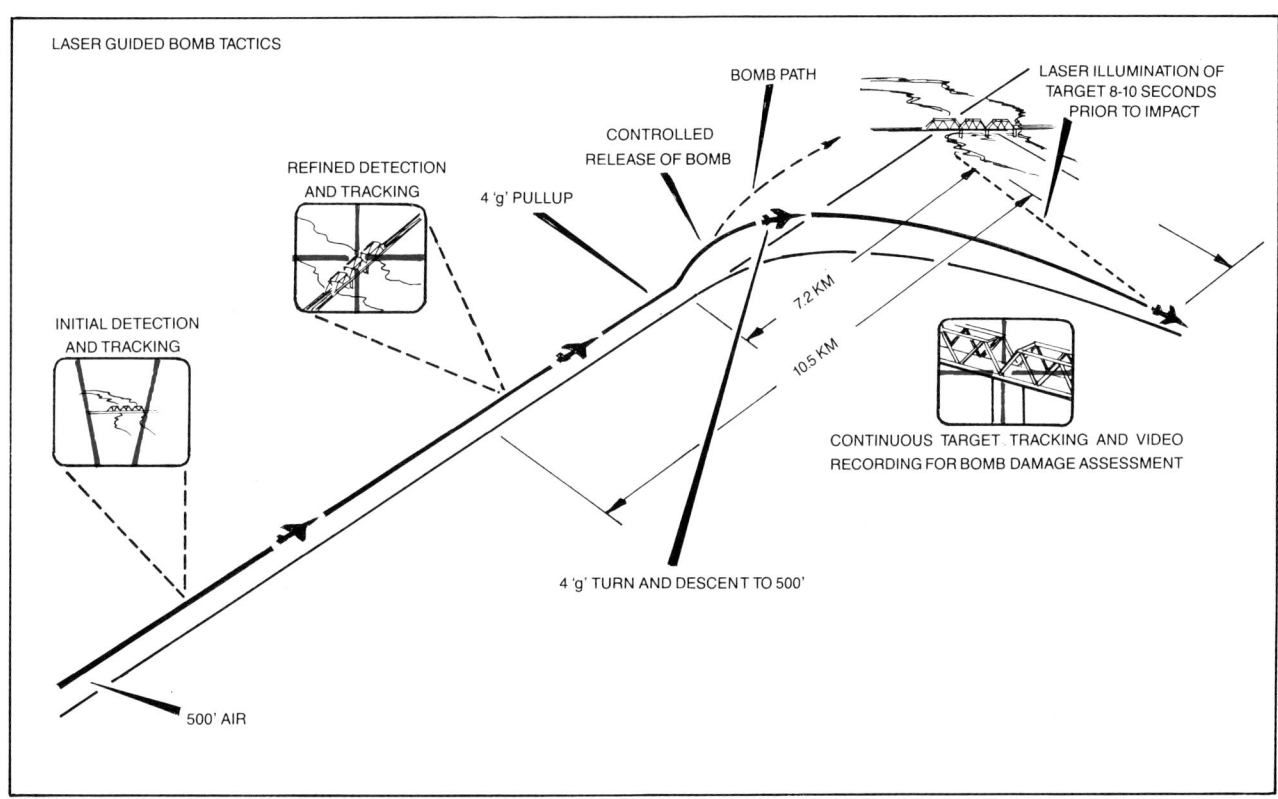

Using Pave Tack for bomb delivery, an F-111 makes a low-level run at 500 feet into the target area, locating the target bridge by infra-red imaging. While still out of hostile radar range, the plane guides a laser beam onto the target, climbs quickly, "tosses" the bomb towards the bridge and turns away, descending to 500 feet again. The Pave Tack then swivels around and sends a second pulse to the target to guide the bomb in the last seconds of flight.

Collings went on to test fly the first Australian-built Mirage. "On high speed runs I had to take them out to Mach 1.8 and get between 3.6 and 3.8G. It was a magnificent machine to fly," he recalled. "In handling terms, it was a simple aircraft. The only time you needed utmost precision was on approach to landing, because it had a very fast approach speed — and we didn't have very long runways."

Although it was the time of the Vietnam War, the Mirages were not utilised there. However, they were formed into four squadrons, two in Australia and two as part of a garrison flying and training out of Butterworth in Malaysia. In both ground attack and interceptor roles during exercises there, the aircraft performed admirably, and its presence contributed greatly to the stability of the region south of the war zone.

But, in common with other single-engine, supersonic aircraft, the Mirage was unforgiving when things went wrong. Pilots commented that without power it "glided like a brick", and in emergencies the airmen had to act quickly in deciding to eject or not; by the time the Mirages began to be replaced in the mid-1980s, more than 30 of the aircraft had been lost. They ceased operations at Butterworth in the first half of 1988 and the last RAAF Mirage flew operationally in early 1989.

Despite the Mirage's blisteringly fast speed, it had, however, become outdated. Technology had raced ahead at an increasing pace, and true lookdown-shootdown missile capability had started to appear on the newer fighters used by both NATO and Warsaw Pact airforces. Rather than carrying only one all-weather missile as the Mirage did, they carried four. Huge advances has also been made in air-to-surface capability with the advent of laser-guided bombs, TV-guided air-launched missiles, and stand-off cruise missiles for attacking ships and other surface targets. The performance of the Mirage was still impressive, but as a weapons platform it was obsolete.

The competition to select a new fighter for the RAAF was hard and protracted. Under initial consideration was Dassault's Mirage 2000 from France, the F-15 Eagle and F-18 Hornet from McDonnell-Douglas in the US, General Dynamics's F-16 Fighting Falcon also from America, and from the United Kingdom the Panavia Tornado.

The Mirage lost out owing to a range shortfall when compared to the other contenders. The Eagle and the Tornado were basically air-to-air fighters and not truly multi-role aircraft. Which left the Hornet and the F-16. Two factors pointed towards the Hornet being favoured: it had two engines instead of one, which greatly affected the programme cost over the life of the aircraft; and, importantly, the F-16 did not at the time possess all-weather capability with a laser-guided missile.

The F/A-18s entered service with the RAAF in 1984. Multi-role aircraft in the past were often afflicted by compromises in their capabilities — they were jacks of all trades but masters of none. The high quality of the Hornets, however, their partial carbon-composite makeup giving strength and lightness, their acceleration, their range, their electronic wizardry, gave the pilots who fly them the confidence needed to succeed in high-tech air operations. As well, the RAAF has established a strong infrastructure to support the Hornets in their planned deployment. They fly at Williamtown in NSW and Tindal in the Northern Territory, and they also operate frequently from other bases, particularly those in the north at Townsville and Darwin, and are planned to fly in and out of the bare bases at Learmonth, Derby and Cape York. The Hornets will thus be able to cover adequately the northern half of the continent, fully armed and at short notice. Such effectiveness will be further enhanced by the in-flight refuelling capability of remodelled RAAF Boeing 707s.

The F/A-18s are undoubtedly the spearhead of the RAAF's aim to quickly concentrate combat airpower anywhere in Australia's north. Together with over-the-horizon radar and airborne early warning aircraft, a fully integrated air defence system will be able to cover the continent's most vulnerable airspace,

Once supersonic, now superannuated, French-designed Mirages sit "mothballed" in a RAAF hangar, after their withdrawal from Australian service in 1988. Since 1984, the RAAF's Mirage pilots have been retrained for Hornets.

even with just 75 Hornets at call over such a vast area. And in Australia's part of the world, that capability is unmatched. Together with naval surveillance, and army readiness on land, the F/A-18s are the front line of a defence force that demonstrates strength and combat capability. Their red kangaroo insignias, and those of all the RAAF's squadrons, tell the world that Australia is prepared to defend its approaches and to maintain its region's stability and welfare. The Hornets will take that commitment well into the 21st century.

Flight Lieutenant "Bert" Foster was totally dedicated to his mission now. The Pitch Black commanders had placed the defence of Darwin in his and the squadron's hands.

The combat air patrols were in the best possible position to meet any incoming attack; Foster's formation and two others like it were spread out to cover the northern approaches into the area, their positions controlled by men and women on the ground at the Control and Reporting Unit using a large air-defence radar at nearby Lee Point.

If, however, the enemy came in on the deck as expected, the big radar would not figure in any detection. The Hornet's APG-65 pulse-Doppler radar would most likely get the early contact.

Foster now picked up the incoming hostile aircraft. Two large gaggles were heading straight for Darwin, their prime target the strategically vital dockyards. With no rail link to Darwin, all of the Territory's needs could not be met by road transport alone. Shipping and its support facilities were major targets and needed full protection; even as the battle unfolded, two of the Royal Australian Navy's FFG guided-missile frigates patrolled close to shore as last-ditch defenders in case of air attack.

The attackers continued on their way, and Foster manoeuvred his formation off to one side, aiming to allow the first package through. His on-board electronic support measures, the aircraft's integrated mission computers, had indicated that the first group of incoming aircraft were probably F-15 pre-strike fighters.

The Australians' plan this morning was to take out the A-6 bombers, but the trick would be not to get too close to the Eagles. The F-15s were capable of carrying four AIM-7 Sparrow missiles for medium range attack as well as four AIM-9 Sidewinder missiles for close-in work. The Hornets carried only two of each, and even though the hardware was the same, they were obviously outgunned. The Eagles could afford to launch a missile at maximum range even when a target manoeuvre would trash the

After another day's "fighting" over Williamtown, Hornet pilots of No. 3 Squadron, cross the flight line for a mission debriefing of up to two hours. Regular full-scale international exercises like Pitch Black in northern Australia and Cope Thunder in the Philippines test RAAF pilots' skills and tactics, honed in rigorous daily combat sorties.

weapon — they would still have three left with which to make a kill.

Foster's geometry had worked well. Not wanting to face the Eagles or the Intruders front-on, which would have positioned him as a hittable target, he had offset his formation to enable it to attack in a pincer-like move. The other members of the team then picked up and started to sort the incoming bombers.

The Hornets approached, the pilots working through their various modes of radar to line up their victims. Then, individual bombers were allocated as targets for each of the Australian fighters. It was a vitally important stage of their defence, ensuring that two Hornets did not launch Sparrows against the same aircraft. With only two of the expensive radar-guided weapons per fighter, if the proper sorting was not carried out the enemy could get through.

Foster selected range-while-search mode, readying himself for an attack. First he made sure he had placed himself in the strike envelope — he was just inside his Sparrow's range. The message came up on his HUD, confirming that he was correctly positioned. Then came the next cue: he could now shoot. Foster pulled the trigger.

In a real war, a second and a quarter later the Sparrow missile would have been ejected from its bay and the rocket motor ignited, taking the deadly weapon on its course of destruction. Today, however, the Hornets were flying in simulator mode. All the mid-air moves could be made, even the trigger pulled; the only difference being was that the weapons were not released. The information from the radar was genuine, and the HUD symbology was for real, indicating the imaginary path of the Sparrow as it headed for its Intruder.

Soon after the missile launch, Foster turned away from the direction of the attack, initially through about 50 degrees so that he could keep the bandits illuminated with his radar and continue to direct his Sparrow. Then, his HUD indicated that the missile had timed out, striking the bomber.

He now turned further, heading towards the threat direction and looking for more raiders. The strike on the bombers had yet to be reported by the radar controllers on the ground, but they now passed on the message that relief was on the way for Foster's formation. Another group of Hornets was approaching, and they would be better placed to attack the bombers still flying. Foster and his mates were directed back towards the tankers to once again top up their fuel tanks. Only four missiles had been fired, so after refuelling they would probably be directed to another patrol position.

The pressure was off for the moment. Exercises so often went this way, and as Foster brought his Hornet around to its new heading, he wondered if the RAAF's rigorous training would prepare him for any real battle. It was hard to say. Although the Hornets and Eagles had met earlier in previous wargames, undertaking pure air-to-air battles, such exercises could never fully put the aircraft through their paces. Thankfully, the two fighters would never meet in mortal combat.

With missiles not leaving their fighters when exercising, the outcome of the air-to-air engagements was often inconclusive. And in a genuine stoush, having aircraft going down in smoking wreckage would certainly raise anxiety levels. Absent mates in the bar at night would also greatly affect the squadron's morale. These were the unknown elements that the men and machines of the RAAF might never face. Still, they worked long and hard to be the best in the sky, so that the Australian continent below could remain forever secure.

SPECIAL OPERATIONS

A Zodiac boat is launched from an RAAF Hercules as a six man Special Air Service (SAS) Regiment team prepares to parachute into the sea.

COMMANDO ELITE

During World War II, the Australian Army raised and operated a number of independent companies and commando squadrons to wreak havoc behind Japanese lines with aggressive raids and sabotage strikes. These important missions and specialised combat skills continue today in the Army's regular and reserve special action forces.

The inheritors of this commando tradition are the men of the Army's 1st Commando Regiment, organised as two volunteer reserve companies based in Sydney and Melbourne. Highly trained in both airborne and amphibious operations, the commandos operate in strengths of up to a hundred men. They can be sent in ahead of regular troops to sieze and hold or find and destroy enemy installations. Or they can be dropped far behind enemy lines on scores of missions, from rescuing prisoners to attacking power plants or radars.

The regulars of the Special Air Service Regiment, or SAS, train for situations requiring a small team of dedicated professionals. Their elite reputation is well deserved. In Vietnam, over a six year period, the SAS conducted more than 1,300 patrols, killing nearly 500 enemy for the loss of only two men by hostile action, and gathering information on enemy activities in the Australian area of operations.

Today, the SAS are based at Swanbourne Barracks in Western Australia, where they train to operate in teams of four to six men for long-range reconnaissance and surveillance, and raids deep in enemy territory. On such missions, SAS teams are covertly inserted by parachuting from high altitudes into the sea or rapelling from a hovering helicopter into jungle. In amphibious operations they are transported by submarine from which small craft such as kayaks or Zodiac inflatable boats, with silenced outboard motors, quickly take them ashore.

Once on the ground the SAS man relies largely on his skills of camouflage and fieldcraft for concealed observation and reporting. His weapons are usually silenced versions of standard infantry weapons but he can select from a worldwide arsenal for a particular job: from a rugged Soviet AK-47 assault rifle to a stubby little German Heckler and Koch submachine-gun. At night, SAS marksmen can use ambient light and infra-red goggles to find their way. The SAS are also trained in the art of winning the allegiance of disaffected locals and training them for guerilla warfare — used in both Vietnam and the Pacific war.

The growth in international terrorism has created a new peacetime role for the SAS, whose skills make them ideal to counter hijackings and other hostage situations. A squadron of the SAS are on permanent stand-by and train for all possible terrorist scenarios in an indoor training complex at Swanbourne, grimly named the "Killing House". Here encounters are at short range, often in dim light, as SAS teams shoot live ammunition with only a split second to distinguish "terrorist" from "hostage".

In all their roles, the SAS maintain the proud tradition of Australian special operations. "He who dares, wins," is their motto and their techniques are nothing if not daring.

Disguised by balaclavas, SAS troopers parachute from a Hercules during an exercise. Even in official photographs, SAS members' identities are kept secret for security reasons.

Exhaustion shows on a young soldier's face during a gruelling SAS selection course which includes a daily 20-kilometre run with rifle and 40-kilogram pack. The SAS demands exceptional intelligence, physical stamina and skill.

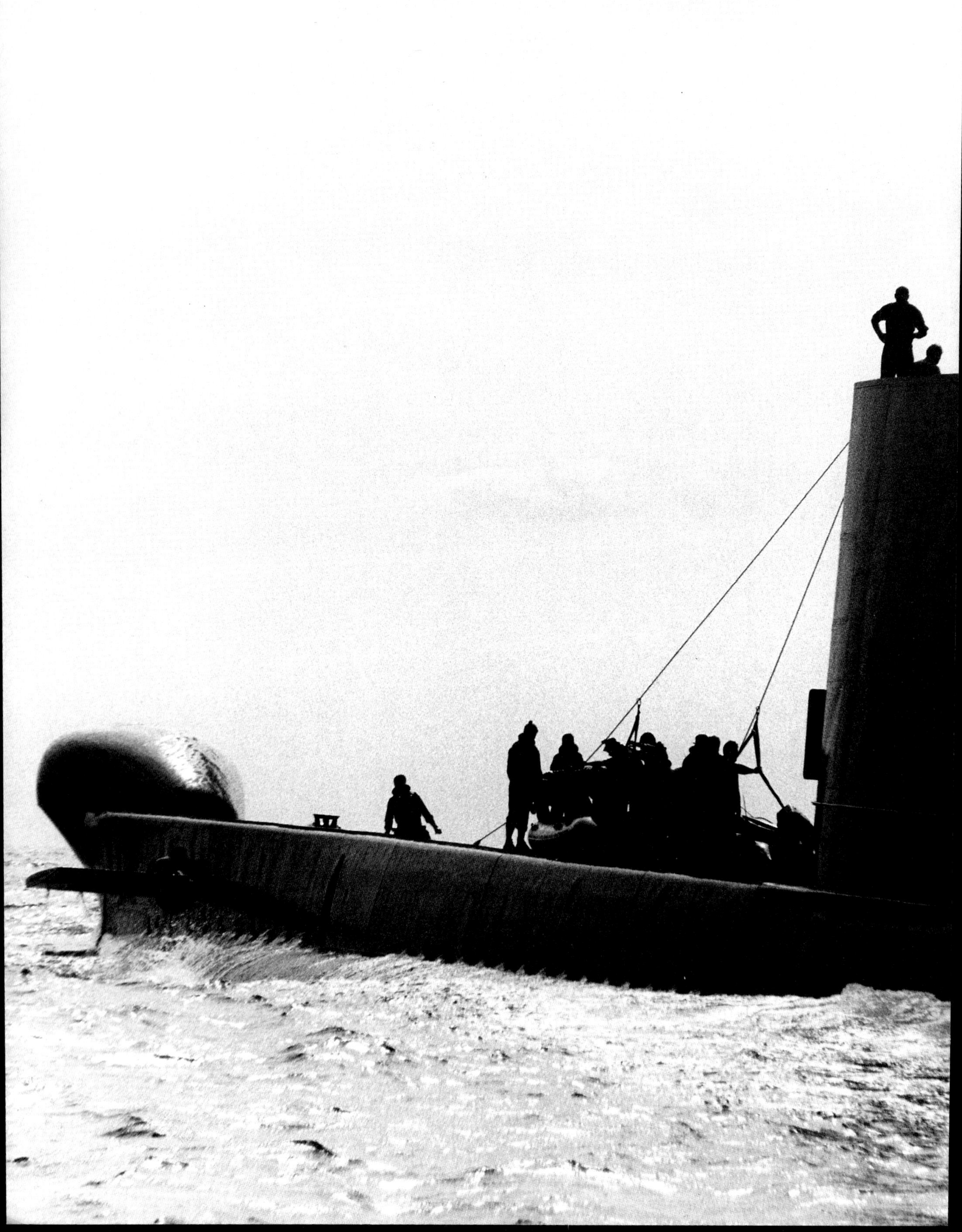

Left: During a seaborne operation exercise, an SAS patrol launches an inflatable boat from an Oberon submarine to quickly go ashore on a reconnaissance or sabotage mission in enemy territory. Above: Similarly trained for covert amphibious landings, commandos of the reserve 1st Commando Regiment storm up the beach from their Zodiac craft. For both SAS and commando patrols, the objective of such missions is to preserve secrecy and, unless ordered, avoid engaging the enemy.

Above: During counter-terrorist training at Swanbourne Barracks, SAS troopers enter the "Killing House" where, in a real-life exercise involving live ammunition, they must kill "terrorists" and rescue "hostages". There is no margin for error. Right: A heavily laden SAS team rapels from a hovering helicopter to begin a long-range reconnaissance patrol through the rugged Stirling Ranges in Western Australia.

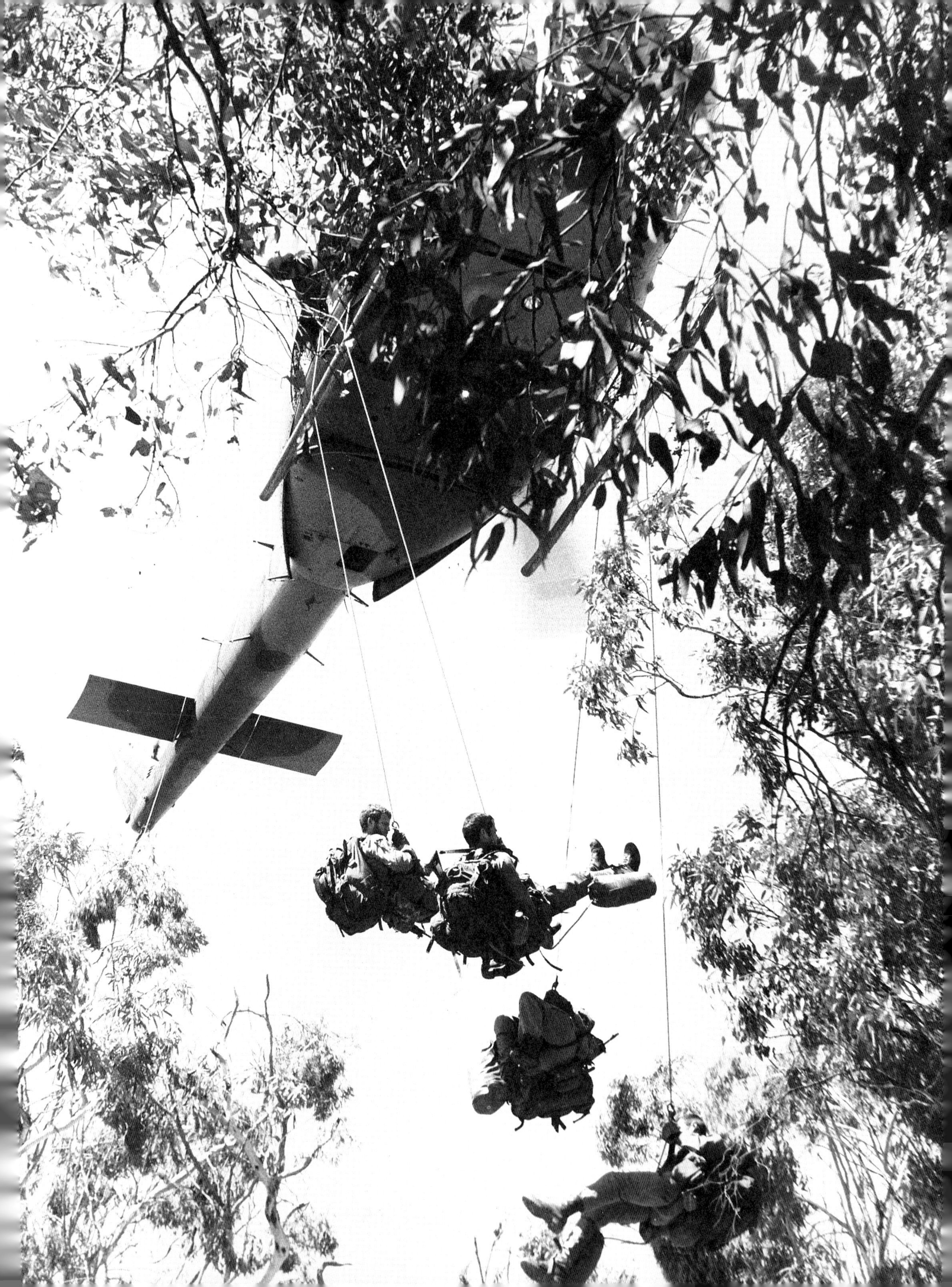

4
A MOBILE ARMY

Having perfected jungle warfare in Malaya, Borneo, and Vietnam, the Army today has changed its tactics and strategic shape for defence of Australia's vast north. Modernising its inventory of weapons from helicopters to small-arms, the modern Army is a mobile and flexible force.

It was noon and the sun beat down mercilessly on the backs of a six-man patrol steering their dinghies through the quiet waters of the Jackson River in North Queensland. Only the sound of the outboards and the occasional birdcall cut through the throbbing hum of cicadas and the buzz of mosquitos in the heat. Platoon commander Sergeant David Whitehead was satisfied with his patrol's progress so far but there was no time to relax. The soldiers nursed their rifles, watching intently for any movement on this crocodile infested river. The big fresh-water crocodiles in this area strike unexpectedly and with frightening speed.

The task of this surveillance and reconnaissance patrol from the Army's 51st Far North Queensland Regiment, was to find a crossing point on the river for an overland route to the northern tip of Cape York Peninsula. It was their second day out on a four day patrol in this remote and inhospitable country. Each man had specialist skills as medic, radio operator or driver and all were trained riflemen — skills needed for survival on such long treks. The

A kangaroo on crossed swords, surmounted by the Crown, comprises the Australian Regular Army's official insignia.

previous day, their two Toyota Landcruisers, packed with personal gear, rations, jerry cans of water, two 12-foot aluminium dinghies and a radio set, had negotiated the rough inland route from Weipa, 80 kilometres back down the coast. At Cullens Point the Landcruisers were unloaded and camouflaged in a hide before the patrol set out on its trip upstream.

It had been a long hot day out on the river when late in the afternoon, the waters became shallower. Satisfied they had found a suitable crossing, the patrol went ashore and checked their position on their maps. Sergeant Whitehead contacted the Regiment's headquarters at Cairns on his high-frequency AN/PRC-F1 radio and reported the patrol's location. At some later date, another patrol will come forward to confirm this route, but for Dave Whitehead and his men the job was done and as dusk approached they set up camp for a night under the stars.

The 51st Far North Queensland Regiment is one of the Army's three regional force surveillance units operating in the deep north. Manned by reservists, these units are gradually, patrol by patrol, gaining an increasingly detailed picture of Australia's Top End from the Kimberley mountain range in the west to Cape York Peninsula in the east. This is the poorly charted and unfamiliar country that the modern Australian Army is preparing to defend and must get to know intimately. During the 1950s and 1960s, Australia's political stance demanded and maintained a forward defence policy which strategically postured all three of its forces towards South-East Asia. Since then, military thinking has altered from fighting an enemy in that region's forests and rice paddies to defending the Australian continent itself.

It is in the north that threats of minor incursions by possible enemy forces are foreseen by today's military planners and the Army's tactics and organisation are being concentrated in the Top End for just such a contingency.

The surveillance units, like the 450-strong 51st Far North Queensland Regiment, play a key role in preparing the Army for northern defence. Their patrols record every natural and man-made feature of military interest — hills, roads, bridges, private airstrips, river and creek crossings. They note where tracks lead, what traffic they can carry, where vehicles can be hidden, what hills give observation over the coastline, what valleys give access to the hinterland. They also note sources of drinking water and take samples back for testing. Depots are being established in most of the major towns, aboriginal settlements and remote homesteads of the Top End. Over half of 51 FNQR's strength comes from aboriginal recruits with invaluable knowledge of their local areas and of "bush tucker" skills for soldiers living off the land on long patrols. For the soldiers who will operate in these remote parts, the patrols are preparing new maps, called "snack maps", which include photographs and descriptions of edible plants and animals to be found in particular areas.

"The country is rugged and variable in the extreme", said 51 FNQR's operations officer, Major Steve Ferndale, "with heavily wooded islands and dead flat coral atolls in Torres Strait, and on the Peninsula, patches of rainforest, mudflats and dry savanna. Tyranny of distance rules here and with only one north-south road, most troops will have to be airlifted into the area. Our task is to find where the helicopters and aircraft can get in and do the job."

Darwin is the focal point of the new activity. The concrete buildings of Larrakeyah barracks, which survived Japanese bombing in World War II, became a sleepy outpost during the years of Australia's forward defence posture, but the base is now bustling with military activity. A new command has been set up there, known as Norcom, which directly covers the Northern Territory and the Kimberley region of northwestern Australia. As the nucleus of joint operations, supported by navy and airforce units, Norcom will be able to quickly mobilise a military response in case of an emergency in the far-flung reaches of the north.

Vital in that chain are links with local authorities that now have to be forged. Any successful land operation to counter harassment, raids and

116 *Watchful for crocodiles, a Norforce patrol cruises a remote river in Queensland. The 51st Far North Queensland Regiment, one of three Norforce surveillan*

nits has an operational area covering 448,000 square kilometres and 1,700 kilometres of coastline.

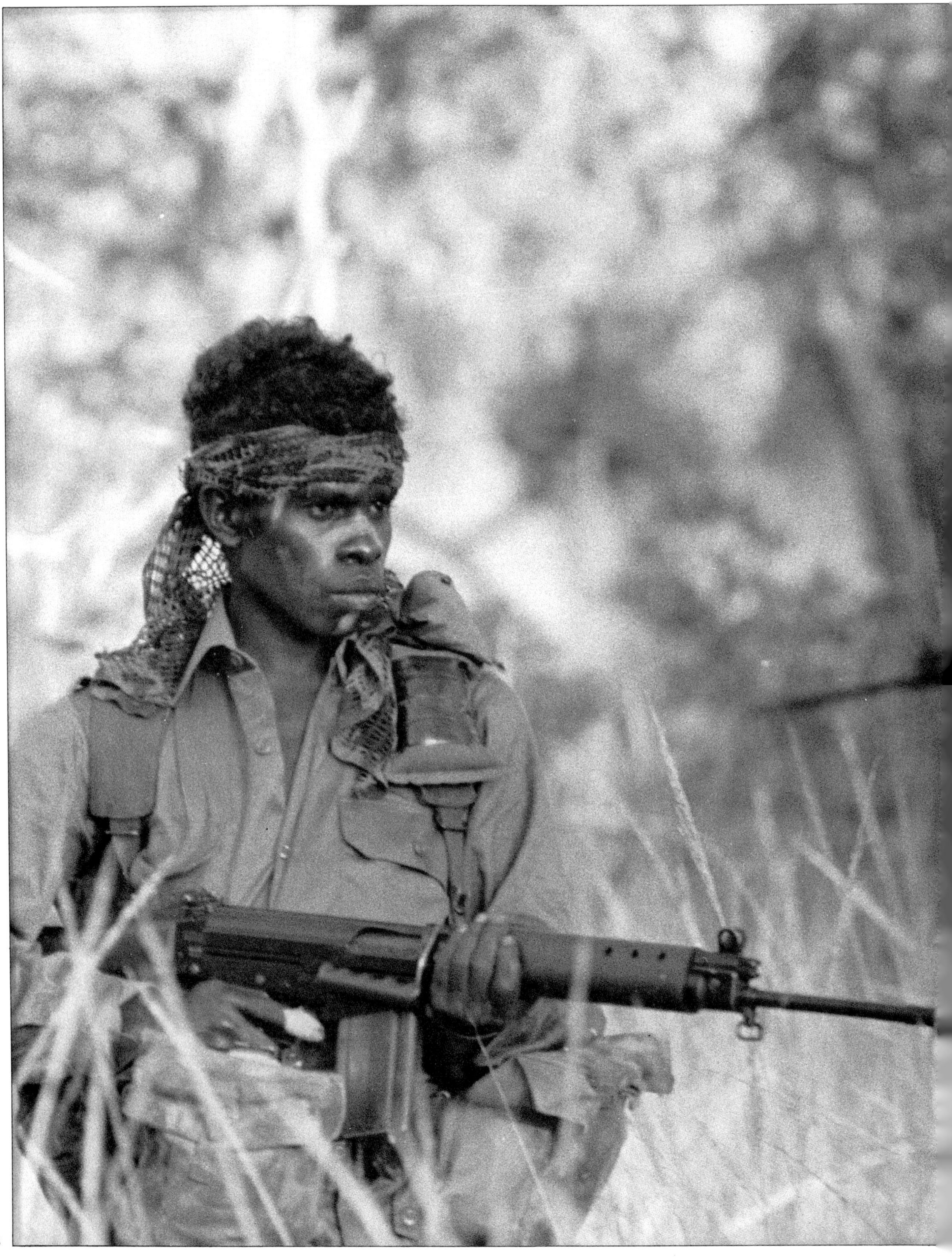

An aboriginal recruit of Norforce, patrols through scrub in the Northern Territory. While the Norforce units, with regular cadre staff, recruit reservists locally, other reserve contingents are sent north for their annual training in key areas they may be called to defend in the future.

incursions will require cooperation with the civilian community and local services will have to be secured. Above all, good Intelligence is vital, and Army Reserve combat units are being given the task of gathering information in the local area and protecting local assets of military value.

"Many of our assets, such as power generation, water supply and the transport and communications systems are vulnerable because of their location near to the coast and their natural openness as civilian services," said Colonel Peter Daniel, Commander of Divisional Engineers of the Reserve 2nd Division based in Sydney, NSW. Applying their civilian technical expertise of how particular industries operate to the problems of defending civilian installations, reserve soldiers have been engaging in mock attack and defence exercises on such targets near their bases in NSW and Victoria. "The next step", said Daniel during one such recent exercise, "is to familiarise these units with similar problems in the Top End. By training in the area, we can maintain our ability to react rapidly to any possible threat."

With the work of the surveillance units and the local knowledge and training of reserve units in the north, Norcom is able to determine the size and composition of the Army's regular forces to be established there and of those to be earmarked for rapid reinforcement in the area should the need arise. To meet the new needs, reorganisation of the Army's regular units is well underway. The first punch to any northern incursion would be delivered by the so-called Operational Deployment Force, focused on the 1st Division's 3rd Brigade, based at Townsville in North Queensland. In addition, battalions of the 1st Division's 1st Brigade, based in NSW and Victoria, are trained and ready as a back-up if a conflict should broaden beyond the capability of the ODF to contain it.

The ability to deploy and reinforce forces rapidly is essential to the new defence plan. Once on the ground in the north, manoeuvrability of men and weapons in all kinds of terrain and climates is the password to survivability. Most army units are now reequipped

Soldiers brave the gruelling confidence and obstacle course at Canungra Land Warfare Centre during the 1988 Regional Skills Competition. Australian troops of 2/4 RAR tested their stamina and aptitude against soldiers from New Zealand, Hong Kong, Malaysia, Papua New Guinea, Thailand and Hawaii — and won.

and reorganised to be lightweight and air portable, a need which became clearly defined in Vietnam when not only infantry but engineers, gunners and signallers were called upon to get personnel and equipment into inaccessible areas very quickly. The terrain in Australia is very different, with greater distances to cover, but the availability of a highly mobile force capable of rapid deployment at short notice remains a major defence priority.

With these major changes in the Army's organisation and strategic planning have come major changes in training and equipment since the heady days of Vietnam. For that generation of soldiers, their keenest and most painful memories of combat training were on Battle Ridge at the Jungle Training Centre at Canungra in southeast Queensland, where final preparations were made before leaving for the terrifying reality of war in Vietnam. In those frantic days of the 1960s, Battle Ridge was training battalion and company groups in the art of fighting and survival in the Asian jungle. Here the skills of ambush and counter-ambush, contact drills and patrolling were honed to a keen edge.

This was the stuff that the Jungle Training Centre had become famous for. It was established during World War II to train soldiers for fighting in the islands north of Australia and as well as the Diggers, many US servicemen also came to appreciate the rigours of Canungra. An aura and mystique grew up around this training school — the total blackness at night under the jungle canopy with the only glimmer of light coming from the fluorescence of the rotting leaves on the jungle floor, haunted many a soldier. Stories spread of US soldiers going into the jungle around the Centre and never finding their way out.

Canungra was closed at the end of hostilities but the Centre was reopened in 1954 to train the Australian contingents for service during the Malayan Emergency. From then on it has continued to serve as an important part in strengthening the battle readiness of Australia's infantry.

The training has always been necessarily tough. One exercise track was made up of rope climbs, low barbed wire and log walls with several surprise mud and slime pits, finishing with a jump from a high tower into the river. It was called the "Confidence Course", but many a young officer in its midst had cause to ponder his future if this was to typify life in the army. One of them later recalled: "It was a most inaptly named piece of bastardry designed to destroy any confidence you had in your own physical abilities."

The training methods and philosophy developed at Canungra have been proved effective over and over again, and never more so than by the advisers of the Australian Army Training Team sent to Vietnam in 1962 to work with the Army of South Vietnam throughout the whole period of hostilities until the team was withdrawn in 1972. The techniques of patrolling, harbour discipline for night-time defence around a patrol's position, and security and silent cordon kept casualties to a minimum and were critical to warfare in the Asian jungle. The lessons of the Malayan and Borneo operations only a few years earlier had convinced the Australians of the value of small-scale operations training. As the war continued, ambush and counter-ambush and contact drills were modified to suit the new weapons and conditions in Vietnam and the Australians began learning new tactics, termed counter revolutionary warfare, to match the guerilla-style tactics of their enemy. The advisers concentrated on junior leadership skills, navigation and patrolling, stealth, marksmanship, combat discipline and close-encounter battle techniques. Australian infantry used the slow, painstaking but effective cordon and search method for entering villages suspected of harbouring Viet Cong. They also began to catch on to the enemy's tricks in order to uncover hidden caches of arms and supplies and cleverly camouflaged tunnel entrances.

As the requirements of training have changed from counter-revolutionary warfare and jungle warfare to defence of the Australian continent itself, Canungra today has become the Land Warfare Centre. With a greater emphasis on

On patrol, a soldier keeps alert watch as he talks to base on an HF/VHF Plessey-Raven back-pack radio set. The Raven field radio network is the combat end of the Army's new communications system.

TALKING BATTLEFIELD

With such an enormous area of responsibility, Australia's key to northern defence will always be mobility. And the only way for the Australian Army to coordinate the movement of military units over thousands of kilometres in the Top End is through a super-sophisticated communications system.

The requirements are complex. In the event of hostilities, orders from the ADF commander in Canberra must pass swiftly and securely down the chain of command through land headquarters and all Divisional levels ultimately to each section in the field. The distances to be covered are great. The Army envisages that in time of war, its brigades and battalions may have to travel as much as 70 kilometres a day, with distances of up to 250 kilometres between units. For managing air strikes, supply flights, or naval support for land operations it will be vital to have constant communications between all three services as well as connections with allied forces using NATO or equivalent protocols. The communications system which will meet these challenges is being developed now by the ADF and Australian industry and will be widely in service by the mid-1990s.

For communication links between Army headquarters and units in the field, the concept under development is AUSTACCS, the Australian Tactical Command and Control System. At the sharp end of combat will be the tactical radio network called Raven, consisting of back-pack radios and larger sets mounted in vehicles. This integrated system will replace the current range of radio sets with a single family for communication between battalion commanders, company commanders and COs down to platoons and field sections. Raven will use both VHF, line-of-sight signals and HF, or shortwave signals to cover vast distances and it will convert both voice and data signals into digital impulses for speedier communication and information storage. Though all messages will be encrypted, Raven will also use a unique frequency management feature to keep signals hopping from frequency to frequency so quickly that it will be virtually impossible for an enemy to jam or eavesdrop on field communications.

To talk to the next level of the command structure, AUSTACCS has Parakeet, a compact version of what a telephone exchange will be like in the year 2000 or beyond. Fully digital and capable of being airlifted and mobilised, like Raven, Parakeet will use UHF, VHF, HF and optical fibre links and tie into the civilian telephone system and the Syracuse military satellite system. It will carry voice, telegraph, data and facsimile traffic to and from higher command levels and provide connections to allied forces in the operational area.

Parallel to the Raven and Parakeet networks is a computer terminal link-up which will automate the marking of battle maps, the compilation of intelligence material and the updating of logistics planning data — all presently done by hand. In Divisional and Brigade headquarters computers will act as word-processors for preparing operational orders and provide an updated symbolic display of the battlefield. These computers will talk to battlefield computers housed in specially sheltered vehicles. At the unit level, soldiers will carry rugged lap-top computers to store and feed data into combat radios and to retransmit this data to other radio sets. Operational orders will be disseminated throughout a Divisional size force in about an hour. If any of these devices should fall into enemy hands, information can be wiped far quicker than destroying paper records.

The top, nationwide layer of Australia's military communications system is DISCON, the Defence Integrated Secure Communications Network. This system will tie together all military units and communication installations in Australia largely through civilian landlines and satellite links. All communications will be encrypted for security and users will have terminals to give them pictures, voice or computer data. By the mid-1990s, the ADF commander or the Prime Minister in Canberra will be able to pick up his desk phone and communicate directly through DISCON, then Parakeet and Raven to an Army officer, pilot or ship's commander anywhere in Australia or its immediate region.

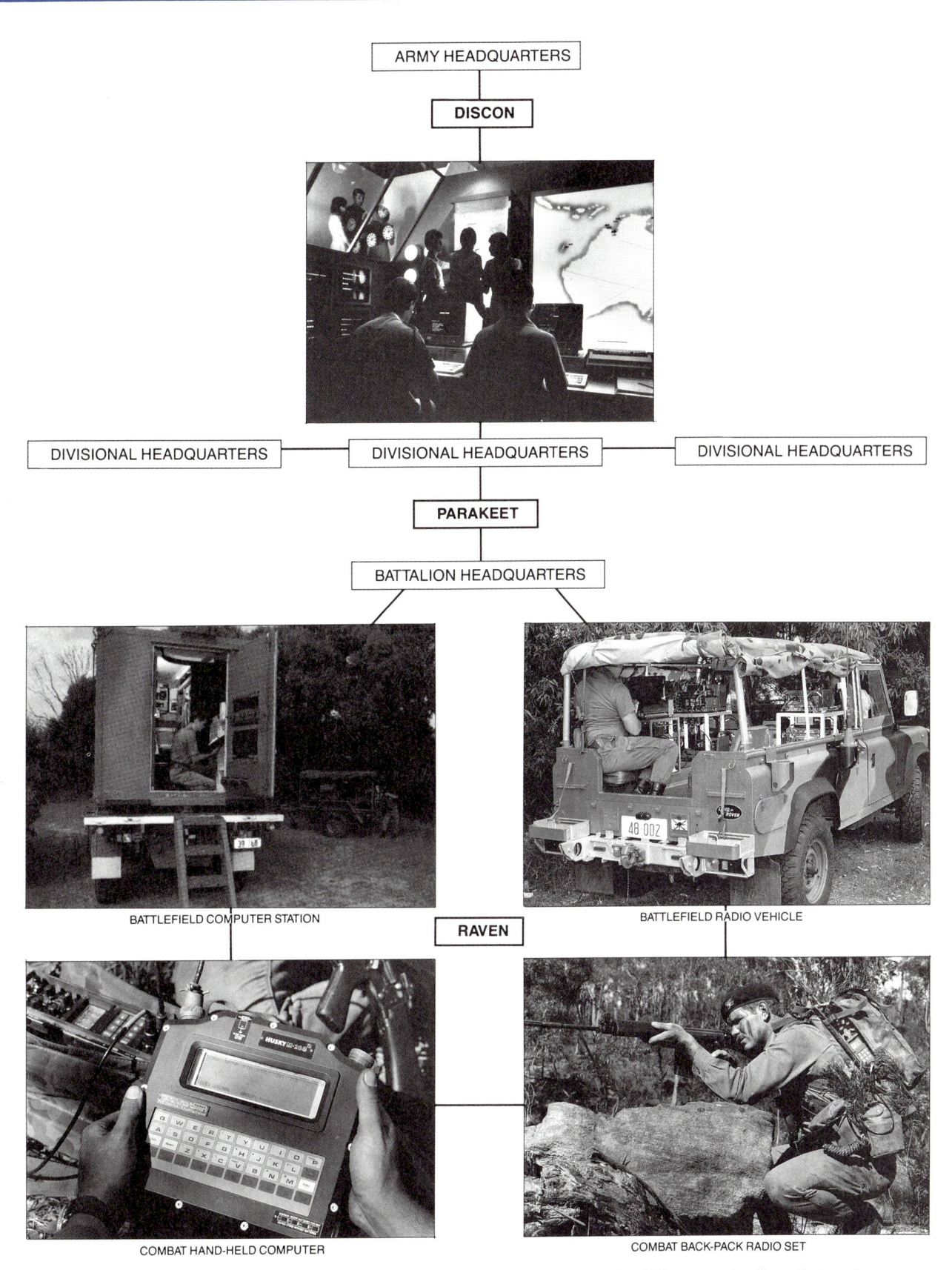

```
                    ARMY HEADQUARTERS
                          |
                       DISCON
                          |
                    [photograph]

DIVISIONAL HEADQUARTERS — DIVISIONAL HEADQUARTERS — DIVISIONAL HEADQUARTERS
                                    |
                                PARAKEET
                                    |
                         BATTALION HEADQUARTERS
```

BATTLEFIELD COMPUTER STATION BATTLEFIELD RADIO VEHICLE

RAVEN

COMBAT HAND-HELD COMPUTER COMBAT BACK-PACK RADIO SET

Military communication goes through three networks: battlefield back-pack and vehicle-mounted radios talk through Raven; a digital telephone trunk system, Parakeet carries messages to a higher level and DISCON is a nationwide communication network. A computer link-up passes data from combat lap-tops to battlefield data stations to HQ computers.

more open manoeuvres, Canungra's courses teach a gamut of tactics needed in all Australian climates and terrain from the steep and rocky Kimberleys in northwestern Australia to the harsh bushland of the Northern Territory and North Queensland. But the Army has not forsaken the skills of jungle training which are developed and taught at the new Land Force Battle School at Tully in North Queensland.

As the Army's tactical training has evolved to meet new challenges, so too has the Army's weaponry had to keep abreast of technological change, affecting the very core of the soldier's life, his personal weapons. In the late 1950s, the .303 inch Lee Enfield, the Australian infantryman's basic assault rifle since World War I, was replaced by the 7.62 mm L1A1 self-loading rifle. By 1960 all Australian Army units were equipped with the SLR, produced in Australia as a semi-automatic version of the Belgian Fabric Nationale. During the Vietnam War, Australian soldiers were armed with a new array of US weapons including the M16A1 5.56 mm Armalite rifle and its variant, the M203 with a 40 mm grenade launcher attached in an under-and-over configuration. These new weapons greatly increased the firepower of the basic rifle sections. While the grenade launcher on its own did not give a soldier enough firepower if a contact occurred, and carrying two separate weapons was obviously clumsy, the combination M203 grenade launcher/rifle proved a particularly useful combat weapon.

Both these rifles, though reliable and long-serving, are now at the end of their battle-efficient days and will be replaced over the next few years by the Austrian-designed Steyr AUG 1 rifle, produced for the Australian Army

About to be airlifted by chopper, a soldier nurses his M16A1 Armalite rifle. First acquired by Australian troops in Vietnam, the US-produced Colt M16A1 5.56 mm Armalite is a magazine-fed, gas-operated rifle capable of automatic and semi-automatic fire with 300 metres effective range and 60 rpm practical rate of fire.

as the F88 compact assault rifle. In its standard format, the Steyr has both semi-automatic and automatic fire capability and an effective range of 300 metres. An optical sight, built into the handle, gives 1:5 times magnification, allows aiming with both eyes open and is particularly useful in low light conditions.

Also due for updated weaponry are the machine-gun sections. During World War II, the standard light machine-gun for rifle sections was the .303 inch Bren while the machine-gun companies had the Vickers heavy machine-gun. In Vietnam both these weapons were replaced by the American GPMG M60, lighter than the Vickers and heavier than the Bren, but, with a rate of fire of 550 rounds per minute, much faster than both its predecessors. With a tripod attachment and optical sights, the M60 could handle the longer range tasks of a heavy

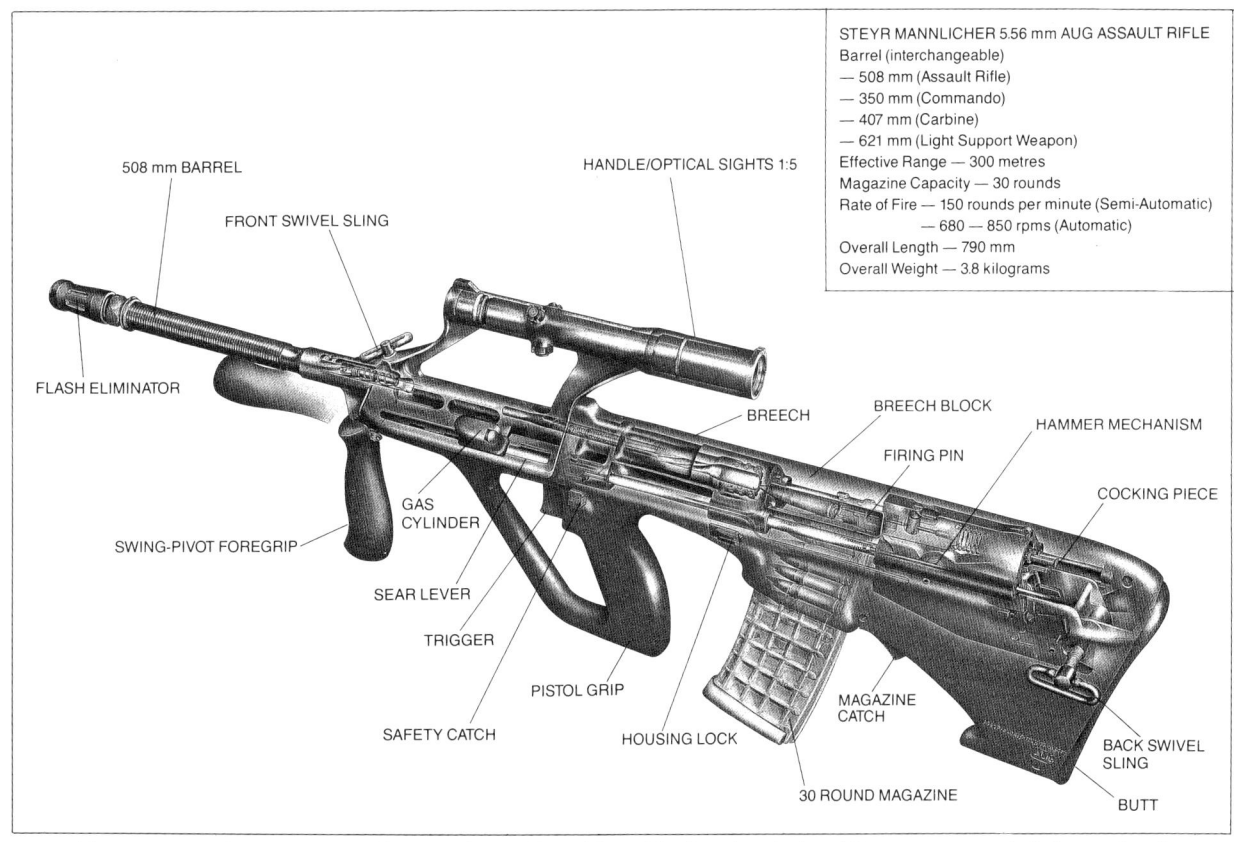

STEYR MANNLICHER 5.56 mm AUG ASSAULT RIFLE
Barrel (interchangeable)
— 508 mm (Assault Rifle)
— 350 mm (Commando)
— 407 mm (Carbine)
— 621 mm (Light Support Weapon)
Effective Range — 300 metres
Magazine Capacity — 30 rounds
Rate of Fire — 150 rounds per minute (Semi-Automatic)
— 680 — 850 rpms (Automatic)
Overall Length — 790 mm
Overall Weight — 3.8 kilograms

Above: With both eyes open, a soldier uses the excellent sights of the Austrian-designed Steyr gun, currently being produced under licence at the Lithgow Small Arms Factory, NSW, as the new standard Army assault rifle. Below: Configured here as an assault weapon, the Steyr easily converts to a shorter, 9 mm-barrel, silenced commando rifle.

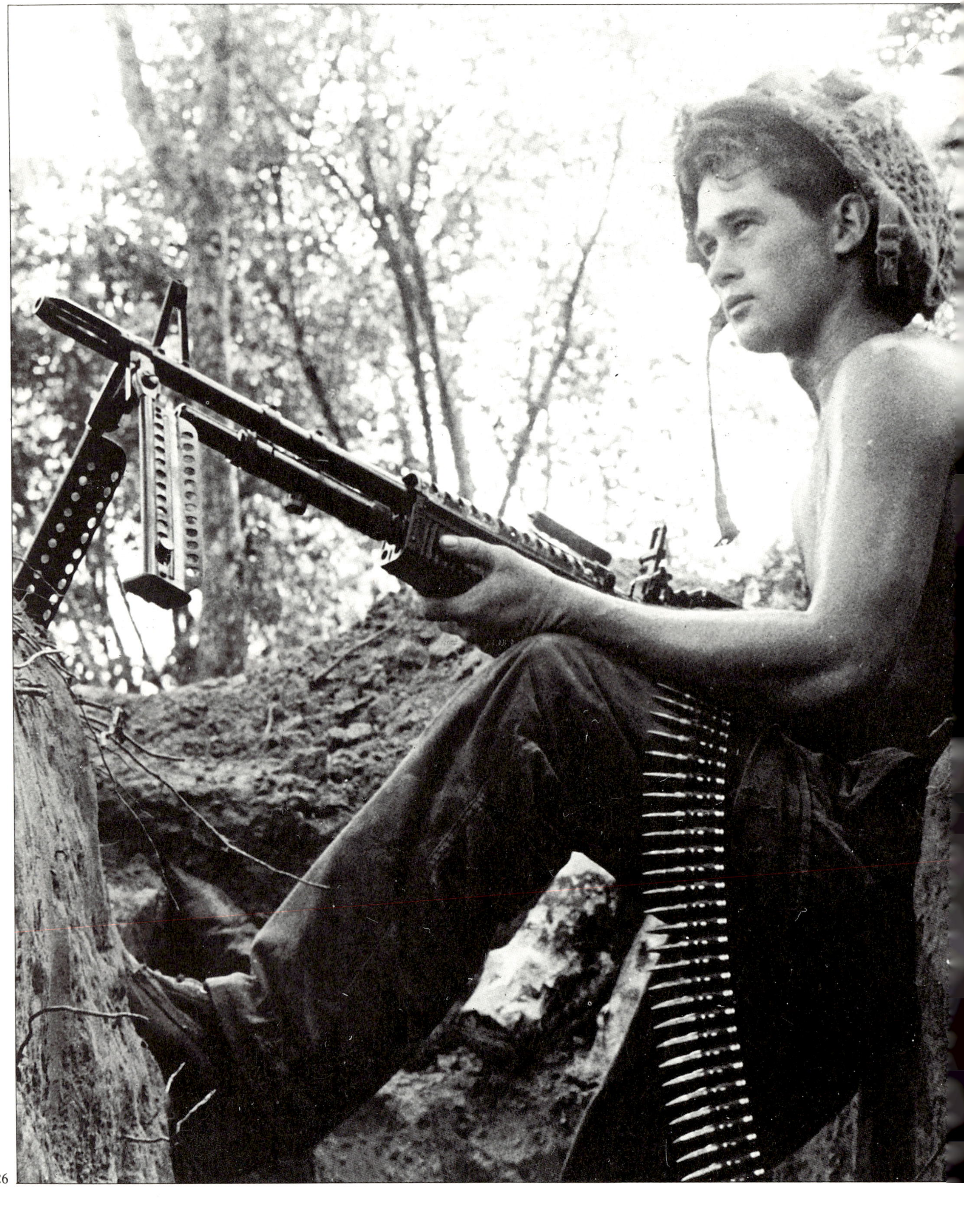

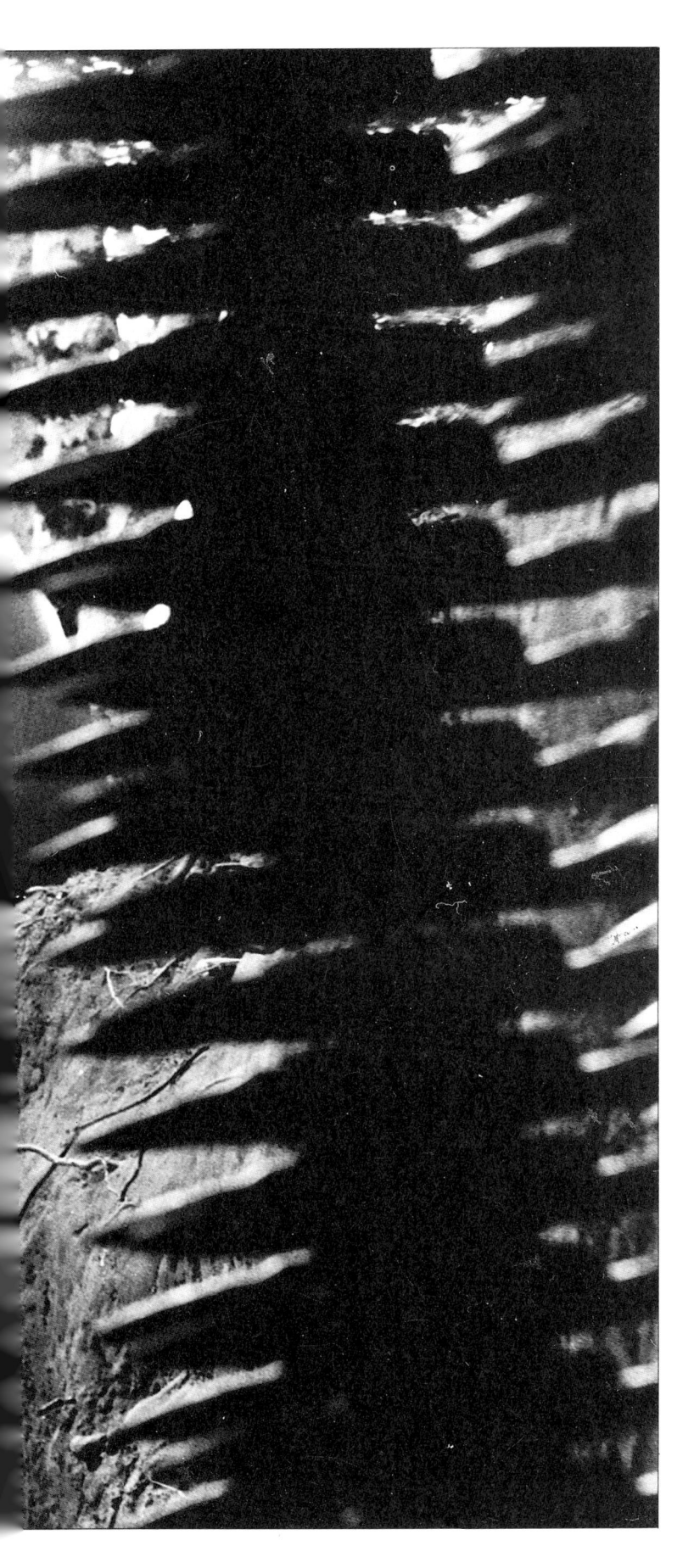

At Coral fire-support base in Vietnam, a young Digger keeps vigil with his GPMG 7.62 mm M60 machine-gun. Gas-operated, belt-fed and air-cooled, the M60 was employed in a light role on a bipod, with an effective range of 500 metres, or as a medium weapon on a tripod with 1,100 metres range.

machine-gun and with belt-fed ammunition and quick-changing barrels, it proved a worthy improvement. After Vietnam, the standard machine-gun became the belt-fed 7.62 mm Belgian-designed MAG 58. With a range of at least 800 metres at over 750 rounds per minute, the MAG 58 has proved a capable and willing workhorse for Australian machine-gunners, but weighing 13 kilograms it was always far too heavy for an infantry section and was only ever considered an interim weapon to replace the obsolete M60. Although some MAGs are being retained as general support weapons, it in turn is to be replaced by another Belgian-designed gun, the 5.56 mm belt-fed Minimi, which at 6.8 kilograms is a little more than half the weight of its predecessor and can give an effective range of 600 metres at a similar rate of fire. With the introduction of the Steyr and the Minimi, all the small arms of Australian infantry will use the standard NATO 5.56 ammunition, enabling the Army to mesh easily with other international forces when needed in the world's hotspots.

The Vietnam era saw other items of armoury introduced to the Australian Army. The American Claymore mine, a thin curved metal case containing thousands of tiny steel balls packed in an explosive charge, could be fired by a trip wire or command-detonated by a magneto switch. Also added to the list was a new anti-personnel mine, largely constructed from plastic and extremely difficult to detect. The 81 mm mortar replaced the older 3-inch mortar and the M26 grenade replaced the old-fashioned Mills grenade.

Its direct involvement with US forces in Vietnam led to further "Americanisation" of the Australian Army. American military jargon was picked up and began to spread through the ranks. The starched, shaved and shiny image of the "British-style" soldier which had long dominated Australia's military tradition gave way to a more pragmatic modern Digger, most dramatically expressed in his unironed, soft, camouflaged clothes.

In a broader sense, the Army's units themselves began to change shape at this time, adapting in size and structure to meet different needs. Units are now pegged at under strength size to allow for rapid expansion, when the occasion demands, into well-staffed and organised structures. Battalions, for example, are kept at around two thirds strength and most major units do not have the complete complement of operational sub-units. This contains costs to affordable levels while keeping enough staff to maintain the required range of skills for tactical training.

Perhaps the most revolutionary influence of the Vietnam war on the Australian Army was the helicopter. Still rare and novel items in Korea, Malaya and Borneo, the helicopter came of age in Vietnam as an essential component of battlefield mobility. The ubiquitous Australian Iroquois utility choppers which served in Vietnam performed many roles well: troop and equipment transport, medical evacuations, search and rescue and, configured as gunships, close ground-support firepower. The big, ugly, twin-rotor American Chinooks also performed valuable service for the Australians, with large troop and cargo lifts to inaccessible areas.

Since the withdrawal from Vietnam, three rotary-wing transport RAAF squadrons have been operating Iroquois, Chinooks and Bell Hueys in support of the Army as well as fulfilling multiple peacetime roles. Agriculture, flood relief, rescue, firefighting and police work have all benefited from the expertise of the RAAF's helicopter pilots and crews.

In 1989, however, the RAAF's Chinooks and older Iroquois began to be phased out and a new era in Australia's land helicopter force began with the introduction of the powerful Sikorsky Black Hawk. With a lift capacity of over 1,200 kilograms, a ferry range of about 300 kilometres which can be doubled with auxiliary fuel tanks, and armed with two MAG 58 machine-guns, the Black Hawk will be a valuable asset to the Army's mobility. A significant change in defence force thinking has accompanied the introduction of the Army Black Hawk. While it was the RAAF that operated helicopters in support of ground forces in Vietnam, the new fleet of Black Hawks will be flown by Australian Army pilots. The 5th Aviation Regiment based in Townsville will form part of an aviation squadron for the northern based Operational Deployment Force. Able to provide company-strength airlifts and rapid deployment of troops anywhere in the Top End, the Black Hawk is the key to the high mobility required of the ODF to meet threats at short notice.

As well as being able to rapidly mobilise the infantry battalions of the ODF in time of crisis, the Army must also have available forces with greater combat power — tanks, medium and heavy guns, and mechanised troops.

Already a number of southern-based units are earmarked for redeployment to the north to boost this capability. In the early 1990s, the 2nd Cavalry Regiment will move to the Darwin area from its present base at Holsworthy, NSW. A reconnaissance unit capable of providing mobile surveillance over extended areas and conducting offensive, defensive and delaying actions against incursions, the 2nd Cavalry Regiment with its 300 cavalry troopers and 80 or so armoured reconnaissance vehicles will add a powerful punch to the Darwin command.

Because the Top End is so vast, it would be impossible for the 2nd Cavalry Regiment to provide general surveillance over the entire area. Instead it will operate in any threatened area from a forward operating base and deploy its troops in response to intelligence information. The North West Mobile Force, another regional force surveillance unit covering an area across the Northern Territory into the Kimberleys, may report positive sightings of hostile landings or advances. The 2nd Cavalry Regiment would respond by dispatching a small force, probably a troop of five vehicles initially, to investigate the reports and deal with the situation as it evolved.

The regiment's armoured fighting vehicles are based on the Vietnam-era M113 Armoured Personnel Carrier. These vehicles are still highly regarded for fast and efficient movement

ARMY ASSAULT CHOPPER

An Australian Black Hawk, in RAAF colours, undergoes combat loading trials for the Army, at Townsville. To stop power-lines fouling the rotors in low-level flight, cable-cutters are mounted above the cockpit and on the front wheels.

If the helicopter did not exist, the strategists of today's Australian modern military would have to invent it. For its ability to reach out swiftly with men and weapons over vast distances, to provide pinpoint fire-support, to search and rescue and evacuate casualties, the helicopter's value as a battle asset is critical to Australia's planning for northern defence. The machine that will meet all these needs is the new versatile Sikorsky UH-60 helicopter, coming into wide service with both the US and Australian armed forces.

Of a total initial procurement of 53 Sikorskys, the Navy will acquire 14, specially fitted out as S70B Seahawks, to be operated from the RAN's super-sophisticated, guided missile FFG-7 frigates. For the Army the Sikorsky chopper is the S70A Black Hawk with 39 on order and an option to buy more later. Australian troops got their first taste of Black Hawks during the US-Australian "Diamond Dollar" exercise in Queensland in 1987. Flying numerous missions, American Black Hawks airlifted over 800 troops, transported about 108 tonnes of internal cargo and personnel and lifted nearly 22.5 tonnes of external cargo on slings including 105 mm howitzers. Despite harsh dry conditions and long supply lines, the Black Hawks maintained a fleet readiness rate of 98 per cent. It was an impressive Australian debut for the chopper which won the confidence and respect of its ultimate customers — the infantrymen on the ground.

In January 1989 control of the land helicopter force was officially handed from No. 9 Squadron RAAF to the 5th Aviation Regiment in Townsville from where the Black Hawks will be flown to provide air support for the northern based Operational Deployment Force (ODF).

Each helicopter can carry 10 combat-equipped infantrymen over a distance of about 160 kilometres at a maximum cruising speed of 145 knots, and a fleet of 16 Black Hawks can insert a company of 160 soldiers in one lift. With this kind of speed, range and capacity, it would take no more than a morning to deploy an entire battalion on the northern coast to meet an invading force. The Australian Black Hawk has an operational radius of about 100 kilometres and a ferry range without payload of about 300 kilometres. On extended range missions, it carries an external 874 litre fuel tank.

The Australian Black Hawk is flown by a crew of four — two pilots and two gunner-dispatchers, who act as loadmasters and man the door-mounted machine guns to give suppressive fire during landings and extractions. For protection in the combat zone, the Black Hawk's Hover Infra-Red (IR) Dispersion system masks the heat from its two 1,560 h.p. General Electric T700-GE-701A engines to reduce the target area for any enemy heat-seeking missiles. Critical areas of the ship are armour plated to withstand multiple hits from 20 mm cannon fire. On rescue missions, an external hydraulic rescue hoist can pluck a man from the jungle or sea.

While the Black Hawk will be the key to the Army's flexible mobility, it will not be the only chopper in Australia's modern helicopter inventory. The Army is currently upgrading the famed Vietnam-era Bell Hueys as modern gunships with rapid-fire gatling-style mini-cannons and rocket pods, and it will continue operating its swift nimble Bell Kiowas as reconnaissance and command and control aircraft. With its modernised helicopter force, the Australian Army will be ready to face any future threat.

SIKORSKY S70A BLACK HAWK

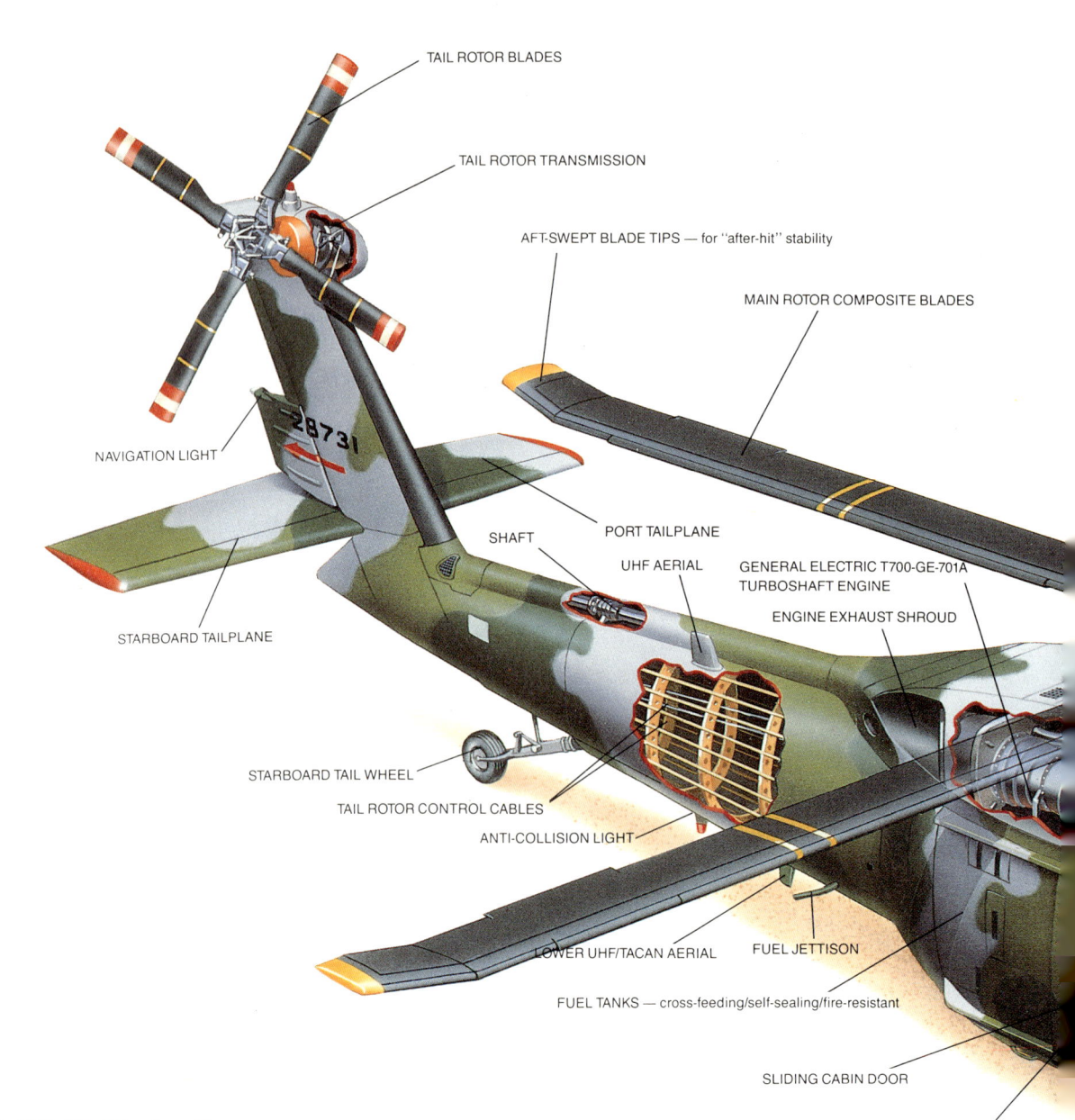

- TAIL ROTOR BLADES
- TAIL ROTOR TRANSMISSION
- AFT-SWEPT BLADE TIPS — for "after-hit" stability
- MAIN ROTOR COMPOSITE BLADES
- NAVIGATION LIGHT
- SHAFT
- PORT TAILPLANE
- UHF AERIAL
- GENERAL ELECTRIC T700-GE-701A TURBOSHAFT ENGINE
- ENGINE EXHAUST SHROUD
- STARBOARD TAILPLANE
- STARBOARD TAIL WHEEL
- TAIL ROTOR CONTROL CABLES
- ANTI-COLLISION LIGHT
- LOWER UHF/TACAN AERIAL
- FUEL JETTISON
- FUEL TANKS — cross-feeding/self-sealing/fire-resistant
- SLIDING CABIN DOOR
- ENGINE DRIVE SHAFTS
- GUNNER FLOOR ARMOUR

The basic airframe of the UH-60A Sikorsky utility helicopter, shown here in its factory combat colours, is adapted for Australian service with additional features: external cabin steps with grab handles, avionics access door, external hydraulic hoist, hover IR suppression, gunner floor armour and armoured pilots' seats, rotor brake, overhead powerlines wire-strike protection, and tinted overhead glazing. The Black Hawk's flight-critical systems and components can provide 20 minutes minimum flight time after worst-case ballistic damage. If both tail rotor cables are disabled, a separate rotor servo drives the rotor blades to a preselected safe flight pitch angle.

Characterised by its high twin-engine cowlings, a Black Hawk in dark combat disguise, appears a deadly and menacing machine of war.

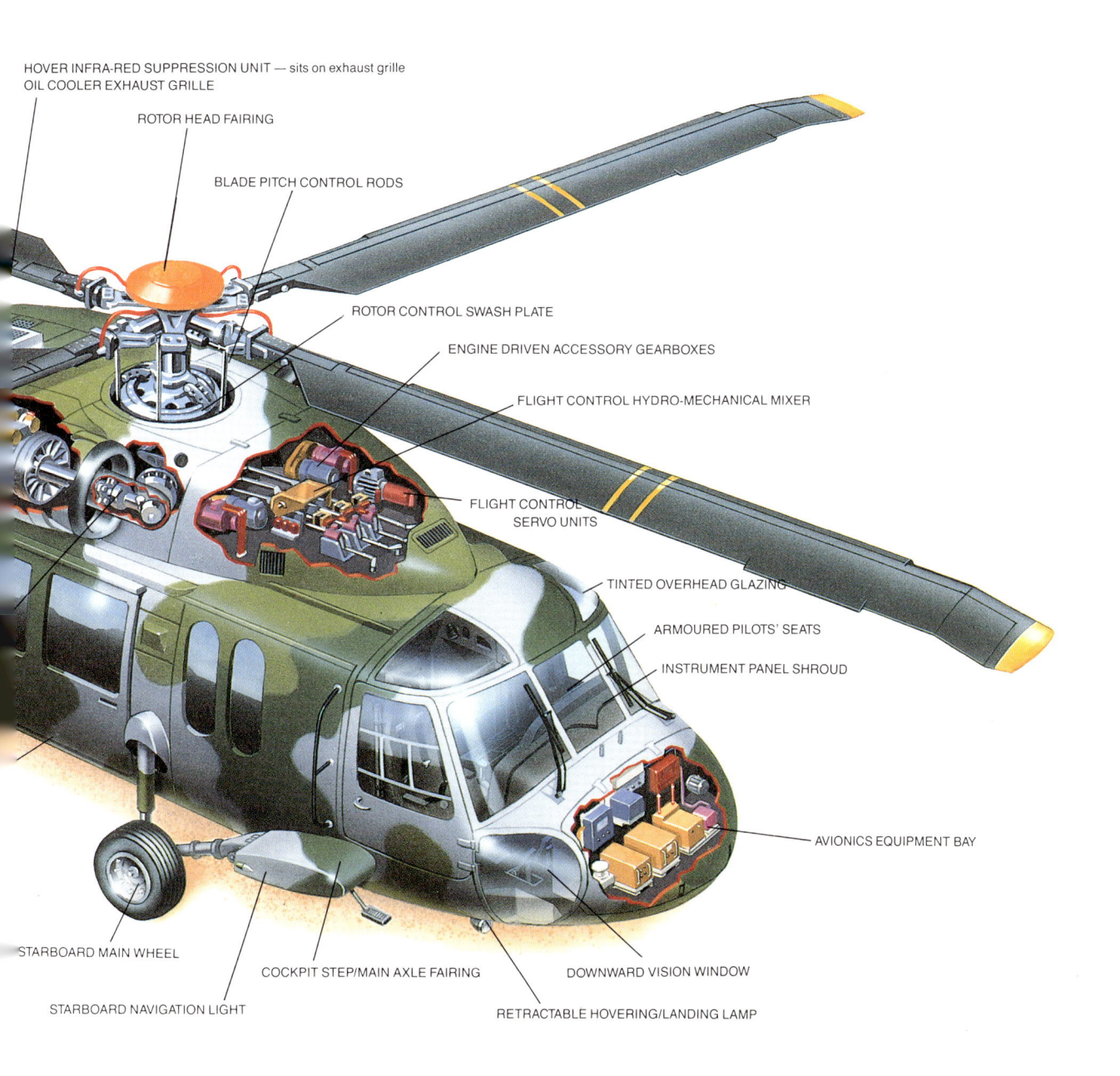

- HOVER INFRA-RED SUPPRESSION UNIT — sits on exhaust grille
- OIL COOLER EXHAUST GRILLE
- ROTOR HEAD FAIRING
- BLADE PITCH CONTROL RODS
- ROTOR CONTROL SWASH PLATE
- ENGINE DRIVEN ACCESSORY GEARBOXES
- FLIGHT CONTROL HYDRO-MECHANICAL MIXER
- FLIGHT CONTROL SERVO UNITS
- TINTED OVERHEAD GLAZING
- ARMOURED PILOTS' SEATS
- INSTRUMENT PANEL SHROUD
- AVIONICS EQUIPMENT BAY
- STARBOARD MAIN WHEEL
- COCKPIT STEP/MAIN AXLE FAIRING
- DOWNWARD VISION WINDOW
- STARBOARD NAVIGATION LIGHT
- RETRACTABLE HOVERING/LANDING LAMP

Armed with a heavy .50 calibre machine-gun, an Australian armoured personnel carrier sets up a checkpoint on a Vietnam road as local traffic plods past. Later in the war, some APCs were fitted with 76 mm guns.

across most terrains and have alloy hulls for good protection from small-arms fire in the battle-zone. Manned by a crew of two, the M113 can carry up to 10 combat-equipped troops at speeds of more than 60 kilometres per hour to a range of 480 kilometres. With a front splash-board fitted to protect the engine, it can also "swim" across water obstacles — the fire-support variant of the APC has to offset the weight of its heavier gun and turret with front and side flotation pods.

The scout version of the M113 is armed with turret-mounted .30 and .50 calibre twin machine-guns while the fire-support vehicle has the APC chassis with a 76 mm quick-firing gun mounted on a rotating turret, borrowed from the Scorpion tank. As well as firing the normal high-explosive and armour-piercing rounds, this 76 mm gun also fires HESH (high explosive squash head) rounds for use against other armoured vehicles. The fire-support version of the APC also carries two .30 calibre machine-guns and discharge tubes for smoke and anti-personnel canisters.

Versions of both these vehicles saw active service in Vietnam. As the main equipment of the 3rd Cavalry Regiment, the APCs were the workhorse of the Australian Task Force, performing such diverse roles as convoy escort, carrying infantry and stores, and engaging in cordon and search operations and close combat with the enemy. "They were everywhere, in every operation", recalls Brigadier Peter Badman, who served as a Major with the Australian forces in Vietnam, commanding tanks of the 1st Armoured Regiment. "The noise of the M113 was as familiar as the sound of the Huey helicopter and is ingrained in the memory of every veteran of the Vietnam war."

With their high speed, cross-country mobility and good communications essential for surveillance operations, the armoured personnel carriers fit well into the Australian Army's tactical plans. And with its assault troop-

Patrolling through thick Vietnam jungle, soldiers of 9 RAR are supported by a Centurion tank of 1st Armoured Regiment. The Centurions provided close-fire support for attacks on bunkers, in village fighting and in defence of Australian bases.

carrying capability and firepower and attack capacity, the M113 can deal independently with any small enemy groups it might encounter on dispersed operations. Although the M113 is getting old, instead of a replacement it will be updated, possibly with a bigger engine, self-sealing external fuel tanks, and wheels, rather than tracks, to better equip it for northern conditions. It may also be upgraded with the latest in weapons and surveillance gear.

The M113 can also be used as an armoured command vehicle. Based on the basic carrier chassis, the command variant has a higher silhouette and comes with an array of communications systems to allow a field commander to have a mobile tactical headquarters that can stay close to the action. In Vietnam these mobile command posts proved that such mobility is a great step forward from the static headquarters or the constant setting up and pulling down endured by commanders in the pre-Vietnam era.

The queen of the battlefield since it made its first tentative crawl across the fields of France in 1916, has been the tank. Although Australia had an armoured division during World War II, it never saw action as a distinct formation. The main battle tanks then were the Matilda, the Grant and Sherman, and while they turned the tide of the tank battles in the open deserts of North Africa, and provided armoured power to the Allied offensive in Europe, the Pacific theatre was not conducive to tank warfare. The Japanese had light and medium tanks, but they largely failed in the island campaigns. With the exception of some actions, such as those of Australian-manned Stuart tanks at the battles of Buna and Gona in northern Papua in late 1942, the tactical role of tanks in the Pacific was limited by the thick vegetation and soft ground of the jungle. The same problem also existed to some extent in Vietnam; even so, when the Centurions did get through, many a platoon and company commander considered them "bloody handy".

As Commander of Australian Centurions in Vietnam, Peter Badman remembers the marvellous toughness of these tanks: "In particular, their ammunition stowage and mine protection was much better than the Americans' M48 Pattons. This survivability factor made up for their questionable mechanical reliability in the minds of their crews who came to respect the sound British design and workmanship in the hull and turret of the old 'Cents'."

The Centurion tank served Australia with various upgrades until its final retirement in 1978. The project team to evaluate and decide on a replacement tank had been looking at the options for several years and by 1974 the competition was down to the American M60 tank, a big tough machine cast in the same mould as the M48 Patton, and the latest German Leopard 1, then in service with West German armoured units. Australian crews were trained in each type of tank and became vehemently loyal to their own machine when the tanks were put through a rigorous series of automotive and gunnery trials, in temperate, tropical and desert conditions in Victoria, North Queensland and Western Australia. Both tanks proved to be extremely tough and reliable but in the end the greater mobility of the agile, light-armoured Leopard won out over the heavy-armoured M60. A key factor in the decision was also the fact that the smaller, lighter Leopard could be more easily transported by road, rail or ship to meet the Army's need for high mobility within Australia.

The Leopard has an impressive radio communications system which allows compatibility with other army radio networks as well as aircraft operating within its range. The whole reason, of course, for the Leopard tank's existence is to be a powerful mobile gun platform and in this aspect the Leopard is daunting. Its main gun is fully stabilised in traverse and elevation and has sophisticated infra-red target-acquisition and fire-control equipment. Combined with powerful engines and a suspension system, this enables the tank to operate day or night and to pinpoint targets at several kilometres range while travelling at high speed across rough country.

Such capabilities are tested again and again in battle group training exercises; when the Leopards practise with and against other tanks, APCs and infantry and artillery teams. Most battle group training is conducted at Puckapunyal, the Victorian home base of the 1st Armoured Regiment, 96 kilometres northwest of Melbourne. Australian armoured units are usually comprised in two ways — an armoured-heavy battle group consists of three tank squadrons each of 14 tanks, and a company of mechanised infantry, in a troop of APCs, while an infantry-heavy battle group has three mechanised companies and a single tank squadron.

As the second battalion of the southern-based 1st Brigade, the 5/7th Battalion trains as a mechanised battalion for reinforcement of the Operational Deployment Force in the north. Depending on the nature of the exercise, it can be configured as an armoured-heavy or infantry-heavy battle group with Leopard tanks on detachment from 1st Armoured Regiment. At Puckapunyal or in the dry, dusty west of NSW, tactical skills are learned the hard way, so that if battle groups are needed in the north they will be ready to add their weight to the Army's defence.

Even before the dawn chorus of kookaburras announced the rising sun over the scrub near Sofala, central western NSW, the tired but alert sentries of the 5/7th Battalion heard the rumbling sound of tanks of 1st Armoured Regiment in the darkness. Now, in the rosy dawnlight, the combat-laden troops climbed aboard their armoured personnel carriers, or "tracks", ready for the battle group's advance. The two lead tanks of the troop came thundering through the scrub, followed by the troop leader's tank which disappeared briefly from sight as it plunged into the muddy creek behind the battalion's perimeter. Water streaming from its sides, the tank clambered up the near bank and raced forward. Using its snorkel exhaust, the Leopard can easily ford deep waterways and climb out again unassisted if the banks are not too steep. The infantry-heavy battle group formed up and the advance began.

A POTENT CAVALRY

Churning up a dustcloud, a combat-laden, 42-tonne AS1 Leopard tank roars over open ground. The tank's commander, with his turret hatch open (left), directs the gunner (right) and the driver, seated below in the hull.

Inside the cramped, noisy turret, crammed with panoramic and telescopic gunsights and switches for the Leopard's computerised fire-control system, a gunner communicates on headsets with his loader/operator (left).

AGILE AND ACCURATE

When the German designed Leopard main battle tank was introduced into Australian service to replace the Centurion in the mid-1970s, it represented the ultimate in tank design. With development beginning in the late 1950s, the Leopard 1 was produced for West German armoured units. The Leopard 1A3 tank, developed in 1970 with improved protection and fire control systems, was further adapted for the Australian Army as the AS1 version. While the Australian Leopard cannot match the latest generation of tanks such as the American M1 Abrams, it is by far the most advanced tank design in Australia's region.

The Australian Leopard, with a weight of 42.4 tonnes when fully loaded for combat, can achieve a top speed of 62 kilometres per hour powered by its 820 h.p. V10 diesel engine and automatic transmission. Highly mobile and agile in the field, it is able to climb a gradient of 60 degrees, cross a three-metre gap, climb over obstacles to a height of 1.15 metres and cross all but the roughest terrain at speed. Its torsion bar suspension and hydraulic shock absorbers smooth out the bumps.

The Leopard's main armament is its L7A3 105 mm gun capable of engaging enemy tanks at a range of up to 2,500 metres and lesser targets to 8,000 metres. With a maximum capacity of 59 rounds, it can fire a range of ammunition — high explosive squash-head shells, armour-piercing shells, and anti-personnel and smoke canisters. The tank's computerised fire control system measures and constantly updates such variables as air temperature, wind speed, vehicle movement and range to target and uses active and passive infra-red imaging and laser guidance to locate and lock its gun onto a target. Gyro-stabilised and with full traverse and tilt, the gun automatically moves to hold a designated target even as the tank roars cross-country at top speed. The Leopard is also armed with two M63 7.62 mm machine-guns. One is mounted coaxially with the main armament, with a range of 1,600 metres while the other, for the use of the tank commander, is an anti-aircraft gun with a 900-metre range.

Each Leopard has a crew of four — a commander, a driver, a gunner and an operator, responsible for loading the main gun and manning the radios. The commander, gunner and operator occupy the turret while the driver is seated in the front of the hull. The basic formation for armoured operations is the troop of three tanks. Commanded by a lieutenant troop leader, the troop advances with two tanks forward, each with an arc of responsibility right and left of the centre line and the troop leader's tank in the middle, overwatching the forward tanks and acting as reserve. A tank squadron consists of four troops with two additional tanks as part of the squadron's headquarters.

There are two variants of the Leopard in Australian service used as tank support vehicles. The Armoured Vehicle Layer Bridge (AVLB) can lay down a bridge quickly for Leopards or personnel carriers to ford a deep waterway or wide gap. The Armoured Recovery Vehicle Medium (ARVM) uses a 20-tonne crane and a winch with 35-tonne pulling capacity to tow, lift or repair other Leopards and can replace a tank's damaged or disabled power pack in 30 minutes.

The Australian Army's 1st Armoured Regiment, based at Puckapunyal in Victoria, has a full complement of more than a 100 Leopards, including variants, to form a fast and powerful tank force.

Above: Like an aquatic monster rising from the deep, a Leopard tank charges from its heavily camouflaged hiding place in a dam, ready for action. When carrying its snorkelling gear, and with hatches and gun muzzle sealed tight, the tank can ford waterways to a depth of four metres. Left: The Armoured Vehicle Layer Bridge (AVLB) is a basic tank chassis, mounted by an extendable launcher arm, which lays a 22-metre-long bridge strong enough to support a Leopard tank.

As their two-man crews await orders for the next assault, a squadron of 4th Cavalry Regiment fire-support APCs forms an impressive line-up of firepower. The combined operations of scout and fire-support variants of the M113 will provide a strong and highly mobile force for long-range reconnaissance patrols in Australia's north.

Covering a kilometre-wide front, the three Leopard tanks and an advanced infantry guard aboard a troop of APCs led the battle group to clear the main axis of advance. As this armoured spearhead lumbered across the scrubby bushland, scout and fire-support M113s from 2nd Cavalry Regiment were spread out to the far left and right to secure the group's flanks. Pre-warned by aerial reconnaissance of a deep eroded gully ahead, tank bridge-layers and low loaders, carrying engineers' assault-bridge components, stayed close behind the vanguard. When the crossing was reached, two bridge-layers moved up and cantilevered their hydraulically operated trackways across the gully. The Leopards crossed quickly, with the two lead tanks taking up covering positions for the third. The infantry guard had dismounted from their carriers to set up all-round cover fire while a small bulldozer cut into the bank to level out other crossing points for the APCs. The engineers laid an assault bridge within minutes and the troops climbed into their carriers. Soon the armoured spearhead moved off, followed later by the other vehicles and artillery units of the battle group.

The exercise was progressing to the satisfaction of the umpires and the battle group commander. The lead APCs with the three Leopards on the left flank halted on the rise of a high ridge. Commanding this lead infantry company of 5/7th Battalion, Major Steve Kelly received a report on the radio in his APC, that the rest of his lead company's "tracks" had cleared the ridge, designated 'bound "acorn"' as a code-named map checkpoint on his route. The only features on the sparsely wooded plain were a few homestead buildings and a private airstrip in the distance. While the tanks kept a low profile, known as being in "hulldown" position, Kelly's lead platoon arrived and the advance guard cautiously rolled out across the plain towards the homestead.

Suddenly there was a small explosion and the rattle of heavy machine-gun fire. Within three

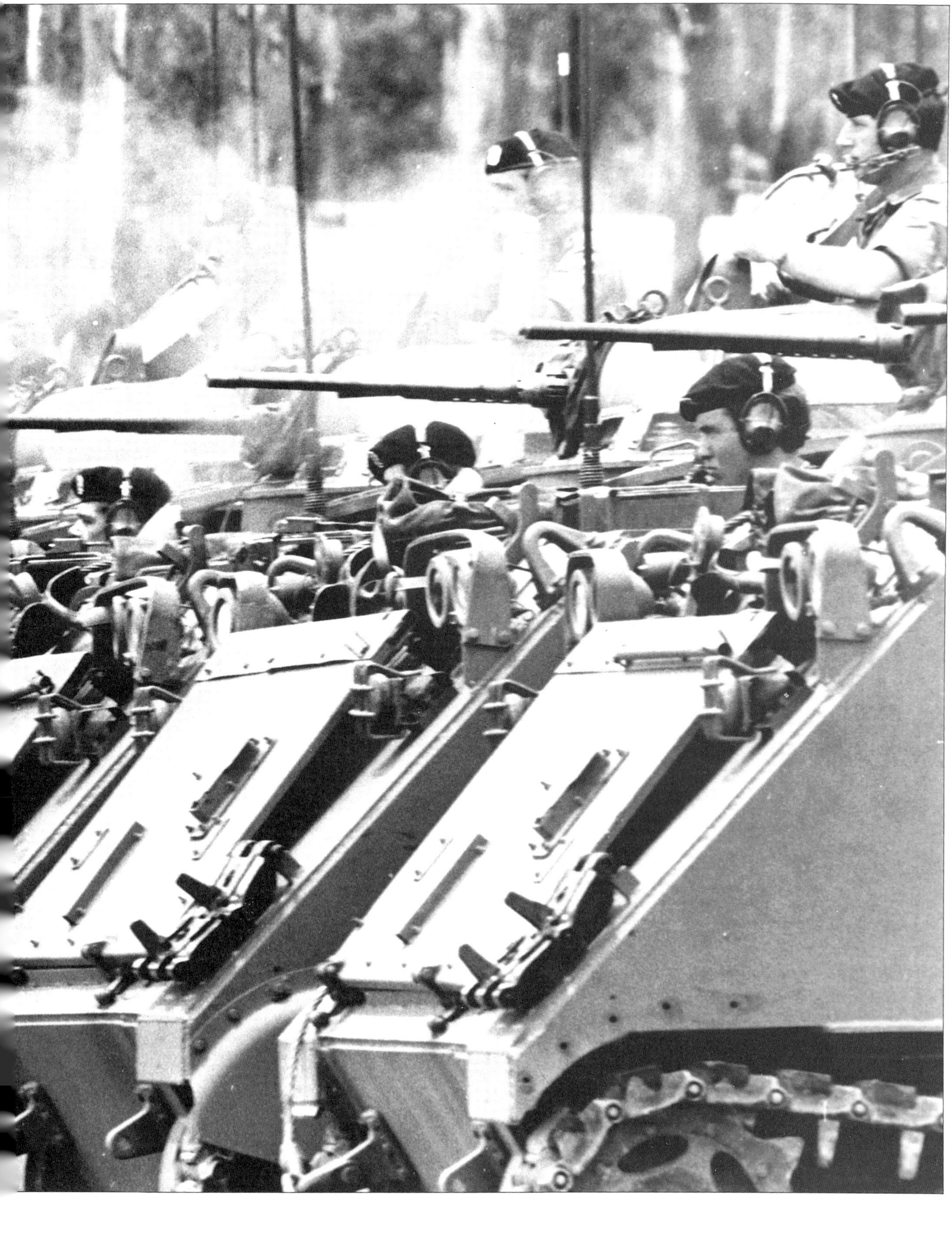

Army engineers grapple with the components of a pontoon assault bridge. Assault bridges range from aluminium floating bridges, able to carry Land Rover-size vehicles with trailers, up to heavy ferries for Leopard tanks and APCs.

hundred metres of the outer buildings, the group had come under fire. Discharging smoke as a cover, the tanks and APCs quickly withdrew to a small nearby ridge and returned the fire with their .30 and .50 calibre machine-guns. Kelly's men leapt into action from the carriers and worked their way up the ridge line to establish machine-gun posts. Kelly reported the contact to battalion HQ and the Forward Observer, the gunnery officer in the vanguard, called for battery fire from the direct support field artillery.

Now the officers of the exercise control group, consulting on a separate radio network to the participants but able to feed messages into the battlefield communications network, threw in another surprise element. Kelly received a report that one of the tanks had been hit by an RPG2 anti-armour missile and had been immobilised. The fictional enemy in this exercise were armed, it seemed, with the deadly Russian-made anti-tank missile launchers.

Back in his armoured control vehicle, the battalion commander anxiously awaited more news about the advance guard's contact. Judging from the siting of the enemy's RPG and heavy machine-gun fire, Kelly estimated an enemy force of reinforced platoon strength was holding the homestead. Also operating from the ACV, the battery commander of 8/12th Medium Regiment, in direct radio contact with his field battery of six 155 mm guns, had received the Forward Observer's request and ordered guns to be deployed behind the high ridge "acorn", about 20 kilometres to the rear of the armoured vanguard. As instructions came through from the Forward Observer to the battery command post, accommodated in a camouflaged Land Rover parked near the guns, they were fed into the Field Artillery Computer Equipment, or FACE, and relayed to the guns themselves. The ranging gun put away its first shot.

Introduced in the 1970s, FACE combines with other computer devices to significantly enhance artillery operations. It is another step forward from the days of the traditional artillery plotting

Gunners clear a smoking shell from the breech of the Army's latest artillery piece, the British-designed Hamel gun. Manufactured in Bendigo, Victoria, 105 Hamels are on order to replace Italian L5 pack-howitzers and American M2A2s.

board. The long-serving plotting board was an accurate method for calculating the angle and direction of guns to hit their targets; in the late 1960s, a small, hand-held programmable calculator was added which greatly sped up the process and integrated well with the current computers. Now, as technology races towards the end of the 20th century, the FACE is to be superseded by an even smaller and lighter system which is more powerful and faster and easier to operate. Radar ranging equipment has already been introduced, which can lock onto a target and provide gunners with all the ranging data they require. It can even lock onto an airborne projectile, predict its trajectory and accurately calculate the position of the gun, vehicle or ship that fired the round, in order for the gunners to retaliate decisively.

Australia's gunners have been in the forefront of the Army's modernisation in the past two decades. The change began in the late 1950s with the phasing out of the British 25-pounder field gun which had served Australia well in World War II and through the Korean and Malayan Emergency period. By the mid-1960s, all Australian artillery units were equipped with two new field guns, the heavyweight American 105 mm M2A2 howitzer and the Italian 105 mm L5 pack howitzer, a mountain gun that can be stripped quickly to man-pack loads for carrying into inaccessible terrain. The ballistics and size of 105 mm ammunition have proved to be the optimum for field artillery throughout the world, and these models of the 105 mm have seen service in Malaya, Borneo and Vietnam. The pack version, lighter and with a shorter range than its towable big brother, is still in service with the Operational Deployment Force which must be able to rapidly transport its guns to remote areas. But with a maximum range of only 11 kilometres for their 15 kilogram shells, the older 105 mm guns will be replaced over the next few years by the British-designed but Australian-manufactured Hamel gun, which can fire the same weight projectile up to a range of 18 kilometres.

During the joint Australian-American Diamond Dollar Exercise in 1987, paratroopers of 3 RAR leap from the skies over northern Queensland in operation Far Canopy, the largest parachute drop attempted to date. The parachute battalion maintains a high level of readiness as a rapidly deployable strikeforce.

In 1983, medium artillery units also updated from their World War II vintage British 5.5 inch guns to the new American M198 medium 155 mm gun. With a range of 24.5 kilometres, a high angle of fire, and ordnance including high explosive, smoke, white phosphorus, and illuminating rounds and rocket-propelled projectiles, it is an awesome artillery piece. With its long range, the M198 does not need to be continually redeployed to reach its targets. This is just as well, for with an overall weight of more than seven tonnes and a length of 12 metres including a split trail in the firing position, it is not an easy gun to handle or camouflage for its crew of 10.

Back at the gun position behind the high ridge, the ranging gun fired its first shots, making adjustments called for by the Forward Observer and relayed to each of the gun crews. As the last guns were towed into position the gunners worked frantically, pulling out the trails and bedding their weapons in to get them ready. With the final adjustments communicated to all crews from the ranging gun's officer, the order was given to fire for effect: ''Let 'er rip!''. The guns roared in unison and each gun crew went into its well-drilled routine of loading, firing and clearing the smoking shell from the gun breech. Behind the small ridge out on the scrubby plain, the tanks had been keeping hulldown positions with just enough exposure to bring their main guns to bear on their targets. Their furious rounds of fire had kept the enemy quiet until the main artillery barrage began in earnest.

Kelly's APC probed forward so that he could make a personal recce. Satisfied that he had the enemy pinned down, he relayed his orders over the combat group's radio network for an attack. The troops clambered into their carriers and they moved out. The tanks also moved up on Kelly's left flank, easily negotiating an eroded creek bed, and found a good firing position. As the artillery barrage continued to rain down on the homestead buildings, Kelly took two

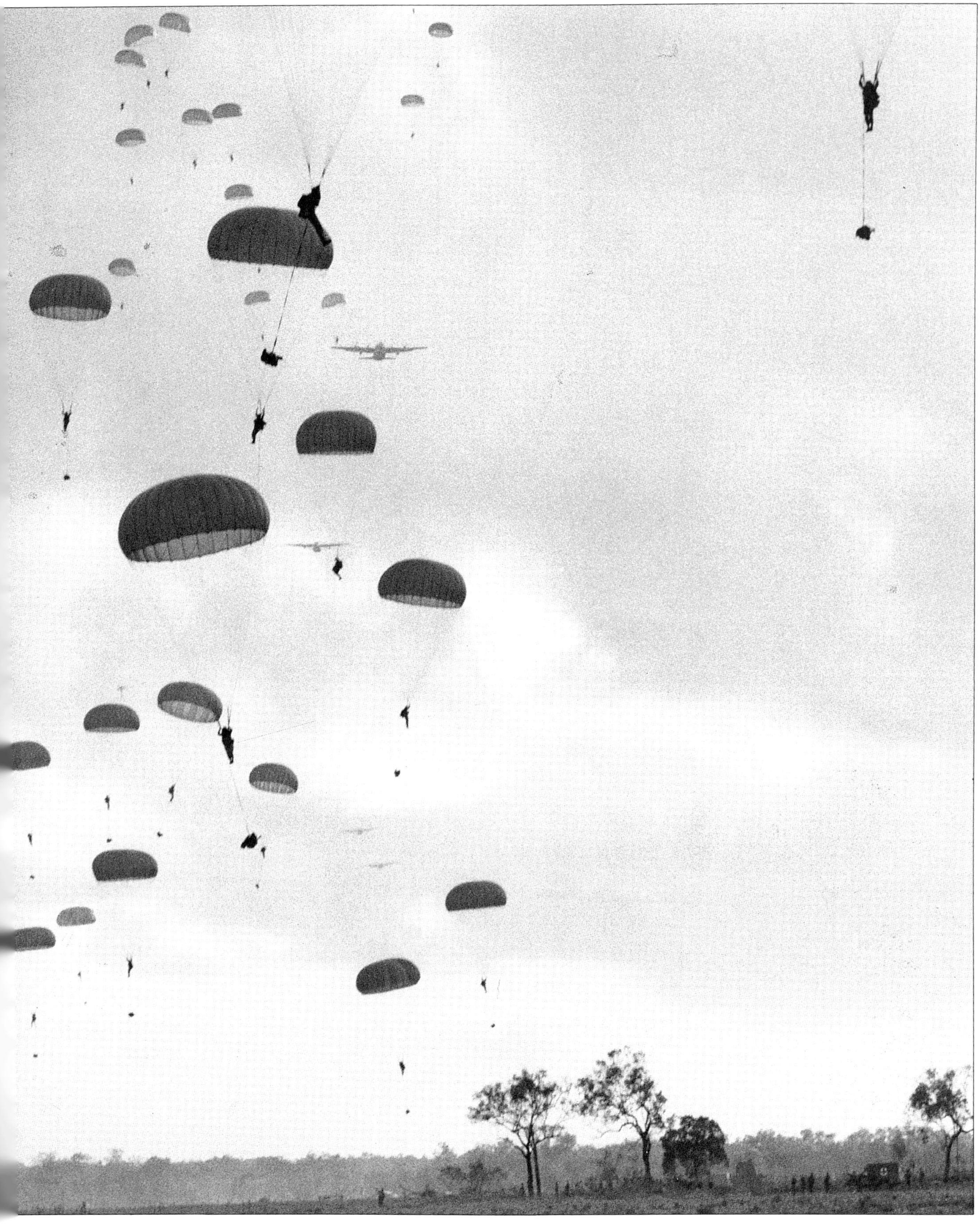

At the 1st Recruit Training Battalion at Kapooka, young women recruits learn weapons drill under the watchful eye of an instructor. After 12 weeks of basic training, they will be allocated to specialist courses in different branches of the Army.

WOMEN IN UNIFORM

Women have a long and proud history of service with Australia's armed forces but it is only in the last few years that the role of women has been expanded to the point where they can now train alongside men in most tasks of the modern soldier.

Australian women first served in a war zone as volunteer nurses with the second contingent to the Boer War in 1900. In World War I, they were officially enlisted and commissioned into the Army's Nursing Corps while back home women demonstrated they could take on "men's work" in both rural and industrial jobs. In World War II, women's wartime involvement expanded with home defence roles such as drivers, mechanics, clerks, searchlight operators and anti-aircraft crews, enlisted in the Australian Women Army Service (AWAS) which by 1944 exceeded 25,000 staff. The Women's Land Army, an organisation that recruited women in all areas of rural work, kept Australia's economy running and its troops and civilians fed and clothed.

Numbers dwindled after the war, but in 1950 a nucleus of women recruits was established as the Australian Women Army Corps (AWAC), able to be expanded as the occasion demanded. In 1951, this small unit became the Women's Royal Australian Army Corps (WRAAC), which by 1959 had earned permanent status in the Army structure. Throughout the 1950s and 1960s it provided mostly clerical services to the Army. Career advancement and promotion were extremely limited and resignation was automatically required on marriage. For a long time women recruits were unable to carry weapons even on the parade ground. Change came slowly.

With the Sex Discrimination Act introduced in 1984, the Australian Defence Forces reviewed their employment policies and opened more positions to women. Largely as a result of these new policies, the proportion of women in the services has risen dramatically with an overall figure of 10.9 per cent in February 1989 compared to 6.0 per cent in July 1981. This represents the highest percentage of female employment in the armed services in any country of the Western world. As for women officers, in the Army in 1989 there were 96 women Majors (as opposed to 54 in 1984), 11 Lieutenant Colonels (as opposed to four) and one Colonel. In 1989, the percentage of women officers in the Army stood at 8.8 per cent while in the Navy it is 11.1 per cent and in the Air Force 11.8 per cent. The highest rank to be achieved by women in the Navy is Commmander of whom there are 10 and in the Air Force there are seven female Wing Commanders and one Group Captain.

Women train for combat alongside other recruits but they cannot perform combat duties, defined as "direct participation in acts of violence against an enemy in time of war" or combat-related duties. In the Army they are eligible for a wide range of jobs, including supervisory positions, in all support services such as intelligence, signals, stores, drivers, mechanics and electrical technicians, military police, medical, catering, computers and clerical. In the Navy and Airforce they are similarly employed in support roles including naval instructors, aircraft engineers, welders and fitters, radio operators and air traffic controllers. With a review of policy in June 1989, more positions may soon be opened for women.

The realisation is dawning that a large country with a limited population like Australia cannot afford to ignore or waste such a valuable defence resource as women recruits.

platoons forward in APCs over the open ground with a third platoon close behind. The APCs' rear ramps slammed down and, in a cloud of dust, the troops spilled out of the carriers and quickly formed up for an assault. As they advanced with their rifles and light machine-guns pouring fire into the enemy positions, the carriers' heavy machine-guns thumped away, firing over their heads.

Having sighted their guns on the enemy's RPG section in a ramshackle barn, two of the tanks rolled forward from the left flank. As they bounced and swerved over the rough ground their guns automatically swivelled and tilted, keeping them in the same azimuth and elevation programmed into the fire-control computers by the gunners. The tanks closed in, their guns booming and flashing with unerring accuracy as their rounds exploded into the barnhouse. The artillery now lifted from the objective and began to drop a curtain of fire behind the next rise to cut off any enemy retreat to the airstrip. The infantry had worked their way round the outer buildings and were clearing out the last of the opposition while the tanks took up positions to engage any enemy attempting escape in armoured carriers. The battle for the homestead was over, the position secured. An echelon of track-load carriers and recovery vehicles moved up to retrieve any damaged vehicles. While casualties were treated and evacuated and prisoners herded aboard the trucks, the tanks left with a new advance guard of infantry and the advance of the battle group continued on schedule.

The battle group's operations had been fluid and fast-moving, taking advantage of the shock action and firepower that can be delivered by such forces. The Leopard tanks and APCs had combined all the techniques of the Army's

At the forefront of the Army's modern technology, a Rapier anti-aircraft platform launches its guided surface-to-air missile. The Rapier can engage any target below 10,000 feet to a range of 6.5 kilometres, while the Swedish, man-portable RBS-70, successor to the Redeye, can engage aircraft at up to five kilometres range.

KEEPING THE PEACE

Across a wind-swept desert battleground, riddled with mines and unexploded shells, Iranian soldiers carry stretchers of plastic-wrapped corpses in a solemn exchange of war dead with Iraqis. The atmosphere of mutual hatred is palpable. On this silent battlefield between two armies, now in a state of cease-fire, stand three Australian officers, wearing the blue berets of the United Nations. Theirs is a delicate, dangerous and often thankless task — they are there to keep the peace.

Since August 1988, a multinational peace-keeping force of 350 observers, called the UN Iran-Iraq Military Observer Group (UNIIMOG), has been policing the Iran-Iraq cease-fire in the hope of paving the way for a more permanent settlement. The 15 Australian Army officers serving with this force form part of Australia's ongoing contribution to the UN presence in the world's trouble-spots.

The United Nation's peace-keeping role began in 1948 and over the years no fewer than over 500,000 military and civilian personnel from more than 50 countries have taken part in 15 UN operations of this kind. Australia has played an active part from the start. When the Dutch colonial government clashed with the native independence movement in the Dutch East Indies, Australia lobbied hard in the UN Security Council to resolve the conflict. Between 1947 and 1950, Australia had 15 military observers serving with the UN Committee for Indonesia (UNCI) which oversaw the creation of the present nation-state.

Australia also has had a long association with UN efforts in the Middle East. After the Arab-Israeli cease-fire of 1948, the Security Council set up a UN Truce Supervision Organization (UNTSO), staffed by professional military observers including Australians. Since 1956, Australian Army officers with UNTSO have been seconded for tours of duty in this volatile region including the UN Yemen Observation Mission (UNYOM) in 1963. They continue to serve with the UN Disengagement Observer Force (UNDOF) in the Golan Heights buffer-zone, supervising the Syria-Israel cease-fire of 1974; with UN Interim Force in Lebanon (UNIFIL), formed in 1978 to oversee the withdrawal of Israeli troops from Southern Lebanon; and most recently with UNIIMOG on the Iran-Iraq border. Forty RAAF officers, four Army officers and a detachment of Iroquois helicopters joined the UN Emergency Force (UNEF II) in the Sinai from 1976 to 1979 to supervise the Egypt-Israel cease-fire. When the conflict over the border state of Kashmir erupted between India and Pakistan, Australia contributed six Army observers, an RAAF detachment and a Caribou transport to the UN Military Observer Group in India and Pakistan (UNMOGIP), serving from 1949 until 1986. Today, Australia still has 20 Federal police assigned to the UN Peace-keeping Force in Cyprus (UNFICYP), patrolling a tense cease-fire line between the Greek and Turkish communities on the island.

In March 1989, engineers of 17th Construction Squadron board a US Galaxy transport as members of the Australian contingent to the UN Transition Assistance Group (UNTAG) in Namibia.

Under strict orders to use force only in self-defence, blue beret soldiers find the peace-keeping role very demanding, especially when threatened by the people they are meant to protect. More than 700 blue berets have been killed over the last 40 years. Indeed in 1988, four Australians lost their lives on Cyprus and another was killed by a land mine in Southern Lebanon.

Yet Australia continues to meet her UN obligations. In early 1989, 300 Australian engineers and support staff were sent to Namibia as part of the UN Transition Assistance Group (UNTAG) to police the withdrawal of Cuban, South African, African National Congress and SWAPO troops from the border regions and oversee elections for an independent Namibia. Undertaking engineering projects and mine-clearing in support of the UN force, the Australian contingent has a dangerous job. They will be armed, ready for any trouble but aware that their first duty is to keep tempers cool and avoid conflict.

In December 1978, an RAAF Iroquois chopper in United Nations livery flies low over jeeps of a Swedish battalion. As part of the UN Emergency Force in the Sinai Desert to supervise a cease-fire between Egypt and Israel, Australia contributed Army and RAAF personnel and four Iroquois.

Only minutes after hitting the deck and quickly stowing their canopies, parachutists of 3 RAR, are alert and ready for combat, fingers on the triggers of their rifles and machine-guns. Even with all the sophisticated hardware money can buy, the backbone of a modern Army remains well-trained, disciplined and determined soldiers.

heavy combat units, backed by both field and longer-range medium artillery, to give mobility with strength for a powerful punch when and wherever it may be needed. As the mechanised battalion of the 1st Division's 1st Brigade, the 5/7th had demonstrated they can provide an effective counter to enemy land attacks.

The other battalion of the 1st Brigade, the 3rd Battalion Royal Australian Regiment, trains as a parachute force. All its equipment is lightweight, and as such can be rapidly deployed to seize any vital objective, such as an airfield, and to hold the area for the arrival of heavier-armed forces to pre-empt or counter an incursion. In a typical scenario, the battalion would parachute in and secure an airstrip which could then be used to fly in extra ground troops along with the artillery, armour, engineers and communications needed to quickly establish a complete, balanced fighting group. Though Australia has no amphibious assault capability of its own, the paratroopers of 3 RAR can still practise parachute assaults to secure beachheads for amphibious troop landings during full-scale exercises like "Kangaroo" manoeuvres held every year in northern Australia with allied forces.

In the event of an enemy incursion in Australia's north, the nation's land combat force will depend on faster reaction times than either of these battalions, based in NSW and Victoria, can give. The first line of northern ground defence is the Operational Deployment Force, built on the 1st Division's 3rd Brigade at Townsville. The 3rd Brigade consists of two infantry battalions with their associated field artillery regiment and field engineer squadron. Fully trained and equipped with stocks to sustain it in action for six months, the ODF has one company held at seven days' readiness, a battalion at 14 days' and the rest of the force on 28 days' readiness. It has a parachute battalion and the 2nd Cavalry Regiment available as back-up and can also call on the 5th Aviation Regiment and an anti-air squadron equipped with the Rapier guided-missile system.

Australia's anti-air defences have for a long time lagged behind the technology of her aircraft. Even in World War II, Australian anti-aircraft gunners were using World War I vintage Lewis heavy machine-guns to supplement the 40 mm Bofors. Australia's first taste of Surface-to-Air-Missile (SAM) systems was the Bloodhound missile, which was questionably old technology when purchased for the RAAF in the 1950s. In the 1970s, the Redeye infra-red, heat-seeking missile, launched from a shoulder-mounted rocket-launcher was introduced as a deadly anti-aircraft weapon for the Australian infantryman. Today's Army, in an era when the most potent and sophisticated aircraft give close air support to ground forces, must have an up to date anti-aircraft capability. The Rapier guided-missile system is rapidly transportable by air and land, where it is towed on a trailer behind a heavy-duty Land Rover, and can be quickly set up for action. With a dazzling array of electronics to direct the missile onto its target, it can ensure one-shot-one-hit accuracy.

The Rapier is the ultimate high-tech system in the Australian land force's crew-served weapons and it demonstrates how sophisticated the world's modern armies are becoming. One of the great military adages has always been: "While the navy and airforces man the equipment, the army equips the man." But this is fast becoming less true as new, smarter, and more sophisticated machines of war are introduced to the late 20th century battlefield. Still, the Army's most vital asset remains its manpower. The battlefield may become more lethal, complex and stressful, but Australia's soldiers must be ready to meet the challenge — and win.

5

INTO THE FUTURE

Revolutionary designs and concepts for tomorrow's military communications, weapons and hardware are already on the drawing board or in the experimental phase. With a more modest budget than the superpowers, Australia must still plan for modern warfare of the 21st century.

It has been a common cry throughout the history of modern warfare, that generals spend their time preparing to fight the last war rather than the next. More accurately, they have often been called upon to fight wars with equipment left over from previous conflicts.

As the business of war has become more and more affected by the march of technology, most modern defence hierarchies employ officers whose task is to look into the future. Their work is called combat development, and their minds soar over all the possibilities, no matter how fantastic, or unlikely. They leave no tactical or technical stone unturned.

At any time, the combat developers' filing cabinets are full of many futuristic concepts, most of which will never see the light of day. They are not required to fetter their imaginations or limit their enquiry by such practical considerations as cost or available resources. That is the province of the defence analysts, planners and budget makers, who must achieve the best possible selection of equipment within the prevailing strategic,

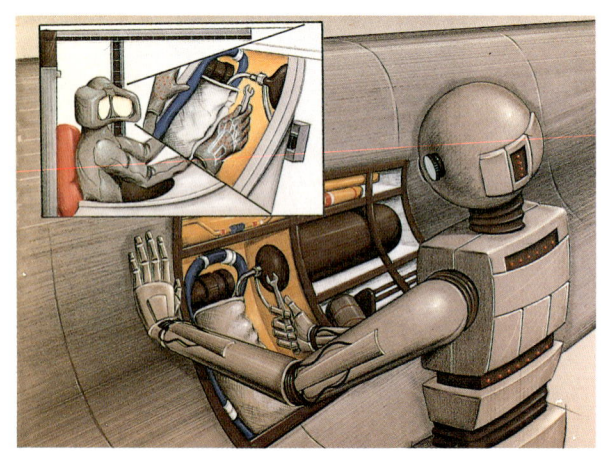

Doing repairs by remote-control, a technician views the task in a visor as a robot "mimics" his hand motions.

economic, social and political constraints. Ultimately, they are the ones who determine the military's future.

What then, does the 21st century hold for Australia's defence forces? A good place to start would be to look at a few of the less fantastic concepts residing in the combat developers' bottom drawer. Many of the technological dreams there might be awesome and indeed relevant only to a superpower such as America; certainly they will not always be achievable or affordable by a country of Australia's size. But the military concepts they predict and the tactical possibilities they herald affect all the world's battlefields. And there is no certain guarantee that Australia will remain forever isolated from future conflicts inside and outside of its strategic surrounds.

Australia has in the past based its defence on a policy of limited self-sufficiency within the framework of alliances involving a major partner, firstly Britain and then the United States of America. Since the Vietnam War, that defence policy has evolved to be more self-reliant and more concerned with a regional defence posture. The risk scenarios flowing from such an evolution are that Australia may be drawn, as in the past, into a war in support of its larger allies or that it may become involved unilaterally in a local conflict despite her alliances. The assessment of these risks determines the future shape and equipment levels of the Australian Defence Force.

It is most likely that the RAAF and RAN will continue to attract significant expenditure, remaining relatively well-equipped compared with other air and naval forces in the region. This would be consistent with a defensively sound maritime strategy. Moreover, widening concerns about events on Australia's maritime flanks create the possible need to develop a capability for power projection into both the Indian and southern Pacific Oceans.

In the meantime, the full-time component of the Army is unlikely to grow any larger and may well decline in combat power when, as seems likely, heavier equipment such as tanks and lighter armoured vehicles grow old and are not replaced. The Army, in fact, has only a minor role to play in Australia's maritime strategy. Still the question remains: if an "enemy" did, in the future, land in Australia, what force structure, capabilities and training are required to deter or defeat him?

Australia finds itself in the unique position of being an island nation with a vast continental land mass and a small population spread right around it. All three military forces are vital in the defence of the territory, its approaches and surrounds. And all of the three environments, the land, sea and air, fit closely together in Australia's defence posture.

Perhaps the most fearsome aspect of future wars is the speed at which events will occur in all environments. The rate of information exchange in some areas is expected to increase by as much as 1,000 per cent, while the speed and volume of incoming weapons and data will be potentially paralysing.

To meet such contingencies, the growth of computer technology will be a major part of the ongoing modernisation of any military force. Super mini-computers using parallel and adaptive processing techniques, superconductivity-based hardware and high-speed, low-loss, fibre-optic networks will all take over the processing of the massive amounts of incoming data, and in doing so they will revolutionise tactical command and control systems at all levels — from the fighter pilot's cockpit to the frigate's bridge to the army corps' headquarters.

In parallel, improved data integration, superb computer-generated graphical displays and tactical decision-making aided by the artificial intelligence of expert systems will help future military commanders make their plans and control their battles.

To maximise the ADF's moves into joint-service operations, steps have already been taken to replace antiquated single-service command arrangements with a joint-service command structure. Computer-based support systems to take the new headquarters into the next century will appear in the 1990s.

Command and control systems will also use photonics, operating with photons instead of electrons at the heart of their sensing, computing and transmitting systems, thereby providing reaction times in the "speed of light" magnitude. In the extreme, the fighter pilot of the future is likely to find his tactical information projected directly onto his eyeball by the photonics of his battle helmet.

This pilot will also find himself in a super cockpit operating without conventional head-up and panel-mounted displays. Control of his aircraft may be partly augmented by voice commands, recognised and interpreted by one of many on-board microprocessors. His craft may be capable of computer-controlled "un-aerodynamic" behaviour such as flying sideways to better engage targets to a flank. Among its extraordinary repertoire of subsonic and supersonic manoeuvres will be a capability to take off and land vertically from concealed positions. Without doubt, his aircraft will employ so-called "Stealth" techniques of low-profile design, radar absorbing materials and electronic counter-measures to make it invisible to electronic detection and interception.

Below the fighter, much closer to ground and the land battle, are the highly manoeuvrable scout and attack helicopters. They are capable of all-weather operation because of their sophisticated avionic fits and advanced airframes. These helicopters will employ thermal and electronic sensors and smart weapons to bring close support to the combat soldier.

The battlefield helicopters of the future will be lighter, more powerful and have dual engines. The lightweight airframes will allow the light reconnaissance helicopter to climb at speeds in excess of 500 feet per minute and travel horizontally at speeds of 200 knots or more. Like its sisters, the utility and attack helicopters, it will employ an automated cockpit with helmet-mounted displays, wide-field-of-view optics, digital terrain maps and worldwide navigation capability. Target acquisition and night vision sensors will be incorporated in an electronic or photonic architecture which will allow rapid and accurate transfer of data and targets between aircraft, while reliability and crashworthiness will be significantly improved by the use of the new materials and engines.

The fighting man on the ground is likely to be wearing clothing that provides not only a measure of ballistic protection but also cover from electronic and optical detection. His personal weapon will be made of lightweight composite materials and ceramics, and it will be self-cleaning. The rifle will fire a small-calibre projectile in deadly salvo bursts using a combustible cartridge case.

The soldier will receive orders from section or squad commanders via inbuilt, short-range, speech-secure radio inside his composite bullet-proof helmet. Beside him on the battlefield will be robotic vehicles which can perform many dangerous tasks such as mine clearing and reconnaissance in contaminated areas. Armoured vehicles with extraordinary cross-country capabilities based on computer-controlled suspension systems will be operating nearby. They will also employ microprocessor-controlled robotics internally to reduce the workload of the crew in tasks such as armament loading and vehicle replenishment. And they will be capable of true 24-hour operation on the battlefield as a result of increased reliability, integrated computer-controlled logistic systems and advanced on-board and imaging equipment.

At sea, many of the most significant advances will not be physically apparent, as they will affect communications and Intelligence based on satellite technology. Even so, the naval surface vessel of the 21st century is likely to look very different from the ships of today. It will have experienced observable changes in hull and superstructure design. Lighter vessels such as frigates may use a catamaran-like Small Waterplane Area Twin Hull (SWATH) concept which will provide increased stability, quieter operation, better survivability and an improved platform for wide-aperture sonar arrays.

The development of vertically launched missile systems (VLS) and advanced cruise missiles will also permit the battlecruiser of the future to carry a huge amount of ordnance. In line with increasing speeds of engagement, there will be a need to launch and control large numbers of missiles simultaneously. VLS can facilitate this, but a large amount of open deck space will be required.

Beneath the ocean's surface, the advantage will go to the side with the edge in fluid dynamics, computer technology and acoustic science. In this extremely difficult environment, the problems of hull and propeller design and the detection and recognition of enemy submarines depend on the ability to deal with computational and analytical problems of great complexity, often in real time. In increasing degrees, the battle at sea will rely on space technology for its command, control, communications and Intelligence.

The future will see new shapes in space other than satellites, space stations and shuttles. It is likely that phased-array radars will be spread over huge areas of space, making unprecedented survivability and accuracy possible. The development of nuclear-propulsion systems and high-energy, stable propulsion chemicals such as tetrahydrogen will provide an order of magnitude increase over present systems. Such propulsion systems may permit the development of aircraft which can operate in the upper atmosphere at speeds from 6,000 to 12,000 kilometres per hour and which would be able to accelerate directly to orbit from a runway.

Naturally, as more and more of the defence capability of nations becomes dependent on space-based systems, the greater will be the need to protect these capabilities. A likely means of achieving this is by placing in orbit, in close proximity to critical satellites, defender spacecraft armed with directed-energy weapons. So dependent will all armed services become on space-based systems, it seems probable that, in the final analysis, control of near space will be the deciding factor in any future major conflict. Here at last will be the ultimate tactical high ground.

Depending on Australia's political and strategic climate in the future, and the nature of its alliances with the superpower who may be utilising such technologies, the Australian Defence Force may find itself patching in to the 21st century's tactical satellite systems. Already, astonishingly clear Intelligence can be accessed via space — weapons-based satellites are but a generation of technology away. Whether or not they are politically or economically viable remains to be seen.

Certainly Australia will incorporate advances in military designs closer to the ground. The ADF has a comprehensive lineup of hardware that will take it into the next century. To remain strategically and tactically capable, the F-111s, Orions and Hornets, the FFGs, their Seahawks, and the new 471 submarines, and the Army's Black Hawk helicopters and ground weaponry will have to be kept at their performance peak. Much of their updating will be software based, with weapons and data systems playing a major role in extending the machinery's lifespan.

More and more it appears that the military is being shaped by its technological advances. This is most apparent in the airforce and navy, but even on the ground the humble foot soldier increasingly has to be a master of modern computer-controlled equipment. Still, it is he who must pull the trigger, or it is the fighter pilot who must unleash a devastating array of cruise missiles, or the submariner who must creep silently towards his enemy before firing his deadly self-propelled torpedoes.

The navigation, surveillance and weapons systems are now, and will be ever more so awesomely powerful in the future, but it is the men of war who must ultimately decide the future of military conflicts. Whether the hardware has been proven in past campaigns, or is literally space-aged and untried in the heat of battle, will undoubtedly be telling factors. So too will be the strategic and tactical preparedness of fighting nations. The Australian Defence Force is coming to grips with all that lies ahead — and in doing so it proudly calls upon all that it has achieved in its illustrious military history.

COMMAND AND CONTROL

To help commanders with future battle management, military headquarters will require the best possible information, computation and display technologies.

Massive data bases will move strategic and tactical data quickly and accurately throughout large distributed computer networks. Expert systems will provide automatic response to many military problems, but there will always be the need for human decisions to be made in real time.

The technology will allow the fusion of information from a myriad of battlefield sensors to create virtual-image battle displays within headquarters at all levels of command. Such displays, based on three-dimensional computer graphics and holograms, will give the decision-makers a real-time natural display of the tactical situation over which they must exercise control.

These extraordinarily realistic displays will permit the rehearsal of plans and specific missions with appropriate assessment of their probability of success. But most importantly they will help reduce the remoteness of the higher commander from the feel of the battle.

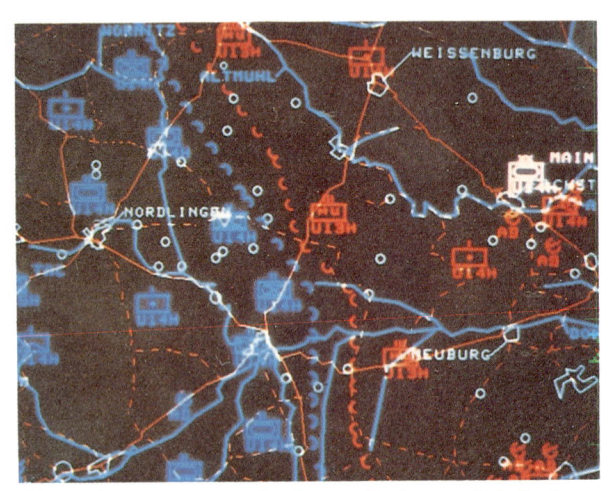

Above: A computer-screen battle-map displays symbols for the status and disposition of military units in a NATO exercise. Data-linked to all land, sea and air assets, computers can display and update progress of a battle in real time. Right: In a futuristic control room, commanders monitor and direct an air strike using a huge computer-generated holographic display.

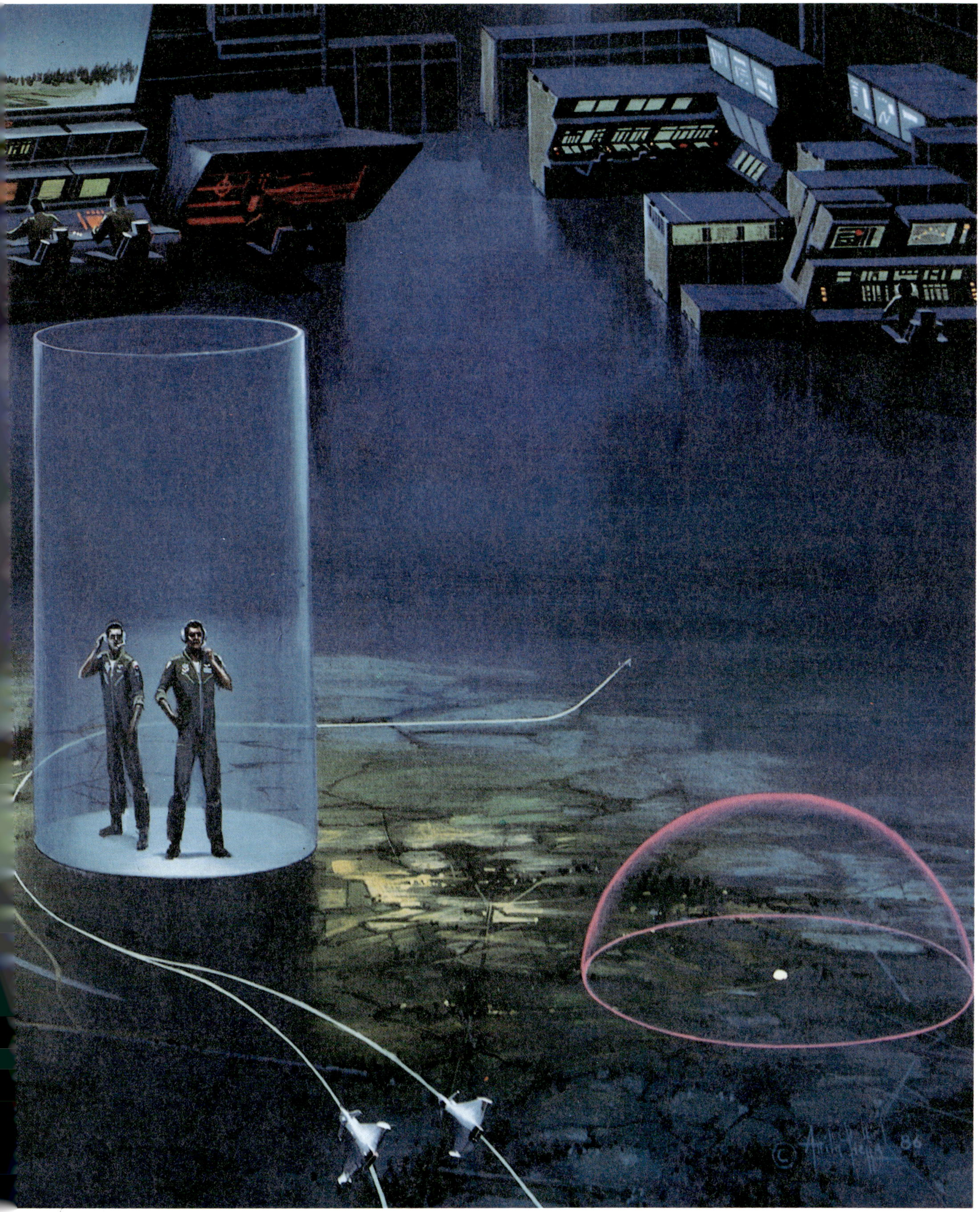

WINGED STEALTH

Of all the advanced aviation technologies none is more revolutionary than "Stealth". It has the potential to neutralise the tactical importance of radar and to restore dominance to attacking fighters, strategic bombers and cruise missiles.

"Stealth" combines three technologies, the first of which is the use of exotic radar absorbing materials in the basic construction of the aircraft. The skeletal elements and the skin are made of layered carbon-fibre epoxies and ceramics with less visibility to radar than any metal.

Airframe design is characterised by curved surfaces with a minimum of sharp corners and protrusions which can reflect radar beams. In the B2 bomber this is achieved by a swept "flying wing" concept, while the engine intakes and air-cooled exhausts are mounted on the top of the wings, invisible to infra-red sensors.

The third technology of the "Stealth" aircraft is that of an advanced level of electronic counter counter-measures. At $500 million each, the B2s deserve all the protection money can buy.

Above: In the supercockpit of tomorrow's aircraft, a computer-graphic display is projected into the eyes of the pilot. The helmet display shows a contour-grid terrain map, the computer plotted flight path of the aircraft and information on enemy aircraft, radars and missiles. Right: Blending into the dusk, the silhouette of a futuristic-looking aircraft symbolises the new age of stealth.

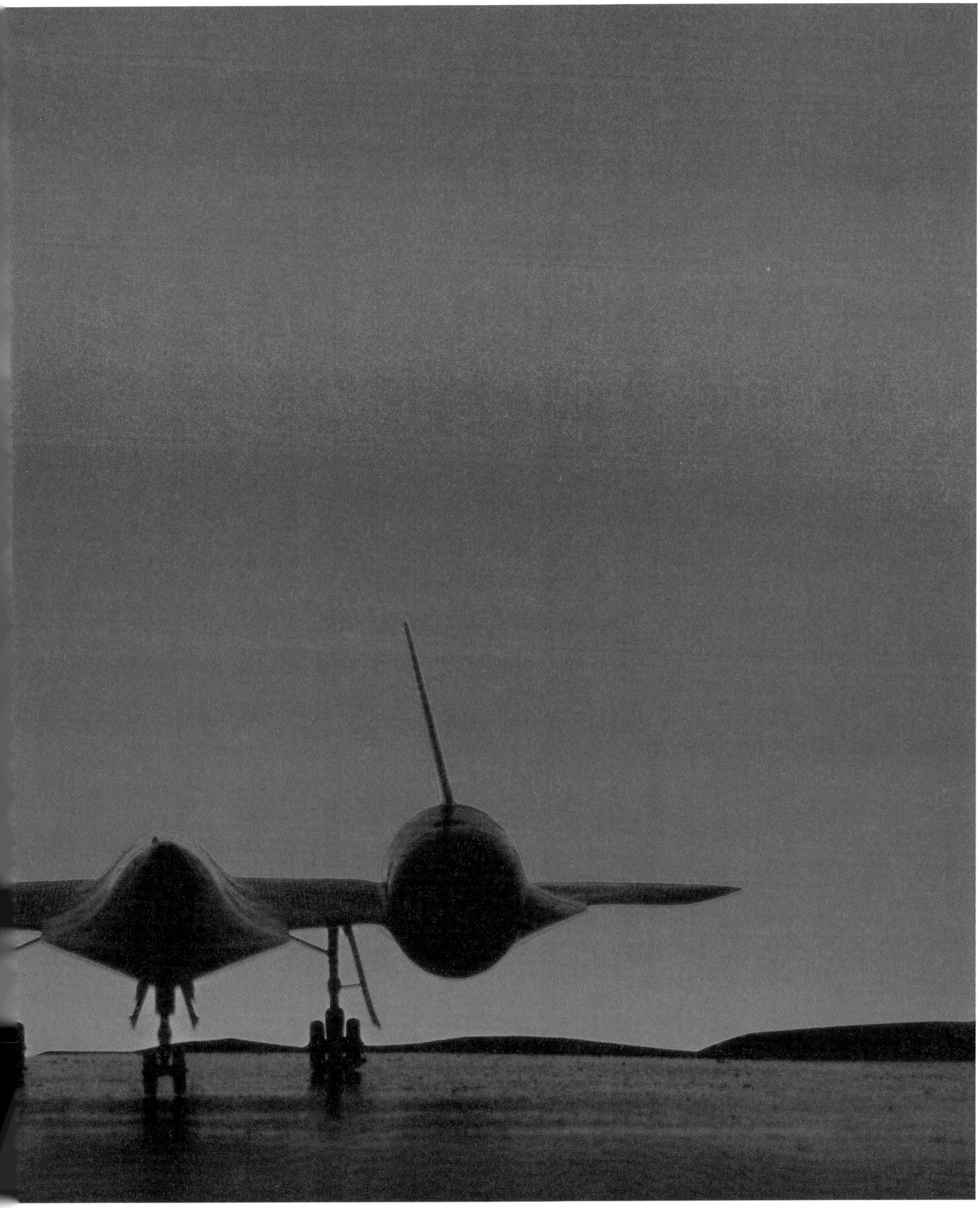

ARMY ADVANCES

Even with computerised communications, robotic or remote-controlled vehicles and computer-assisted armoured vehicles, the soldier on the battlefield of the future will still look to his personal weapon for the fighting edge he needs to survive and win in combat.

The G11 Advanced Combat Rifle made by Heckler and Koch typifies trends in military small-arms. Its design takes into account the fall-off in marksmanship which occurs under the stress of battle. This is offset by firing a cone of three shots in a high-speed burst to improve the chance of a hit. The bullet is embedded in a caseless shaped propellant charge and loaded via a transverse revolving cylinder breech. The resultant very high rate of fire of 2,000 rounds per minute, coupled with hydraulically damped recoil, allows the salvo of three rounds to leave the barrel before any aim-disturbing kick is felt by the firer. The caseless ammunition weighs half as much as conventional ammunition with obvious combat and logistic advantages.

Similar technology to that which permits the infantryman's rifle to use lightweight high-strength composites will be found in the battlefield helicopters of the future. Revolutionary lightweight airframes and engines will enhance the performance and speed of reconnaissance choppers while new concepts in sensors and cockpit design will give attack helicopters a quantum leap in navigation and target acquisition capabilities.

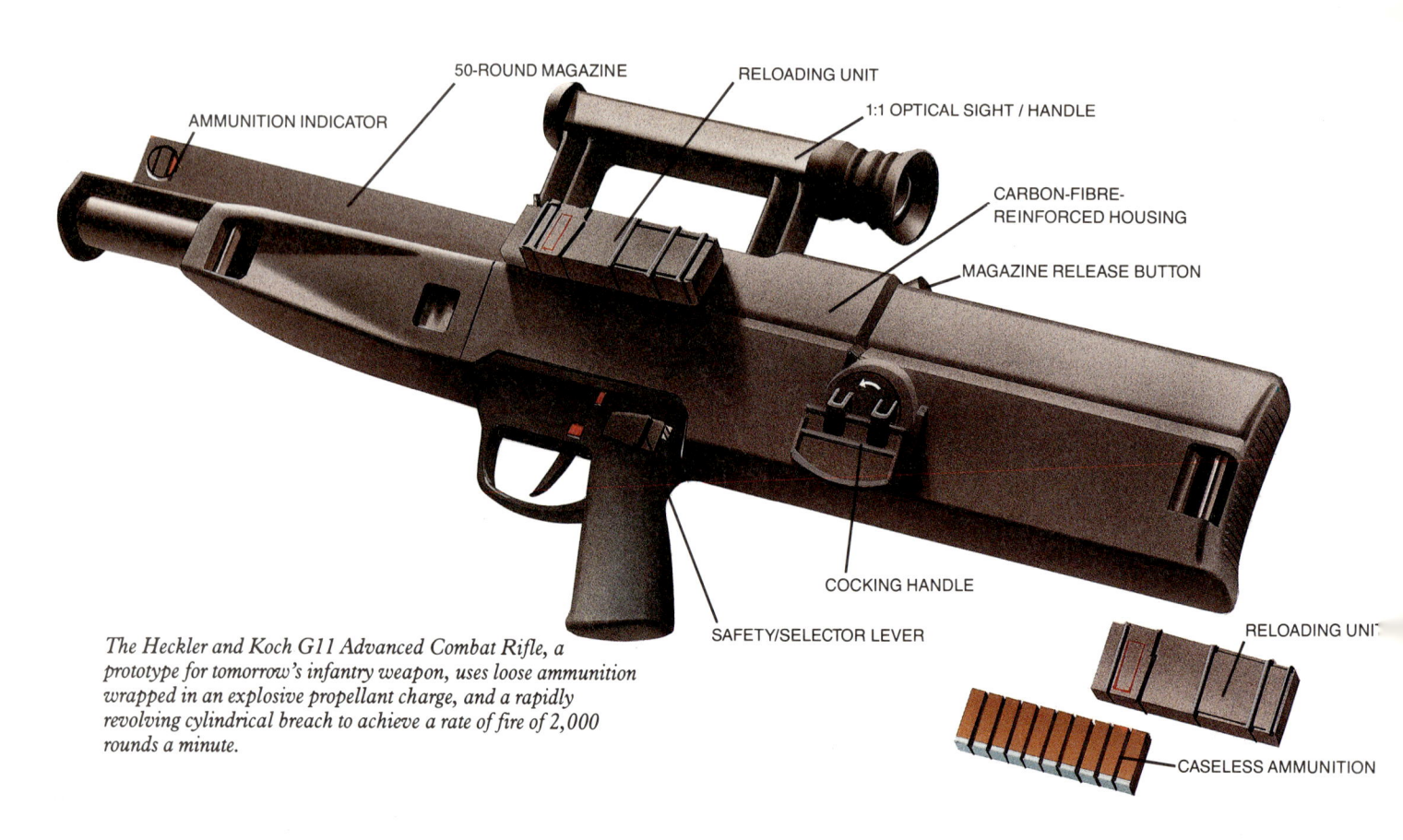

The Heckler and Koch G11 Advanced Combat Rifle, a prototype for tomorrow's infantry weapon, uses loose ammunition wrapped in an explosive propellant charge, and a rapidly revolving cylindrical breach to achieve a rate of fire of 2,000 rounds a minute.

Two futuristic scout and attack helicopters skim low over a battlefield. Though these choppers may seem the stuff of science fiction, the McDonnell Douglas Helicopter Company is currently bidding for a US Army helicopter contract with this space-age design, in competition with a Bell-Sikorsky prototype.

BLUEPRINT BATTLESHIP

The futuristic concept of the Strike Battle Cruiser embodies many advanced naval technologies. Its basic shape is determined not by traditional factors but by the requirements of its main weapon system, the Vertically Launched Missile. The SBC will carry hundreds of missiles ready for instantaneous, simultaneous launching. The weapons may be anti-ship, anti-submarine or anti-air, and will employ advanced non-nuclear warheads, have longer ranges and use stealth techniques to ensure their success. Similar missiles may be capable of rapid adaptation to different roles by changing their payload packages for such tasks as jamming, anti-radar, strike or damage assessment. Guidance to their targets may be effected by any ship, submarine or aircraft in the electronically integrated task group best able to complete the engagement. The SBC's close-in protection may be provided by directed energy weapons using either high-energy lasers or microwaves or charged particle beams. The power for these weapons will come from very powerful, super-conductivity-based generators which may also be capable of augmenting the cruiser's normal propulsion system with an electric drive train.

Above: The shape of tomorrow's surface navy may look something like this futuristic Strike Battle Cruiser equipped with multiple Vertical Launch Missiles (VLS) and high-energy laser guns. The bridge will resemble the cockpit of a 747 aircraft with room for only one or two commanders. Right: A Strike Battle Cruiser of the future launches anti-air missiles against an enemy air attack.

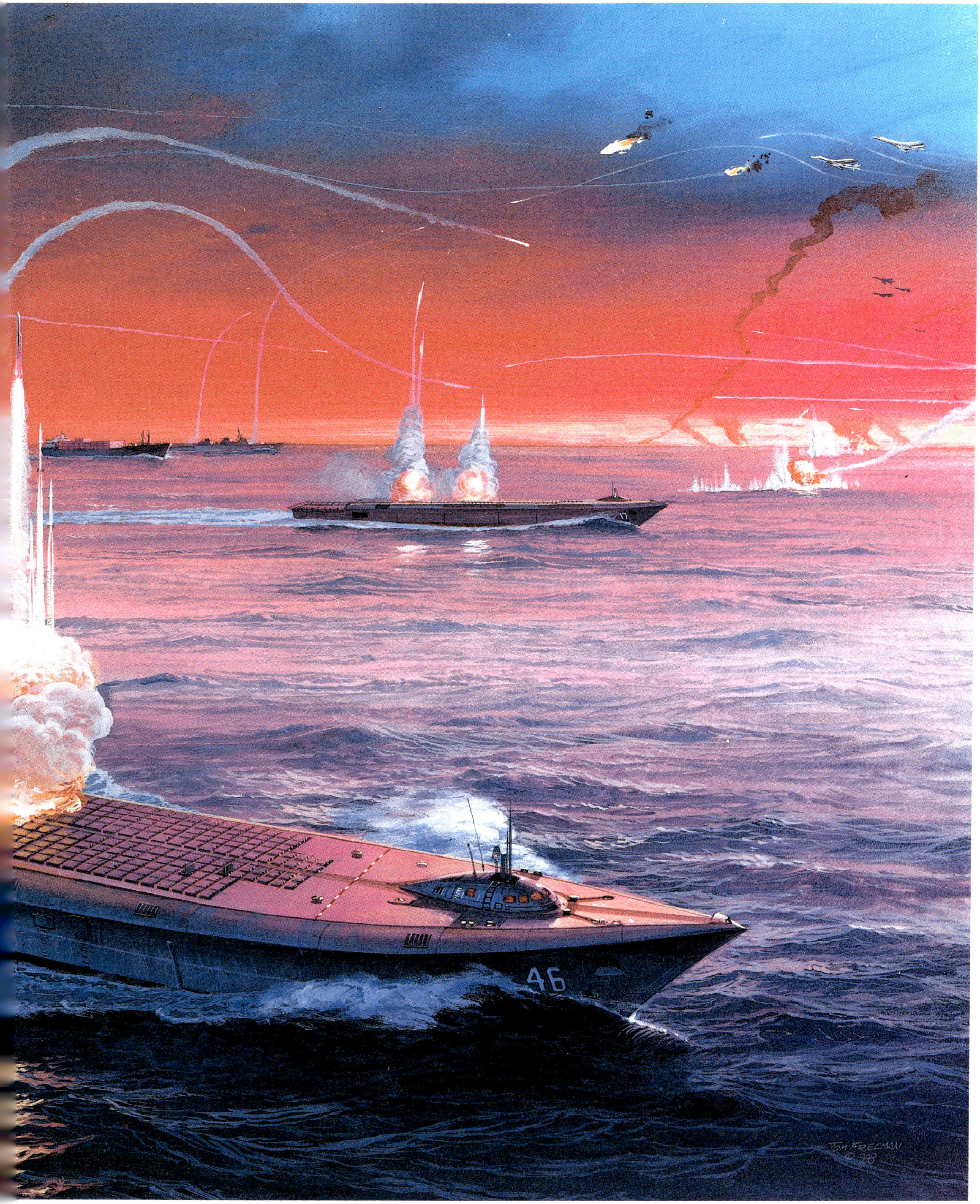
46

HIGHEST BATTLEGROUND

The aerospace plane, capable of operating in the earth's atmosphere and in space, will be made possible by a better understanding of hypersonic aerodynamics, and advances in air-breathing propulsive systems and lightweight, high-temperature resistant materials. These developments will permit efficient flight missions in the Mach 8 to Mach 25 bracket which will include horizontal take-off, orbital space flight and horizontal landings. Such a plane could fill interceptor, transport, space rescue and many other military roles such as special strategic reconnaissance.

The development of directed energy weapons is receiving impetus as more and more military critical payloads are placed in space. As well as the particle beam and high-energy lasers and microwave weapons which can disrupt the guidance systems of incoming anti-satellite missiles, there is a need for very high electrical fields to accelerate very dense solid shot to hyper velocities, to destroy a variety of hardened targets. These weapons offer special advantages both for the spacecraft defender station and for offensive anti-satellite (ASAT) systems.

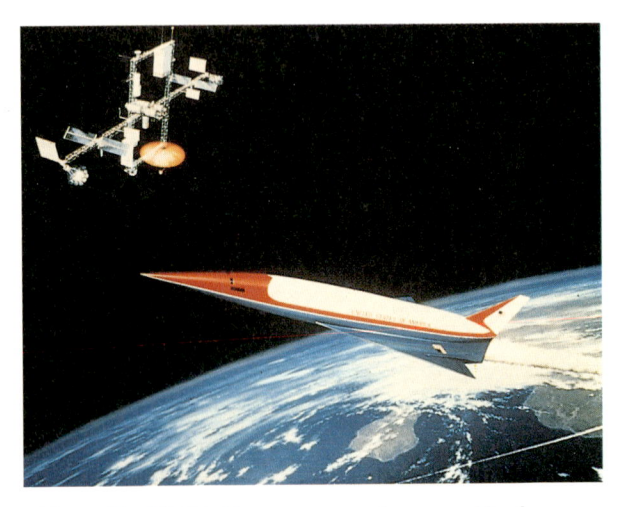

Above: The US Air Force aerospace plane, capable of horizontal take-off from conventional runways to orbital altitude, would enable regular space missions and hypersonic worldwide flight operations. Right: A defender spacecraft acts as an orbiting high-power laser weapon, directing "killer" beams onto hostile targets, to protect satellites, space stations and craft.

163

ACKNOWLEDGMENTS

John Ferguson Publishers and the authors would like to thank the following individuals and organisations for their contribution to *Modern Military: Towards 2000*. Due to the contemporary nature of this title, the following list will act as a bibliography as it was necessary to consult experts within the various fields rather than books.

Brigadier Steve Gower, Peter Young, George Odgers, John Stackhouse, Sheryl Hallam-Eames and Chief Photographer J.G. Sebastian, Petty Officer Photographer Eric Pitman, Sergeant Howard Moffat and Captain Robert Barnes of Department of Defence Photographic Unit.

BUILDING A MODERN NAVY: Lieutenant Des Owens; Captain Simon Harrington, Lieutenant Larry Menin and Lieutenant Commander Hayes, HMAS *Canberra*; Captain Kim Pitt, Commander John Hodges, Lieutenant Commander Sandy Coulson, Lieutenant Commander Rick Shalders, and Photographic Officer Cameron Martin of HMAS *Platypus*; Captain Michael Dunne of HMAS *Watson*; Public Relations Officer Vic Jeffrey, HMAS *Stirling*; Commander P.D. Johnstone-Hall; Rear Admiral Tony Horton; Lieutenant Keith McCarron of the Naval Photographic Unit; Lieutenant Rod Newbold, Naval Publications; Commander Walsh, *Navy News*; Malcolm Burchett and Rod Webb of Silver Advertising Agency; Commander Kerry Stephen, Carrington Slipways; Ross Milton of Australian Submarine Corporation; Ron Tutt, Artistralia Pty Ltd, Western Australia; Yon Ivanovic, Studio One, Cairns; Peter Lindley, F.H. Industries Ltd, United Kingdom; Pamela von Gruber, *Defence and Foreign Affairs*, International Media Corporation.

FROM MUSTANG TO HORNET: Wing Commander Peter Criss, No. 1 Squadron; Flight Officer John Lonergan and Squadron Leader Roger McKay of No. 77 Squadron; Wing Commander Ross Fox, No. 75 Squadron; Wing Commander Peter Kelly, Wing Commander Phil Morel, Sergeant Crawford and the staff of the Central Photographic Unit, Laverton; Air Commodore Richardson; Squadron Leader Walton, East Sale; Wing Commander Dunne, Warrant Officer Buchanan, Flight Lieutenant Prescott and the staff of Williamtown RAAF Photographic Unit; Mal Lancaster, RAAF photographer; Greg Meggs, aviation photojournalist; Langdon Halls and Alan Patten, McDonnell Douglas Australia; James Boddington, newspaper photographer; David Rowntree of Gavin Anderson & Co, for Boeing International Corporation; Commander D. Henry, US Navy Plant Representative Office; Brian Noonan, RAAF Public Relations Office Brisbane; Squadron Leader T.A. Roediger; Anne Evans, *RAAF News*; Mignon Patterson, RAAF journalist; Alison Frost, Department of Defence Public Relations; Miriam Goodwin, Sinclair-Barry public relations for UNISYS; Flight Lieutenant John Terres, Defence Force Recruiting.

A MOBILE ARMY: Australian Defence Forces Public Relations; Barry Barnes, Production Development Facility, Salisbury; Lieutenant Colonel Polk, Major Andy Reynolds, Captain Robert Barnes and Lisa Keen of Department of Defence Public Relations; Major Steven Bender, Tully Land Warfare School; Sergeant Dave English, 5th Aviation Regiment Townsville; Major Charles Worth, War Games Centre Georges Heights; Kathy Grant, Norma Johns and the staff of Marketforce Advertising Agency; Alan Ross and Herma Goppy of Marshall Cavendish Ltd.; Bruce Cameron Office of Defence Production; Carole David, Hawker de Havilland; Don Munroe, Sikorsky USA; E.F. Sanislo, Sikorsky Australia; Warrant Officer Eric Combe, Phil Mayne and the staff of *Army News*; Lieutenant Colonel Wallace, Major Dave Rawson, Corporal Steve Danaher, Special Air Service Regiment Swanbourne Western Australia; Army Public Relations, Victoria Barracks; Lieutenant Fiona Newman, Major Dennis Coffey, Army Audio-Visual Unit; Norm Weber, Weber Advertising for Barra Sonobuoys and Plessey Raven.

INTO THE FUTURE: Scott Tickner and Colonel Tom Hanlin, Military Liaison US Foreign Press Centre; Tom Freeman, Springhouse Art Ltd.; Linda Cullen and Patty Maddocks, US Naval Institute; Major Dennis Coffey and the Australian Army Audio-Visual Unit; Gerda Parr, Air Force Systems Command; Department of US Air Force; Christopher Alan, New Science Publications; I. Gelfer, Elbit Computers, Israel; McDonnell Douglas, USA and The Concurrent Computer Corporation.

Other contributors were David Astle, Jillian McFarlane, Mike Harris, John Laffin, RAAF Wives Association, United Services Institution and United Nations Information Centre in Sydney. For their help with picture research and illustrations we would like to thank Ian Affleck, Australian War Memorial, Mihri Tansley, Alan Puckett, Carolyn Johns of Wildlight Photo Agency and the staff of News Limited photo library.

PICTURE CREDITS

Credits from left to right are separated by semicolons, from top to bottom by oblique strokes. AWM = Australian War Memorial, CPE = Central Photographic Establishment, RAAF Laverton, DOD = Department of Defence Public Relations, Canberra, DSTO = Defence Science and Technology Organisation, NPU = Naval Photographic Unit, Sydney. USAFSC = Public Relations, United States Air Force Systems Command.

COVER and Page 1: CPE

FRONTISPIECE 6-7: DOD. 8-9: Army News. 10-11: Carolyn Johns, Wildlight Photo Agency.

TO AUSTRALIA'S DEFENCE: 12: DOD. 14: Drawn by Jane Tenney, reference courtesy *Defence and Foreign Affairs Journal*. 17: Carolyn Johns. 19: DOD ADE/A86-44-11. 20-21: DOD RAAF # 105. 24: Drawn by Alan Puckett, reference courtesy DSTO, Salisbury. 25: DOD 88.059.21 / DOD CN 87/17. 26: Mal Lancaster. 28: DOD TOWA 81/44/04.

VANGUARD OF THE SEAS. 30-31: Carolyn Johns. 32: Carolyn Johns. 33: Courtesy HMAS *Canberra*. 34-35: Sikorsky, courtesy News Limited. 36: Carolyn Johns. 37: Carolyn Johns. 38: Carolyn Johns / NPU. 39: NPU. 40-41: Carolyn Johns.

BUILDING A MODERN NAVY. 42: DOD. 44: NPU/NPU/NPU. 46: RAN, courtesy News Limited. 48: NPU. 51: NPU. 52: RAN, courtesy News Limited; RAN, courtesy News Limited. 55: NPU. 56: UPI Bettman, courtesy News Limited. 57: Yon Ivanovic, Studio One. 58: Drawn by Alan Puckett, reference courtesy HMAS *Platypus*. 59: NPU. 60-61: Drawn by Alan Puckett, courtesy The Silver Partnership Advertising Agency and Directorate of Naval Recruiting/HMAS *Platypus*; HMAS *Platypus*; HMAS *Platypus*. 62: DOD CANA 88.70.01/Drawn by Alan Puckett, reference courtesy Australian Submarine Corporation. 64: Drawn by Alan Puckett, reference courtesy Carrington Slipways. 65: Carrington Slipways; Carrington Slipways. 67: The Age, Melbourne.

THE ULTIMATE AIRCRAFT. 69: Carolyn Johns. 70: Carolyn Johns. 71: DOD / Courtesy McDonnell Douglas; drawn by Jane Tenney, reference courtesy Commander D. Henry, US Navy Plant Representative Office. 72-73: Drawn by Langdon Halls, courtesy McDonnell Douglas / Drawn by Alan Puckett, reference courtesy McDonnell Douglas. 74-75: Carolyn Johns. 76-77: Carolyn Johns.

FROM MUSTANG TO HORNET. 78: DOD. 81: Courtesy McDonnell Douglas. 82: AWM JK612. 83: RAAF, courtesy News Limited. 85: AWM VN66-104-5. 87: AWM. 89: RAAF, courtesy News Limited / RAAF, courtesy News Limited. 91: Mal Lancaster. 92: Mal Lancaster / Mal Lancaster / Drawn by Alan Puckett. 93: DOD. 95: DOD CANA (K81) / 404/9. 96-97: Drawn by Alan Puckett, reference courtesy RAAF Public Relations / RAAF News: Greg Meggs; Drawn by Jane Tenney, reference DOD. 98: Courtesy Brian Noonan. 99: DOD CANAF 87.047.27. 100: Drawn by Alan Puckett, reference courtesy Wing Commander Peter Criss, No. 1 Squadron, Amberley / Mal Lancaster. 101: Courtesy Wing Commander Peter Criss; Mal Lancaster / Drawn by Alan Puckett, reference courtesy Wing Commander Peter Criss. 103: News Limited. 104: CPE.

SPECIAL OPERATIONS. 106-107: DOD PERA86/020/020. 108: DOD PERA86/019/11. 109: Courtesy Lieutenant-Colonel Wallace, Special Air Service Regiment, Swanbourne. 110: Courtesy Lieutenant-Colonel Wallace, SAS. 111: DOD CANA 81.26.09. 112: Army A/V Unit. 113: Courtesy Lieutenant-Colonel Wallace, SAS.

A MOBILE ARMY. 114: DOD. 116-117: Marketforce Advertising Agency. 118: DOD SYDA 87/056/32. 120: *Army News*. 122: Courtesy Norman Weber Advertising for Plessey Australia. 123: Marketforce Advertising Agency / Weber Advertising: Weber Advertising / Weber Advertising / Weber Advertising. 124: Marketforce. 125: DOD SYDA 86/105/08 / *Army News*. 126: AWM ERR/68/518/VN. 129: *Army News*. 130-131: Courtesy Marshall Cavendish Publishers; DOD. 132: AWM DNE 65/329/VN. 133: AWM COM 69/250/VN. 135: DOD BRIA 84/121/02. 136: DOD 88.293.06. 137: DOD MELA 84/38/29 / DOD CANA 78/085/01. 139: DOD BRIA 81/021/09. 140: *Army News*, SYDA/89/2/29. 141: DOD TOWA 85/100/07. 143: DOD TOWA 87/176/14. 144: DOD CANA 85/093/01. 145: DOD. 146: Claire Corbett. 147: DOD. 148: DOD BRIA 88/26/21.

INTO THE FUTURE. 150: USAFSC. 154: Courtesy Major Coffey, Army A/V Unit. 155: USAFSC. 156: USAFSC. 157: Courtesy The Concurrent Computer Corporation. 158: Drawn by Alan Puckett. 159: McDonnell Douglas, courtesy US Army Public Relations. 160: Drawn by Tom Freeman, Springhouse Art. 161: Tom Freeman, Springhouse Art. 162: USAFSC. 163: USAFSC.

Every effort has been made to contact and acknowledge owners of copyright in illustrative material used in this book. In the case of an omission, holders of copyright are invited to contact:
John Ferguson Publishers
100 Kippax St.
Surry Hills, N.S.W.
2010.

INDEX

Numerals in italics indicate an illustration of the subject mentioned.

A
A-17 Vaster-Gotland class submarine, *62*
Adelaide HMAS, 16, 17, 22, 23, 26, 32, 63
Aerospace plane, US Air Force, *162*
AIM-7 Sparrow missiles, 70, 100, 103, 105
AIM-9 Sidewinder missiles, 70, *74*, 100, 103
Airborne Warnings Control System (AWACS), 25
AK-47 assault rifle, 108
Albatross HMAS, map 14, 45
Amberley, RAAF airbase, map 14, *91*, 94
Anti-satellite systems (ASAT), 162
Anzac HMAS, 49, 50
ANZAM Treaty, 49, 50
ANZUS pact, 49
APC armoured personnel carriers, 142, 145
APG-65 radar, 70, 79, 103
Armoured Vehicle Layer Bridge (AVLB), 136, *137*
Armoured Recovery Vehicle Medium (ARVM), 136
Army's Nursing Corps, 144
Arunta HMAS, 50
Australian Defence Force, 13, 144, 151, 153
Australian Military Bases, map 14
Australian Tactical Command and Control System (AUSTACCS), 122
Australian Women Army Corps (AWAC), 144
Australian Women Army Service (AWAS), 144
Avon Sabre jet fighters, *83*

B
B2 Bomber, 156
Badman, Brigadier Peter, 132, 134
Balmoral submarine base, 45
Battalions, 1st, 18, 19, 22, 26; 3rd, 149; 5/7th, 134, 138
Battle Ridge, 121
Bell 206B-1 Kiowa helicopters, 18, 129
Bell Huey helicopters, 128, 129, 132
Bell Sikorsky helicopter, *159*
Bloodhound missile, 149
Boeing 737-400 aircraft, *25*
Borneo, 84, 121, 128, 141
Bren, .303 inch machine-gun, 125

Brigade, 1st, 119, 134, 149; 3rd, 18, 22, 119, 149
Brisbane HMAS, *52*, 56
Britain, 27, 49, 80, 83, 84, 99, 151
British 5.5 inch guns, 142
Broadmeadows, map 14
Butterworth airbase, 15, 83, 84, 99, 102

C
C47 Dakota aircraft, 82
Cairns, 57, 115
Cairns HMAS, map 14
Canberra, map 14
Canberra HMAS, *10*, 30, 32, 33, 34, 36, *38*, *39*, *40*, 63, 66, 68
Canberra jet fighters, 83, 88, *89*
Canungra, map 14
Canungra Land Warfare Centre, *120*, 121, 124
Cape York Peninsula, 18, 23, 102, 115
Caribou aircraft, 18, 19, 84, 146
Centurion tank, *133*, 134
Charters Towers, 25
Chinook helicopters, 128
Claymore mine, 127
Clearance Divers, RAN, 53
Collings, Squadron Leader Bill, 99, 102
Company, 135th Assault Helicopter, 53
Computer-generated holographic display, *154*
Computer graphics, 154
Computer-screen battle display, *154*
Coonawarra HMAS, map 14
Cullens Point, 115
Curtin, RAAF airbase, map 14

D
Daniel, Colonel Peter, 119
Darwin, 12, map 14, 16, 22, 23, 29, 78, 79, 94, 102, 103, 115, 128
Darwin HMAS, *10*, 16, *17*, 32, 63
Darwin RAAF airbase, map 14
Defence Integrated Secure Communications Network (DISCON), 122, *123*
Defence Science and Technology Organisation (DSTO), 24
Derby, 29, 102
Derwent HMAS, 17, 22, 26, 49, *51*
Dibb, Dr Paul, 29
Division, 1st, 119, 149; Reserve 2nd, 119
Dubbo HMAS, 57
Duchess HMAS, *54*
Dunbar, Pilot Officer Garry, 86

E
Echo-two cruise missile nuclear submarine, 15
Edinburgh, RAAF airbase, map 14
Egypt, 146
Electronic Support Measures (ESM), 95
Enoggera, map 14
Exclusive Economic Zone, 15

F
F-14 Tomcat aircraft, 70
F-15 Eagle fighters, 79, 102, 103, 105
F-16 Fighting Falcon, 102
F88 assault rifle, 125
F86 Sabre jets, 80, 82
F-104 Starfighter, 99
F-111 aircraft, 16, 18, 22, *26*, 90, *91*, *92*, *93*, 94, 98, 100, *101*, 153
F/A-18 Hornets, *6*, 18, 25, 70, *71*, *72*, *74*, *76*, 78, 79, 80, *81*, 94, 100, 102, 103, 105, 153
Fairey Firefly aircraft, 45
Far Eastern Strategic Reserve, 83
Ferndale, Major Steve, 115
Field Artillery Computer Equipment (FACE), 140, 141
Foster, Flight Lieutenant Bert, 78, 79, 80, 103, 105
France, 49, 99, 133
Fremantle HMAS, 57

G
Gannet aircraft, 47
Garden Island, Sydney, 15
GBU-10 laser-guided bombs, *93*, 100
GBU-15 TV guided bombs, *93*
Gloster Meteor Mark VIII fighters, 80
GPMG M60 machine-gun, 125, *127*
Grant tanks, 133
Guided Bomb Units, 100
Gulf of Carpentaria, 16, 18, 23

H
Hamel gun, *141*
HARM missiles, 70
Harpoon missiles, 22, 23, 32, 36, *38*, 44, 56, *58*, 59, 63, 66, 70, *93*, 95, 96, 98
Harrier jump jets, 16
Harrington, Commander Simon, *32*, 68
Hawker Sea Fury Fighters, see Sea Fury Fighters
Heckler and Koch G11 Advanced Combat Rifle, 108, *158*
Heckler and Koch submachine-gun, 108
Hercules C-130, aircraft, *20*, 84, 107, 108
Hobart, HMAS, *10*, *52*, 53, 54, *56*
Holsworthy, map 14, 128

Hover Infra-Red (IR) Dispersion system, 129
Howitzer 105mm M2A2, American, 141
Howitzer 105mm L5pack, Italian, 141
Hughes APG-65 Doppler radar system, 70, 79, 103
HV/VHF Plessey-Raven back-pack radio, *122, 123*

I
Ikara torpedo-carrying missiles, 49, *51,* 52, 68
India, 29, 146
Indian Ocean, 15, 27, 29, 59, 98
Indonesia, 15, 29, 84
Indonesian archipelago, 12, 27, 50
Infra-Red Detecting System (IRDS), 95
Iroquois UH1B helicopters, *19,* 85, *86,* 128, *147*

J
Japan, 15, 27, 50, 80, 82
Jervis Bay HMAS, 17, 56
Jindalee over-the-horizon radar (OTHR), *24,* 25

K
Kapooka, *map* 14, 144
Kelly, Major Steve, 138, 140, 142
Kimberleys, 17, 115, 124, 128
Kockums 471 class submarines, 56, 59, *62*
Korea, 27, 45, 47, 49, 80, 82, 128, 141
Krivac destroyer, 15
Krupp Atlas MWS 80 Minehunting System, 64
Kuttabul HMAS, *map* 14

L
L1A1, 7.62mm self-loading rifle, 124
Lancaster bombers, 83
Larrakeyah, *map* 14, 115
Learmonth, RAAF airbase, *map* 14, 102
Lee Enfield, .303 inch rifle, 124
Leopard 1A3 tank, 136, 138
Leopard AS1 tank, 134, *135, 136, 137,* 138, *140,* 145
Lewis machine-gun, 149
Lincoln bombers, 83, 98
Lockheed Electra airliner, 95
Lonergan, Flying Officer John, *69,* 70

M
M1 Abrams tank, 136
M16A1 Armalite rifle, 124
M16A1 5.56mm Armalite rifle, *124*
M48 Patton American tank, 134

M60 American tank, 134
M63 7.62mm machine-guns, 136
M113 Armoured Personnel Carrier, 128, 132, 133, *138*
M198 American medium 155mm gun, 142
M203 rifle, 124
MAG 58, 7.62 machine-gun, 127, 128
McDonald, Sub Lieutenant Ian, 46, 47
McDonnell Douglas F/A-18 Hornets, *see* F/A-18 Hornets
McDonnell Douglas Harpoon missiles, *see* Harpoon missiles
Magnetic Anomaly Detector (MAD), 95
Malaya, 49, 82, 83, 88, 121, 128
Malayan Emergency, 49, 50, 83, 121, 141
Malayan Peninsula, 49, 50
Malaysia, 15, 27, 29, 94, 98, 102
Mark 48 torpedos, 56, 59, 62, 68
Mekong Delta, 84, 85
Melbourne, *map* 14, 106
Melbourne HMAS, 32, 47, *48,* 50, 63, 67
Meteor jets, *82,* 83
Middle East, 83, 88
Mine Disposal Vehicles (MDV), 64, 65
Minimi, 5.56mm machine-gun, 127
Mirage jets, 80, *99,* 102, *103*
Moreton HMAS, *map* 14
Murphy, Flight Lieutenant Nigel, 19
Murray, Lieutenant K. "Gus", 50, 52

N
Namibia, 146
NATO Pact, 102
Naval Combat Data System, 32
Naval Gunfire Support Unit, 53
Neptune P2V5 aircraft, 98
New Guinea, *see* Papua New Guinea
New Zealand, 49, 83, *120*
Nicobar Islands, 15, 95
Norcom, 115, 119
Norforce, 13, 17, *116,* 118
North West Mobile Force, 128
Northern Territory, *map* 14, 18, 124, 128

O
Oakey, *map* 14
Oberon submarines, 13, 15, 42, 44, 45, 56, *58, 59, 60, 62,* 63, *108*
O'Connor, Chief Petty Officer, 24
Onslow HMAS, 56, 59
Operational Deployment Force, 18, 22, 119, 128, 129, 134, 141, 149
Orion HMAS, 56, 59
Otama HMAS, 56, 59

Otway HMAS *44,* 56, 59
Ovens HMAS, 56, 59
Oxley HMAS, 42, 43, *44,* 56, 59, 66, 68, *95*

P
P-3C Orion aircraft, 12, 13, 15, 16, 22, 23, 26, 43, 44, 63, 66, 68, 94, *95, 96, 97,* 98, 100, 153
P51 Mustang aircraft, 80, *82*
Pacific Ocean, 27, 29, 98, 151
Panavia Tornado fighters, 102
Papua New Guinea, 15, 18, 29, 57, 133
Parramatta HMAS, 49, 50
Pave Tack laser illumination, 26, 94, 100, *101*
Pearce, RAAF airbase, *map* 14, 80
Penang Island, 83, 84
Perth, *map* 14, 25
Perth HMAS, *52, 53,* 56
Phantom F4E fast strike fighters, 90
Philippines, 49, 50, 94
Phuoc Tuy, 85, 86
Platypus HMAS *map* 14
Point Cook, RAAF airbase, *map* 14, 45, 80
Puckapunyal, *map* 14, 134, 136

Q
Quadrant HMAS, 49
Queenborough HMAS, 49, 50
Queensland, *map* 14, 124
Quiberon HMAS, 49
Quickmatch HMAS, 49, 50

R
Radar Homing and Warning System (RHAWS), 91
Rapier anit-aircraft platform, *145*
Rapier guided-missile system, 149
Red China, 27
Regiments, 1 RAR, 22; 2/4 RAR, *120;* 3 RAR, *142, 148,* 149; 9 RAR, *133;* 1st Commando, 108, *111;* 1st Armoured, 132, *133,* 134, 136; 1st Recruit Training, *144;* 2nd Cavalry, 128, 138, 149; 3rd Cavalry, 132; 4th Cavalry, 138; 5th Aviation, 128, 129, 149; 6 RAR, *8;* 8/12th Medium, 140; 51st Far North Queensland, 114, 115, *116;* 107 Field Battery, 20; Special Air Service, *106,* 108, *109, 110, 111, 112, 113*
Richmond, RAAF airbase, *map* 14
Royal Australian Air Force, 12
Royal Australian Navy, 13
RPG2 anti-armour missile, 140
Rushcutter HMAS, 64, 65

S

Sabre jet fighters, 82, 83, 84, 99.
Salter, Lieutenant Colonel John, 18, 19, 22
Satellite technology, 152
Schofields, airbase, 45
Seacats, 17, *51*
Sea Fury Fighters, 45, 46, 47
Seahawk helicopters, 16, *17*, 23, 32, *34*, 63, 66, 68, 129, 153
Sea King helicopters, 47, *48*
Sea Venom jet fighters, 47
Shalders, Lieutenant Commander Rick, 43, 44, 66, 68
Shelvey, Lieutenant Mark, 66
Sherman tanks, 133
Shoalhaven HMAS, 64
Sidewinder missiles, *see* AIM Sidewinder missiles
Sikorsky Black Hawk helicopters, 88, 128, *129*, *130*, 153
Singapore, 24, 50, 84
Singleton, *map* 14
Skyhawk fighter bombers, 47, *48*
Small Waterplane Area Twin Hull (SWATH), 152
South China Sea, 12, 50, 53, 98
South East Asia, 27, 29, 50, 53, 82, 98, 115
South East Asian Treaty Organisation (SEATO), 49, 50, 83, 84
Soviet MiG-15 jets, 80
Soviet MiG-23, 70
Sparrow missiles, *see* AIM Sparrow missiles
Squadrons, No 1, 83, 91, *98*; No 2, 88, 90; No 3, 70, *83*, *99*, *104*; No 6, 91; No 9, 84, *86*, 129; No 10, *95*; No 35, 84, *85*; No 38 Transport, 82; No 75, 70, 79, 99; No 77, 70, 80, *82*, *99*; No 78 Wing, 83; No 79, 84, *99*; No 805, 45; No 808, 45, 47; No 816, 45, 47; No 817, 45, 47; 17th Construction, *146*; 20th Carrier Air Group, 45; 21st Carrier Air Group, 45
Stalwart HMAS, 58
Stealth aircraft, *156*
Steyr assault rifle, *8*, 124, *125*, 127
Stirling HMAS, *map* 14
Strike Battle Cruiser, *160*
Stuart HMAS, 49
Stuart tanks, 133
Submarine Weapons Update Programme (SWUP), 59
Success HMAS, *10*, 58
Sukarno, President, 50, 83
Supply HMAS, 53, *54*, 58
Surface-to-air-missile (SAM) systems, 149
Swan HMAS, 17, 22, 26, 49
Swanbourne, *map* 14, 108
Sycamore helicopters, 47
Sydney, *map* 14, 45, 49, 108
Sydney HMAS, 32, 45, *46*, 47, 53, *54*, 63

T

Tartar anti-air missiles, 52, 56
Teal HMAS, 52
Terrain Following Radar (TFR), 90, 91, 92
TFX Tactical Fighter Experimental, 90
Tindal, RAAF airbase, *map* 14, 16, 25, 29, 70, 79, 102
Tobruk HMAS, 17, 45, 49, 50, 58, 63
Top End, 29, 79, 80, 115, 119, 128
Torrens HMAS, 49, 66, 68
Townsville, *map* 14, 22, 29, 94, 119, 128, 129, 149
Townsville, RAAF airbase, *map* 14, 102
Tracker planes, 47, *48*
Tyrrell, Flight Lieutenant John, 88, 89, 90, 94

U

UN Committee for Indonesia (UNCI), 146
UN Disengagement Observer Force (UNDOF), 146
UN Emergency Force (UNEF II), 146
UN Interim Force in Lebanon (UNIFIL), 146
UN Iran-Iraq Military Observer Group (UNIIMOG), 146
UN Military Observer Group in India and Pakistan (UNMOGIP), 146
UN Peacekeeping Force in Cyprus (UNFICYP), 146
UN Security Council, 146
UN Transition Assistance Group (UNTAG), *146*
UN Truce Supervision Organization (UNTSO), 146
UN Yemen Observation Mission (UNYOM), 146
United States Air Force F-15 Eagle Fighters, 79; 35th Tactical Fighter Wing, 88
United States Marine Corps A-6 Intruder Bombers, 79

V

Vampire HMAS, 49
Vampire jets, 83
Vendetta HMAS, 49, 54
Vertically launched missile systems (VLS), 152, 153, *160*
Vickers machine-gun, 125
Victoria Barracks, *map* 14
Vietnam, 27, 50, 52, 53, 54, 84, 85, 86, 88, 90, 102, 108, 121, 128, 129, 132, 132, 133, 134, 141
Voyager HMAS, *48*, 49
Vulcan gatling gun, *36*
Vulcan Phalanx Close-in-Weapons-System, 32, *36*
Vung Tau, 53

W

Warramunga HMAS, 50
Warsaw Pact, 102
Watsonia, *map* 14
Waterhen HMAS, *map* 14
Weipa, *map* 14, 18, 20, 22, 26, 115
Wessex helicopters, 47
Whitehead, Sergeant David, 114, 115
Williamtown, RAAF airbase, *map* 14, 70, 80, 102, *104*
Women's Land Army, 144
Woman's Royal Australian Army Corps, 144

Y

Yarra HMAS, 49, 50

Z

Zodiac, inflatable boats, 107, 108, 111